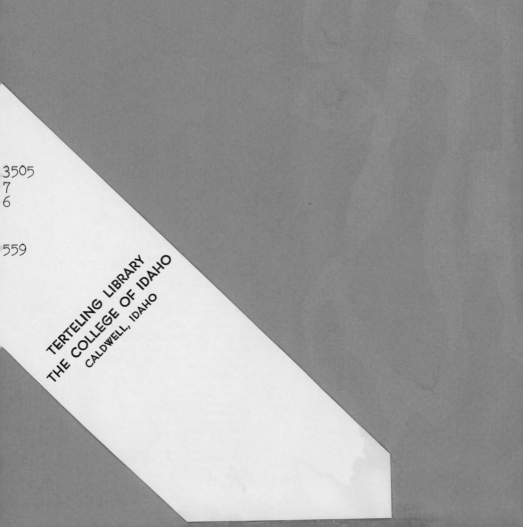

UNCLE VALENTINE

AND OTHER STORIES

Willa Cather Collections
published by the University of Nebraska Press

POETRY

April Twilights (1903)
Edited with an introduction by Bernice Slote

FICTION

Willa Cather's Collected Short Fiction, 1892–1912
Edited by Virginia Faulkner. Introduction by Mildred R. Bennett

NONFICTION

The Kingdom of Art:
Willa Cather's First Principles and Critical Statements, 1893–1896
Edited with two essays and a commentary by Bernice Slote

The World and the Parish:
Willa Cather's Articles and Reviews, 1893–1902
(2 vols.)
Edited with a commentary by William M. Curtin

UNCLE VALENTINE
AND OTHER STORIES

Willa Cather's
Uncollected Short Fiction
1915–1929

Edited with an introduction by
BERNICE SLOTE

UNIVERSITY OF NEBRASKA PRESS · LINCOLN

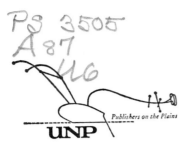

Contents

✻ ✻ ✻

Acknowledgment

�֎ ✖ ✖

The University of Nebraska Press is profoundly grateful to Willa Cather's literary trustees, Mr. Alfred A. Knopf and the late Miss Edith Lewis, for sanctioning the publication of this volume.

We wish also to express our thanks to the Enoch Pratt Free Library, Baltimore, Maryland, and in particular to Mr. Richard Hart, Chairman, Humanities Department, and Miss Sarah Soltys, for timely help in procuring us reproductions of two stories in the American edition of *Smart Set*.

Introduction

❋   ❋   ❋

Willa Cather herself arranged three books of short stories: *The Troll Garden* (1905), *Youth and the Bright Medusa* (1920), and *Obscure Destinies* (1932). Each of these books had a theme, and at least one, *The Troll Garden*, had an intricate form.[1] More than collections, they were books of fiction with a point. After her death three still unpublished stories were collected in *The Old Beauty and Others* (1948); in 1965 her early stories were gathered in one volume, *Collected Short Fiction, 1892–1912*.[2] Now, in *Uncle Valentine and Other Stories*, are presented the seven remaining uncollected stories published from 1915 to 1929, five reprinted for the first time and one—"Coming, Eden Bower!"—a publishing anomaly, for it is a modified version of the first story in *Youth and the Bright Medusa*, "Coming, Aphrodite!" These seven are urban stories, but like the Nebraska tales in *Obscure Destinies* they are primarily about little people who matter more than fame. They are, for the most part, deeply ironic. Although the stories are linked mainly by chronology, they are also bound by the geometrics of urban life—streets and offices, workers and firms, the business world of New York and Pittsburgh, the cities which by 1929 Willa Cather had known well for over thirty years.

The five New York stories were published first, in the period from 1915 to 1920 which also produced the four stories of artists Willa Cather included in *Youth and the Bright Medusa* ("The Diamond Mine," "A Gold Slipper," "Scandal," and "Coming, Aphrodite!"). In the years from 1912 to 1915, after Willa Cather left her position as managing editor of *McClure's Magazine* to devote her time to writing, she had

1. See discussions in *The Kingdom of Art: Willa Cather's First Principles and Critical Statements, 1893–1896*, edited with two essays and a commentary by Bernice Slote (Lincoln: University of Nebraska Press, 1966), pp. 93–97; and in E. K. Brown, *Willa Cather: A Critical Biography*, completed by Leon Edel (New York: Alfred A. Knopf, 1953), pp. 113–22.

2. *Willa Cather's Collected Short Fiction, 1892–1912*, edited by Virginia Faulkner with an introduction by Mildred R. Bennett (Lincoln: University of Nebraska Press, 1965; rev. ed. 1970).

published three novels—*Alexander's Bridge* (1912), *O Pioneers!* (1913), and *The Song of the Lark* (1915)—but, after 1912, no short fiction. The relatively large number of sophisticated, urban stories of New York and artists after 1915 contrasts with her one novel of the period, *My Ántonia*, and its material—though in fact the art of *My Ántonia* is far more sophisticated than that of any of the short pieces. Willa Cather was writing (or revising) and selling stories in this period before 1920 because she needed to make her living with her pen. Even so, her output of signed fiction was not great. What we do have are stories that show an even wider range of interests and techniques than readers have thus far been able to recognize.

Perhaps the most unusual of these stories is "Consequences." There is nothing quite like it anywhere in Cather's work, though it has elements of writers she admired—Poe, Hawthorne, James. It is assumed in the story that there has been a compression of time as Kier Cavenaugh's future self takes form alongside him with casual, everyday familiarity. The old man who haunts Cavenaugh is no ghostlike presence or other-worldly figure or some evocation of the mind—at least in the tone of the telling; he is flatly specific and real, a figure in place and time with dirty white gloves; one who turns to the wall the picture of Kier's twin brother, an athlete dead at sixteen; and one whose appearances are witnessed, to some degree, by the skeptical lawyer and narrator, Henry Eastman. The situation is at least distantly related to that in James's "The Jolly Corner," in which a man pursues the embodiment of the self he would have been if another chain of circumstances had operated. James's effect, however, is of an intense focus of consciousness in which the protagonist almost wills his other self to appear, and the figure does resolve out of the shadows: "He saw, in its great grey glimmering margin, the central vagueness diminish, and he felt it to be taking the very form . . . spectral yet human, a man of his own substance and stature waited there . . . ."[3] In Cather's story the alter ego is real, not spectral; it pursues the protagonist and is not, like that of James, willed to appear.

The concern in "Consequences" is of cause or chance, the moral question one of self-determination. Why do some men commit suicide? Kier Cavenaugh, "a young man of pleasure," and Henry Eastman, a lawyer, take unlikely sides. The lawyer says that some suicides are in-

3. *The Novels and Tales of Henry James*, New York Edition, vol. 17 (New York: Charles Scribner's Sons, 1907–17), p. 475. The quotation from "The Beast in the Jungle" in the next paragraph is from the same volume, p. 72.

explicable; the young man of pleasure argues for a logical cause, "if one knew all the facts." In the context of the story the facts are there but inexplicable. "I believe people can be chilled by a draft from outside, somewhere," says Cavenaugh. From the "far outside," indeed, the laws of cause and effect are affirmed. Perhaps another line from James's "The Beast in the Jungle" is pertinent: John Marcher waits for something that will happen to, or with, him, something which might, among many possibilities, simply alter everything, "'striking at the root of all my world and leaving me to the consequences, however they shape themselves.'"

Like *Alexander's Bridge*, "Consequences" is strongly theatrical, arranged almost perceptibly in scenes. And they have more than a touch of the theatre of the absurd, from the opening quixotic scene near the Flatiron Building on a rainy afternoon, "people tilting at each other with umbrellas," to the figure of a stunned chauffeur surrounded by luggage and his master dead just at the hour of departure for Montana. His crisis, as one puts it, is that "'Harry don't know what to do with the ticket.'"

Both "Consequences" and "The Bookkeeper's Wife" have the flat ending, the throwaway last line, that in context restores perspective. Henry Eastman, after bewildering encounters with the Mystery, "thought of his office as a delightful place." Percy Bixby, at the end of "The Bookkeeper's Wife," must be left to his personal tragedy—"one never did do anything for a fellow who had been stung as hard as that." What happened to Percy is no more than what happens to others—too little money, too much desire, and the closing of the inevitable gates. Like Henry Eastman, Percy grew/ to love his office, though the routine of his carefully unbalanced books could not save him from his self-imposed disaster. Both stories are moralities, if only with a suggestion of a Bunyan parable in names like Stella (the star), who in the end prefers the more spectacular Charley Greengay; Percy is saved from disgrace by Oliver (the peacemaker) Remsen. The story does not go far from this central play of moral conditions (they are hardly choices). Almost helplessly absorbed into the manipulation of his books, committed to his desk without pause for fear of discovery, Percy is in a sense reminiscent of Bartleby, though without Melville's aura of mystery. The eviscerated Mission clock in his empty house is Percy's symbol: a hollow man, indeed, and years before Eliot's. Stella, his wife, for whom he stole and by whom he is discarded, is the hard "new woman" of 1916, liberated enough by selfishness to go her own way in business and in love, capable, beautiful, and cold. She is one of the deadliest women—and wives—in Cather's fiction, slipping easily from one alliance to another, counting position and pleasure worth the sacrifice of any other life. If Percy Bixby is a man who has been stung, Stella is the serpent who did it.

One of Willa Cather's most attractive stories in this period before 1920 is "Ardessa," still ironic but with a satisfying turn. In "Ardessa" we see a magazine office and editor, a magazine something like *McClure's* and an editor transparently the image of S. S. McClure. Though not all of the circumstances fit that magazine or the life of McClure, there are enough to establish the relationship. Among them: the creation of a vibrant new magazine by a swift-moving, intense editor from the West, a disturbing man but one of ideas and grace, of sympathy and firm will (he was always kind, said the late Edith Lewis, who also worked for him);[4] and the collection of writers made famous by the editor's hand, isolated like Buddhas in order to muckrake and write. To catch S. S. McClure in the very gestures of life, hearing almost the inflections of his voice, is one of the charms of reading this story. Another is the quick view into a part of Willa Cather's life which elsewhere is not shown—her nearly six years as a full-time editor of *McClure's*. Her experience with publishing (and familiar matters like demanding writers, or the inevitable moat between editorial and business operations) was longer than that. She had also spent a year as managing editor of the *Home Monthly* in Pittsburgh (1896–97), and several more on the staff of the Pittsburgh *Leader*. Perhaps, then, it is a little strange that we have no more than "Ardessa" as an imaginative record of that world. Once in 1908 Sarah Orne Jewett remarked on Cather's backgrounds: "your Nebraska life, —a child's Virginia, and now an intimate knowledge of what we are pleased to call the 'Bohemia' of newspaper and magazine-office life," and then she commented: "These are uncommon equipment, but you don't see them yet quite enough from the outside,—you stand right in the middle of each of them when you write."[5] No signed stories of a child's Virginia or of "newspaper and magazine-office life" had been published by 1908. If there were others known to Miss Jewett, at least they have not been recorded under Willa Cather's name.

4. Edith Lewis, *Willa Cather Living: A Personal Record* (New York: Alfred A. Knopf, 1953), p. 46.
5. Letter to Willa Cather, December 13, [1908], *Letters of Sarah Orne Jewett*, edited by Annie Fields (Boston: Houghton Mifflin Company, 1911), p. 248.

INTRODUCTION

That Willa Cather wrote under other names, and for other people, brings her own experience closer to "Ardessa" in a slightly different way. If we are sympathetic with hard-working, eager Becky Tietelbaum who wants, more than overtime pay, to get ahead in her work, we can draw into our view the Willa Cather who was also determined to succeed in business, to win out; who worked hard and skillfully. How skillfully she worked as McClure's right hand is revealed in some surviving letters to authors. Though personally she was drawn tight on hair-trigger emotions and sensibility, as the voice of *McClure's* Willa Cather was as calm, firm, kindly, and efficient as any Platonic idea of an editor. The letters to Hugo Munsterberg, who was making life difficult for *McClure's* in 1910 and 1911, is a case in point.[6] The Willa Cather who was a writer, columnist, reviewer, and sometimes reporter and feature writer on Lincoln and Pittsburgh papers could, like Becky, perform faster and better than anyone else—though, unlike Becky, she did it apparently without breathing hard. Sometimes, like Becky, one had to do the work of others without credit. Sometimes she did not mind, when the pleasure of the idea and the acting made it all a game (she could be a consummate actress in language and print, and even more important, she enjoyed doing things mysteriously, by herself, in secret); or when in 1913 she wrote S. S. McClure's autobiography because she loved him. But inescapably there was much of drudgery in rewriting, in substantive editing, in doing the work of others. The end, however, was not unlike Becky's. In Willa Cather's experience there may not have been an Ardessa Devine to defeat, but it was Cather and not somebody else who in 1908 was made managing editor of *McClure's*. "The best magazine executive I know is Miss Cather," S. S. McClure once said.[7]

Should there be more than "Ardessa" from the magazine years? No one can determine the proportions of experience to art. But the fact is that Willa Cather's publishing career did not mesh with her most creative forces, her most creative self. My conjecture (and it has been supported by everything I have so far encountered in relation to Willa Cather), is that she had three not wholly compatible drives: one was to win out with a career, to be a success in a world of mostly men, in a time when women rarely tried and even more rarely succeeded; another

6. Archives, Boston Public Library.
7. Peter Lyon, *Success Story: The Life and Times of S. S. McClure* (New York: Charles Scribner's Sons, 1963), p. 390.

was to be the artist, as great an artist as she might be; and a third was to be a Virginia lady, like her mother. Only the first two are pertinent here—the other story is for another time. Though she achieved both ends—both power and art—the first was behind her in 1912 when she permanently separated from *McClure's* after having reached a very high position indeed. That success had a life of its own; it was a twin destiny not wholly joined to that of the artist. Like two selves, within her world they jostled, and were not one.

Although Willa Cather's two stories in the *Smart Set*—"Her Boss" and "Coming, Eden Bower!"—have been overlooked, each has considerable importance both in her own development and in literary history. They appeared in 1919 and 1920, but Willa Cather's relationship with the *Smart Set*'s editor, H. L. Mencken, began before that. He had reviewed all four of her novels up to that time and considered *My Ántonia* one of the best of American novels. In their correspondence, with each other and with others, there are references to the reviews, Mencken's books, and Cather's current writing, perhaps including "Her Boss." "Coming, Eden Bower!" is certainly the story Mencken meant when he wrote to Louise Pound on April 23, [1920], that he had "bought a capital novelette" from Willa Cather.[8] That story, in a censor-proof version, appeared in the *Smart Set* in August 1920, a month or so before the publication of *Youth and the Bright Medusa*, which included the Eden Bower story, titled "Coming, Aphrodite!," in the version which Cather certainly meant to be definitive.

"Her Boss," uneven as it may be, is important in Willa Cather's fiction because in it she put down for the third time a situation which by its recurrence takes on a kind of archetypal significance in her imaginative world. The situation is of a mature or older man, divided somehow from a wife whom he loves but with whom there is not complete understanding, who turns for emotional harmony to a youthful figure—himself in memory or another who represents to him youth or creative force. The story was told first in *Alexander's Bridge*. It reappeared in *My Ántonia* with Jim Burden's return to his youth. There the wife was very remote, the youth all-encompassing. Now, in "Her Boss," we have Paul Wanning, a business man of sixty, and dying, whose wife and family do not meet

8. *Letters of H. L. Mencken*, selected and annotated by Guy J. Forgue, with a personal note by Hamilton Owens (New York: Alfred A. Knopf, 1961), p. 183. Unpublished letters of H. L. Mencken are in Enoch Pratt Free Library, Baltimore, and the New York Public Library.

his need and who turns to writing the story of his life, especially of his youth in Wyoming, with the help and sympathy of a young secretary, Annie Wooley. It might be noted in passing, though the subject cannot be discussed fully, that the situation reappears in part in "Uncle Valentine"; in *The Professor's House* (1925), in *Lucy Gayheart* (1935), and in *Sapphira and the Slave Girl* (1940). "Her Boss" may be more important as a thematic repetition than as a single story, for it leads directly to *The Professor's House*. There are only sketched lines in the short story, however, mere indications that will be modified and developed in the later novel. Paul Wanning is not the Professor. In the first place he is physically ill, doomed to a death that none will accept but Annie Wooley, a poor girl from a large family who knows how to face deaths and funerals. He admires the things his wife has gathered in his house, all the material objects; he has only the beginning of a creative and intellectual release in the writing done through his last summer. But like the Professor he has a lovely, bosomy wife; he has two daughters, dark and light, hard and soft. In the absence of his family one summer he is comforted at last by the recall of his own youth and his memories, and by the emergence of a dreamlike wonder in his mood. As in "Consequences" there are two stories, the inside truth that only Annie Wooley is left to affirm, and the untruth that becomes, in spite of Annie, the "real" fact. After Paul Wanning's death his law partner knows that his last will is not honored; but no one, not even Annie, will ever know that he had meant what he said when he promised to leave her something as a reward for her help. In death he is distorted and dishonored, and, ironically, all for the sake of "honor." "Rich is tight," says Mrs. Wooley, and there is no way to contradict her.

Aside from the story, in "Her Boss" there are several perceptive passages which foreshadow meditations suited to Professor St. Peter: "His own bed frightened him. In all the years he had lived in this house he had never before looked about his room, at that bed, with the thought that he might one day be trapped there . . . . Now there was something sinister about the bed itself, about its position, and its relation to the rest of the furniture." His wife's "restlessness and her practical turn of mind" had made him a "money-getter." His illness brought "back to him the illusions with which he left college." In his last summer life pours into him, with the sun and air in his office, the boats moving on the river below; as he dictates it is "like living his life over again." Like Professor St. Peter, Paul Wanning does not miss his family when they are away.

"He had become again the mild, contemplative youth he was in college, before he had a profession and a family to grind for, before the two needs which shape our destiny had made of him pretty much what they make of every man." These meditations are refined and deepened in *The Professor's House*.

In the New York stories discussed thus far there is very little use of the city itself as an important part of the action. One rides along familiar streets, notices familiar places, but the urban fact is not a decisive element except for the presence of publishers and firms of lawyers and the general office scene. Paul Wanning, in fact, lived in Orange, New Jersey, though he stayed in New York for much of his last summer. Like Henry Eastman and Percy Bixby, but for quite different reasons, Wanning grew to like his office; he did not feel that he would tire of it in a hundred years. By contrast, one earlier New York story, "Behind the Singer Tower" (1912), depends greatly on the urban concentration of hotels, skyscrapers, and the masses of immigrant construction workers. What does continue from the 1912 story is the recognition of those masses of humanity. In the stories of 1915 to 1920 it is the working girl who is treated sympathetically and realistically. Groups of these girls are mentioned respectfully by Kier Cavenaugh in "Consequences." Individuals like Becky Tietelbaum and Rena Kalski of "Ardessa" and Annie Wooley of "Her Boss" are some of the most vivid characters in the stories. There are also Annie's mother and their friend Willy Steen. The scenes in the Wooley home have a reality that Paul Wanning's dinner table cannot match. When Mrs. Wooley prays for the best, that whatever came to Annie "'might not be in the form of taxable property,'" we know whose feet are on the ground. The same is true for the final New York story; in "Coming, Eden Bower!" the minor characters are barely sketched, but they have life. Caesar III, for example, is one of the most convincing dogs to trot through any work of fiction. He recalls an essay Willa Cather wrote, at about age nine, arguing the virtues of dogs in comparison with cats. The dog, she said then, is "a very intelligent animal," and "kind, noble and generous." Caesar III is the very type of what she considered as "the noble, majestic dog."[9]

"Coming, Eden Bower!" can be discussed interchangeably with "Coming, Aphrodite!": the two are the same story except for matters

9. Archives, Nebraska State Historical Society. See also Mildred R. Bennett, *The World of Willa Cather* (New York, 1951; reprinted with notes and an index, Lincoln: University of Nebraska Press, 1961), pp. 196–97.

of title, text, and publishing history. That "Coming, Aphrodite!" is one of the best of Cather's works of short fiction is undeniable. It also has the interest of twin publication, actually triple, for the English edition of the *Smart Set* has a few minor editorial variants. The chief textual interest, however, is that the magazine version is quite literally clothed for the censoring "Comstocks" and the Watch and Warders. We may begin with whatever facts are known.

The "capital novelette" which Mencken said he had bought—sometime before his letter of April 23, 1920—appeared in the *Smart Set* in August of that year, signed Willa Sibert Cather. With *Youth and the Bright Medusa* (including "Coming, Aphrodite!"), published by Knopf early in the fall, the author began using Willa Cather as her signature. Either because the *Smart Set* version was somewhat different, or because the two were published almost simultaneously, the magazine appearance of the story was not noted in the book. It is quite possible that Willa Cather had little contact with Mencken's novelette after he took it for the *Smart Set*. At least she did not change her signature to her then preferred form. And since she was in France from June to November that year, it is also unlikely that she checked proof for either the American or English edition of the magazine. Some typographical errors in both editions do not appear in *Youth and the Bright Medusa*. A number of stylistic improvements have been made in the book version; at least, when there are variants in style the choice for the final printing is the better one. The chief difference between the two versions is that the *Smart Set* printing has cuts in the more sexually explicit passages and variants that modify certain sensuous details. For example, in what we must consider the true version, "Coming, Aphrodite!," Don Hedger sees Eden Bower nude, exercising in her room and bathed in an almost mystical radiance of sun. In the *Smart Set* Eden Bower wears a pink negligee, thighs are delicately ignored when her body is mentioned, and she even refrains from looking at a mole under her arm. In "Coming, Aphrodite!" the man and woman are unquestionably lovers and keep open the door that has separated their apartments. This whole passage is left out of the magazine version.[10]

Without attempting to guess who made the changes, it is apparent from his letters that Mencken was the fearful one, and with good reason. The holy censoring Comstocks were out to save America, and even

10. See the Appendix for a summary of the variants.

good editors, to protect themselves from jail and their works from burning, had to keep the adversary in mind. Theodore Dreiser's *Titan* had been withdrawn by the publishers only a few years earlier, and because of attacks by censors another Dreiser novel, *The "Genius,"* had been in the same danger. Protests and legal action had helped but not cured. (Willa Cather was one who signed the 1916 protest against Dreiser's treatment.) In February 1920, very near the time he took on Eden Bower, Mencken wrote to Wilbur Cross: "Don't think that Comstockery is dead! It was never more potent." Harper's had been fined $1,000 for a vice-crusade document by Ben B. Lindsey, and another trial was imminent over the printing of James Branch Cabell's *Jurgen*. "Every book publisher is terrified," wrote Mencken, "and every imaginative author has to write with his [this?] sword over his head." A year later, February 11, 1921, Mencken wrote Fielding Hudson Garrison that Tom Smith of the *Century* had told him "the other day" that Cather "had lately sent him a very fine novelette, but that he had to pass it up because of some crim. con. [*sic*] in it. The Comstocks are in violent eruption, and the Century has been taking too many chances."[11] It is not clear what work this might have been—perhaps an early version of *A Lost Lady*, which, it is known, was revised a number of times before its publication in 1923; it was then first serialized by the *Century*. Of all Willa Cather's writings, *A Lost Lady* and "Coming, Eden Bower!" ("Coming, Aphrodite!") are most alike in their use of deliberate and skillful suggestions of sexual passion.

Willa Cather placed the story of Eden Bower with the other accounts of singers and artists collected in *Youth and the Bright Medusa*. But more than any of the others in that group it is a New York story, and place is significant—Washington Square and Coney Island, boarding houses where young artists gathered in the American Bohemia of the turn of the century, fountains and statues and trees, breakfast at the Brevoort, the pigeons rising from the Italian settlement south of the Square, and all this in a lilac spring and easy, moonlight summer. This New York was in Willa Cather's memories: she had lived for a time at 60 Washington Square, a place, no doubt, with hallways, bathrooms, and janitresses like those Eden Bower and Don Hedger knew. On the rooftops of this Bohemia an artist like Don Hedger could watch the moon and shooting stars, and hear from below Eden Bower singing the "tempestuous, overlapping phrases" of Puccini (*La Bohéme*? or more probably, "Vissi

11. *Letters*, pp. 176, 218.

d'arte e d'amor" from *Tosca*?). "Coming, Eden Bower!" is a romantic story, but one held close to earth by glimpses of lame oystermen, basement restaurants with sawdust floors, a dirty sink.

Don Hedger, the painter for whom art has always been enough, and Eden Bower, the young singer on her way to success, are caught for one summer in the ancient ritual of love, deeply sexual and completely absorbing. Briefly, and for this summer, art is subordinate to love and the first principles of male and female. The lure, the commitment, the inevitable quarrel, and the sudden end as Eden leaves with her rich protector for Paris and a career, are drawn with great skill and beauty. Not even the changes in the *Smart Set* version can harm the almost symphonic blend of images, themes, and allusions, or the haunting play of language that rises and falls in the exact rhythm of feeling. As Willa Cather once said of one of Sarah Orne Jewett's stories, it "simply *is the look*"[12]—here, the look itself of man and woman and blinding youth.

With all the immaculate grace of its handling, the story is primitive and is meant to be. The woman's name is a slanting use of Rossetti's poem, "Eden Bower," with its refrains of the first garden: "(*Eden bower's in flower.*) . . . (*And O the bower and the hour!*)." Rossetti's poem is about Lilith, the woman before Eve, who with the serpent plots revenge on mankind:

> It was Lilith the wife of Adam:
> (*Eden bower's in flower.*)
> Not a drop of her blood was human,
> But she was made like a soft sweet woman.[13]

Willa Cather's Eden Bower is both Lilith and Eve, the female principle of beauty and evil without love (or for whom love is a momentary delight). With other allusions in the story she is linked to Diana, to the *belle dame*, to a company of lovely women and cruel lovers. When Don Hedger first sees her in motion in "a luminous mist" in sun and whirling disks of light, the "spot seemed enchanted; as if a vision out of Alexandria, out of the remote pagan past, had bathed itself there in Helianthine fire." For him she was linked with "Crete, or Alexandria, or Veronese's Venice. She was the immortal conception, the perennial theme." In

12. "Preface," *The Best Stories of Sarah Orne Jewett*, selected and arranged with a preface by Willa Cather, 2 vols. (Boston: Houghton Mifflin Company, 1925), 1:xiv.

13. Dante Gabriel Rossetti, *Poems and Translations* (London: Oxford University Press, 1959), pp. 18–23.

Alexandria were Cleopatra and Thaïs; in Crete, Aphrodite—all in the deep pagan past and leading back to "Lilith, the wife of Adam." This archetypal figure is supported by Hedger's story of the Aztec queen and her forty lovers, used and destroyed by her. The figure in such tales is not idealized woman but primitive female. And her beauty is part of the story.

The contrasts of man and woman are heightened visually. Eden is light, golden, flowery. She appears in sun like Danaë in a shower of gold, she identifies with the soaring pigeons (as doves, they stand for love), she rises in a balloon, herself like a bird (or like Aphrodite rising from the sea). Hedger is dark, his rooms are dark and cluttered; he identifies with fish rather than with birds. In one sense he is the observer, his recent interest the painting of fish he has watched in the Aquarium (he knows a lame oysterman, notices fishwomen). His painting is of paradise fish "staring out at people through the glass and green water of their tank." The idea, which he does not quite admit, is "the incommunicability of one stratum of animal life with another." In brief contrasts, the dog Caesar III communicates with Hedger but not with Eden Bower. At the end of their affair Hedger himself and Eden Bower do not communicate; they are on different levels of life, and he is left in solitude, looking up at the stars. In "Coming, Aphrodite!" Willa Cather underscores Hedger's identification with fish by making the phrase not "sitting in solitude" but "sitting in his tank."

But the story is also about two conceptions of success: Hedger's private search for a new art, always changing, rarely profitable; Eden Bower's commitment to fame and money. It is the singer who some eighteen years later returns to New York where signs read "Coming, Eden Bower!" (or, in the other version, "Coming, Aphrodite!," referring to the opera in which she appears). When we last see her, Eden's face is frozen and masklike in the orange light of the street lamps (how far from the moonlight of Washington Square!). The "big career" has taken its toll in the way described by Thea Kronborg in *The Song of the Lark*: She has no personal life; her work has become that. "'It's like being woven into a big web. . . . It takes you up, and uses you, and spins you out; and that is your life. Not much else can happen to you.'"[14] But Eden Bower as actress and artist has another quality Willa Cather often wrote about long before she thought of Thea Kronborg or Eden Bower. What

14. Willa Cather, *The Song of the Lark* (Boston: Houghton Mifflin Company, Sentry Edition, 1963), p. 546.

is dead in the personal self comes alive when the artist creates. Once, interviewing Minnie Maddern Fiske, Willa Cather found her "very pale and weary looking," but as the actress entered into her theme "the color glowed in her cheeks as in live coals when you blow upon them."[15] And of Richard Mansfield's uncanny ability to take on other personalities, she wrote, as if in a letter:

> Each night you seem to wear the livery of a new master and to make your body the receptacle of a different soul. Each night your limbs seem moulded, your cheek seared, your eyes burned by the despotic usage of the particular passion you assume, as a house, long occupied, seems at last to conform to and even share the caprices of its tenant.[16]

So with Eden Bower: her face was hard and settled; "so a sail, that has been filled by a strong breeze, behaves when the wind suddenly dies. Tomorrow night the wind would blow again, and this mask would be the golden face of Clytemnestra," or, in the final version in *Youth and the Bright Medusa*, "the golden face of Aphrodite."

To play Aphrodite, to become Aphrodite, is a more accurate, and ultimate, destiny for Eden Bower than to play Clytemnestra, who fits only as a classic, ancient figure of the pagan past, the unfaithful woman. Clytemnestra is a character in Richard Strauss's opera *Electra*, though the part is not the leading one. Aphrodite has a more likely operatic role. It might be said first that the real-life figure whose career best fits the timing and circumstances of Eden Bower's life is Mary Garden. A girl from Illinois, she went to Paris at about the turn of the century to study and become famous, returning in later years to New York, and, like Eden, not as a member of the Metropolitan but belonging to the Chicago Opera Company. It was Mary Garden who was most identified with parts like Thaïs and Tosca, though Geraldine Farrar sang them, too. One unusual appearance is too close to the timing of Cather's story to be unrelated. On February 27, 1920, Mary Garden sang at the Lexington Theatre with the Chicago company in Erlanger's opera, *Aphrodite*, a work based on Pierre Louÿs's novel of the Alexandrian courtesan Chrysis, who exacted penalties from the sculptor Demetrios as a price of her love, though it was she who eventually was denied by Demetrios and condemned

15. Lincoln *Courier*, January 14, 1899, p. 3. Reprinted in *The World and the Parish: Willa Cather's Articles and Reviews, 1893–1902*, selected and edited with a commentary by William M. Curtin, 2 vols. (Lincoln: University of Nebraska Press, 1970), 2:660.
16. *Courier*, April 22, 1899, pp. 2–3; *The World and the Parish*, 2:677.

to drink the hemlock. The sculptor, preferring his religious worship of the goddess Aphrodite to possession of the woman, and making a model of Chrysis's dead body, devotes himself to his own creation of Aphrodite in art.[17] (Don Hedger, too, found his fingers flexing to draw Eden Bower as he first saw her in naked motion.) Moreover, another version of Louÿs's story, also called *Aphrodite*, had been staged as a dramatic spectacle or pageant in New York a few months earlier, opening December 1, 1919. In what order the parts of Clytemnestra and Aphrodite were given to Eden Bower to play, I am not sure. In the end, of course, the truth of Eden Bower must be that of the immortal goddess, golden Aphrodite; and of the love which is sometimes merely gold.

Was there something in New York that tricked one out of happiness? "Here in New York," Willa Cather wrote in a poem of this period,

> Here in New York, a city full of exiles,
> Short marriages and early deaths and heart-breaks . . . .[18]

No one can sensibly confine such brief, unhappy lives to one place, though it may happen in one life that the sense of exile is strongest somewhere in a city. And certainly as Willa Cather saw it, exile—or alienation, as it would be called in these later years—is one of the most poignant of all human sorrows. It is homesickness, and home-coming, that become themes for the two pieces of short fiction she published in the 1920s—"Uncle Valentine" and "Double Birthday." Both use memories from her Pittsburgh years, which ended only in 1916 with the marriage of her friend Isabelle McClung to Jan Hambourg and the dismantling of the McClung house in which she had lived and even from New York had returned to as a home and as a place to work. She had, then, been part of Pittsburgh for twenty years.

Willa Cather had published three earlier stories with Pittsburgh settings—"The Professor's Commencement" (1902) and "Paul's Case" (1905), which came from her teaching experiences; and "The Namesake" (1907). By the fall of 1905 she had also completed a novel with a Pittsburgh setting. Although, according to news accounts in Lincoln papers, the novel was to be published by McClure's book publishing division, which had just brought out *The Troll Garden* in the spring of 1905, and she was

17. See Pierre Louÿs, *Aphrodite*, translated from the French by Willis L. Parker (New York: Three Sirens Press, 1932). *Aphrodite* first appeared in 1896.
18. "A Silver Cup," *April Twilights and Other Poems* (New York: Alfred A. Knopf, 1923), pp. 62–64.

to deliver the manuscript to the company that September, the book was not published. Perhaps it was this manuscript Willa Cather recalled in a 1931 interview, saying that before she left Pittsburgh to work in New York she had destroyed the completed manuscript of a finished book, because "it wasn't good enough."[19]

What Cather returns to in "Uncle Valentine" are some experiences that had greatly stirred her imagination when she was working on the Pittsburgh *Leader* and met the composer Ethelbert Nevin, whose family owned the newspaper, and visited the Nevins in their home, Vineacre, in suburban Sewickley near the station of Edgeworth. She wrote several articles about Nevin, his music, and their home, as well as a moving account of his untimely death in February 1901.[20] A few years later, in the short story "'A Death in the Desert'" (1903), she suggested the personality and career of Nevin in the character of Adriance Hilgarde. As far as "Uncle Valentine" deals with the house called Greenacre near Pittsburgh, with a composer—Valentine Ramsay—who returns after travel abroad, with his unexpected death, and with his kind of music, it may be said to be about Ethelbert Nevin. Other elements of the story do not follow the facts. Nevin's marriage was, it seems, the opposite of the kind described for Valentine Ramsay, and Mrs. Nevin, according to her pictures, looked a little like the description of Charlotte Waterford, the neighbor and old friend who is most in rapport with Ramsay. Willa Cather once said that Mrs. Nevin was indeed her husband's inspiration.[21] Other factual elements may be related to the story: Willa Cather had also visited a musician friend, Mrs. John Slack, and her family, in their home near Vineacre, and there was a real choir of little girls who practiced with Nevin on Sundays. It is a fact, too, that in several years of friendship Willa Cather admired Nevin, thought him both a fine artist and a lovable man. It is important to realize, however, that whatever individual parts of the whole mosaic of a story may be taken from recognizable fact, the pattern is composed of imaginative as well as objective reality, recombined

19. Alice Booth, "America's Twelve Greatest Women: Willa Cather," *Good Housekeeping*, September 1931, p. 196.

20. *Courier*, February 5, 1898, pp. 3–4; "An Evening at Vineacre," *Courier*, July 15, 1899, pp. 4–5; "The Man Who Wrote 'Narcissus,'" *Ladies' Home Journal*, November 1900, p. 11; *Nebraska State Journal*, March 24, 1901, p. 13. Reprinted in part in *The World and the Parish*, 2:533–38, 626–42.

21. See John Tasker Howard, *Ethelbert Nevin* (New York: Thomas Y. Crowell Company, 1935). Nevin wrote to his wife in the summer of 1899: "I am dependent on you. Miss Cather was right—my melodies are you, my harmony is you, and my discords are yours" (p. 322).

as a kaleidoscope makes a new pattern out of bits and pieces, realigned
and mirrored. This Willa Cather once emphasized to her friend Carrie
Sherwood—about Ántonia, for instance. People found it hard to see
that a character in fiction is not made of arms and legs and faces of actual
people but is the embodiment of a feeling; a story is made of an emotion.[22]
The feeling or emotion that informs "Uncle Valentine" involves two
things: the belief that place is a part of the artist's own personal equipment,
an extension of and identification with his own creativity; and the belief
that, vulnerable as the artist may be in the chances of his world, his art
is inviolable and more lasting than even Pittsburgh steel.

During his year in Greenacre, with friends and children and room
for absorption in woods and fields of his home place, Valentine Ramsay
composes some of his best music. The place "was vocal to him." His
freedom to be and create on Fox Hill comes from a Thoreauvian or
Emersonian feeling that all these fields and woods belong to those that
love them and use them spiritually. They are lost for Ramsay when his
divorced, rich wife intrudes with the purchase of much of the land. To
Ramsay ownership of place is therefore defined: the world belongs to
what is rich and powerful, not to the imagination and spirit. His departure
from Greenacre and, in a few years, his death by accident at "barely
thirty," is another of the world's victories over the spirit. (Nevin himself
was older than that—thirty-seven—when he died. Again Willa Cather
is recreating and recombining. Valentine Ramsay's destiny is in fact,
and perhaps psychologically, more like that of Stephen Crane, another
artist Willa Cather admired. Crane was barely thirty when he died, after
a few last years of work that was not his best.) What prevented Ramsay
from continuing his best work? Things that always prevent, says his
friend Louise Ireland in the opening scene of the story: "marriage, money,
friends, the general social order." The artist works only by himself, in
his own way—if he can.

Valentine Ramsay worked best in his own place, the woods and
gardens and rooms of Greenacre and Fox Hill. Published in the same
year, 1925, Willa Cather's novel *The Professor's House* used as groundwork
the same thesis: Godfrey St. Peter could not leave the house where he had
lived his creative years; he could never work elsewhere, he insisted. The
house was like his body, his garden an ordering of his soul. The very

22. Letter to Carrie Miner Sherwood, January 27, 1934. Archives, Willa Cather
Pioneer Memorial, Red Cloud, Nebraska. Willa Cather stipulated in her will that her
letters should not be quoted.

vehemence of the theme in *The Professor's House* and the lesser but vibrant expression in "Uncle Valentine" suggest its personal importance to Willa Cather and serve as a commentary on one pattern in her life. It is evident from her letters that Willa Cather could write some places and not others. She had worked furiously for twenty years, off and on, in the McClung house in Pittsburgh. Its loss in 1916 was, I think, about as significant as the changing character of her friendships at the time of Isabelle McClung's marriage. She could work in her apartment in Bank Street, at the Shattuck Inn in Jaffrey, New Hampshire, especially well in her own tent in the meadows near the inn. She could not work in special studies created by and hovered over by her friends and family. Her father once wanted to make a study for her in Red Cloud. She did not want it; but on occasion she erected a canvas over the upper porch and worked there in a kind of tent. In 1920 she put up a tent near Hyères on the Mediterranean and worked there for six weeks. In the fall of 1920, says Edith Lewis, she was restless in Paris and "wanted to get home to work."[23] No, in 1923 she did not wish to live with the Hambourgs in the Parisian suburb of Ville d'Avray and work in a study they had prepared. She was ill that summer and could not work well anyway, but she also needed to find some place of her own, some place grown one with her creative history. Her next kind of tent, close to the weather, like her slanting attic room in the old house in Red Cloud, would be a plain cottage high on the cliffs of Grand Manan.

Like "Coming, Eden Bower!," the main story of "Uncle Valentine" is of a time around the turn of the century. The memories are, many of them, Willa Cather's own feeling about her entry into a world of artists and creators in which she first delighted when she came to Pittsburgh, and in which her friendship with Ethelbert Nevin had a particular glow. Charlotte Waterford's day in the city with Ramsay at Christmastime, as imagined by the narrator, is much the same kind of day Willa Cather described to her friends in Lincoln early in 1898: she had lately gone shopping with Nevin, he had carried her bundles, he had given her a bunch of violets big as a moon.[24] Told as a memory, both sweet and bitter, and played out in the mind—not too slowly, as the musical direction states—"Uncle Valentine" perfectly embodies its theme. In the story, which opens with a scene in Paris of the 1920s, Ramsay's songs are being rediscovered, captivating even the blasé young music student. Their

23. *Willa Cather Living*, p. 121.
24. Letter to Mariel Gere, January 10, 1898. Archives, Nebraska State Historical Society.

beauty is imperishable, even though person and place have largely disappeared. As the narrator concludes her memories of Uncle Valentine and the year she was sixteen, she repeats a line from one of the songs: "I know a wall where red roses grow." Although the houses of Fox Hill are all gone, the youngsters still sing that music: "The roses of song and the roses of memory, they are the only ones that last."

In all of her Pittsburgh stories preceding "Uncle Valentine" Willa Cather had used some elements of the industrial ugliness she found there in the early days, for she could remember a Pittsburgh sometimes black at noon from soot and smoke, and in the valleys blackened houses, neglected gardens, and sullen, lifeless rivers. In "Uncle Valentine" she also stresses the inflexibility of stone churches and the "harsh Calvinism" of the city, contrasted by the flowers and color of Valentine's world. But most important to the theme of the story is a closing statement: "The wave of industrial expansion swept down that valley, and roaring mills belch their black smoke up to the heights where those lovely houses used to stand." In both "Uncle Valentine" and *The Professor's House*—in 1925—Willa Cather wrote with considerable irony of America's will to plunder its own body and ravage its beauty. The destruction is described in "Uncle Valentine" as a kind of götterdämmerung, an image appropriately set in a pattern of allusions to Wagnerian story.

On one of their walks with Valentine across the hills, the group of friends see a luminous, ghostly brightness in the mists that have risen from the river, the moon in no solid image but "a flowing, surging, liquid gleaming." In one breath both Valentine and Charlotte murmur, "The Rhinegold!" That evening Uncle Valentine played the Rhine music from Wagner—"Siegmund's love song and the Valhalla music and back to the Rhine journey and the Rhine maidens. The cycle was like a plaything in his hands." The allusion to Wagner's Ring Cycle is specific. But Willa Cather's technique was never to follow a myth or allegory thoroughly and consistently. She wished rather to touch lightly and pass on, letting the suggestions develop as the course of individual imaginations might take them. So one need not look for a retelling of the Cycle here but a reinforcement of meaning and feeling with all the passion and force of Wagnerian music and myth. This kind of allusion is very well described by Gertrude Hall in *The Wagnerian Romances* (for which Willa Cather wrote a preface on its reissue in 1925). She is speaking of *The Rhinegold*: "One feels an allegory. As the poem unfolds, one is often conscious of it. It is well to hold the thread of it lightly and let it slip as soon as it becomes puzzling, settling down contentedly in the joy of simple story." In the same way, Willa Cather lets the Wagnerian allusions be the feeling, not the form, of an allegory. Some elements of the myth relate to "Uncle Valentine" rather directly, however. Miss Hall describes the Rhinegold as being in the river, "where it caught the beams of the sun and shed them down through the waves, brightening the dim water-world, gladdening the water-folk." The conflict in the Cycle is over the possession of the ring made from this mysterious gold. The owner could "force his thralls to mine and forge and so shape" the treasures of the earth "that they might be used to buy and subject the superior peoples," thus making him master of the world. The one condition is that the ring "could by no possibility be fashioned except by one who should have utterly renounced love."[25] Valentine, of course, is destroyed by power, by forces without love, and the ending of the story is a kind of twilight of the gods, Valhalla burned, and a new era beginning: a götterdämmerung, as the fires of industry take the valley and the wooded hills and the houses of the gods.

Observable in "Uncle Valentine" are other elements of theme and form that suggest something of Cather's habit: the intricate modeling under the smooth and fluent surface. We can note the combination of textures and patterns, like the crimson roses flowing over the stone wall. The story will remind us of the idea of a valentine, curved like a heart and patterned with roses, but this design is set with other geometric lines and balances like a Leonardo drawing, strengthening feeling with form. For balance, take the two houses, in one of them a group of men (most of them older, strange, disappointed) and one woman who runs the house, in the other a group of women (most of them young, hopeful) and one man who provides for them. Between them like a bridge (Waterford?) are Charlotte and Valentine, whose names, according to at least one dictionary, both mean "little strong one"[26]— two parts of a whole, identities. We are reminded of the time when both Valentine and Charlotte murmur "The Rhinegold!" in one breath, and the young girls are

25. Gertrude Hall, *The Wagnerian Romances*, with an introduction by Willa Cather (New York: Alfred A. Knopf, 1942; first published 1907), pp. 37–38.

26. Joseph T. Shipley, *Dictionary of Word Origins* (New York: The Philosophical Library, 1945), pp. 416, 428. That such symbolism in Cather is deliberate can be shown by a number of recurrences. For example, in *One of Ours* (1922) it is Gladys Farmer and Claude Wheeler who are spiritually joined; the names Gladys and Claude etymologically stem from one root and both mean "lame."

awed "not so much by the light, as by something in the two voices that had spoken together." For another balance, there is the alternation of inside and outside: rooms are built and torn down even as the weather changes over the hills. But the oneness lasts in a sense of place that is deep and sure, with evocations of the country, of snow and blooming through a golden year, that are like the best of Cather, and in her true voice.

In "Double Birthday" (1929) Willa Cather recalled with loving detail the scenes in Pittsburgh she had known well, from the poor on the South Side to the rich on Squirrel Hill. Judge Hammersley and his widowed daughter, Margaret Parmenter, suggest Judge McClung and his daughter Isabelle, and though its description is different, the Hammersley mansion suggests the McClung house high on a hill. The direction of the story is toward a reknitting of lives, a change of circles, as Margaret eventually goes back to her old friends, Albert Engelhardt, amateur musician and unsuccessful businessman, last of a large and formerly successful family in Pittsburgh and Allegheny, and his Uncle Albert. She goes to their double birthday celebration in their rooms on the South Side. The apartment itself is in every detail that of the George Seibels, so the late Mrs. Seibel once told me. There in her first years in Pittsburgh, especially, Willa Cather met with the Seibels on many warm and friendly occasions.

The most remarkable figure in the story is old Uncle Albert Engelhardt, eighty years old, both opinionated and wise, lover of wine and women, touching but proud in his disappointments. Albert Engelhardt is drawn from life, a salute to a Lincoln man who had been Willa Cather's good friend since 1893 when she was a student and beginning journalist. He was Dr. Julius Tyndale, a man of fifty when they first met and worked as drama critics on Lincoln newspapers. Tyndale also reviewed musical performances and was knowledgeable in all aspects of stage life; he had friends among the famous. He had come from New York in 1893 to practice in Lincoln, the brother of Mrs. Westermann who appears as Mrs. Erlich in One of Ours. His specialty was diseases of the throat and lungs (he had written a book on tuberculosis), and like Engelhardt was much interested in the voices of singers and their care. The identification of Albert Engelhardt with Julius Tyndale is more exact than in most of Willa Cather's portraits from life. In the winter of 1928–29 she apparently wrote him about the story, which was to appear in February, hoping that the portrait would not displease him. He answered on January 10,

1929, calling her "Dear Willa" and saying, "As to your story. How did it ever get into your head that I could or would take offense at anything you might borrow of my characteristics etc. The fact is that I am vain enough to feel flattered by any mention of my person." He closed with "Semper idem / J. H. Tyndale."[27] Dr. Tyndale was then alone in Lincoln, living at the Grand Hotel; he had never married. Five months later, in June 1929, Dr. Tyndale died, aged eighty-six. Willa Cather had for a number of years given him some small checks to help with his expenses.[28]

Very likely the story within the story—Dr. Engelhardt's effort to develop a promising young singer, frustrated by her sudden death—is imagined. The poignance of the Doctor's determined hope, even with its failure, gives his life a particular shine; once he had come that near to greatness, and the importance of his loss gives him stature. And, of course, there is a slight connection with the real life of Dr. Tyndale. He believed that he had helped Willa Cather in the beginning, and so he had—though he had also infuriated her and caused some talk in Lincoln because of his attentions. When he wrote for the *News* and she for the *Journal* there were interesting cross references. He teased her for her expression when she portrayed Electra looking at the dead Clytemnestra in a tableau presented by University students; he joked about her hearty appetite at Chautauqua in 1894; and he sometimes called her in print "the little critic with the potential mind"—using potential in the now rare meaning of potent rather than possible.

"Double Birthday" shows obscure lives with values that come from belief, desire, friendship, and shared memories. It is a positive story, hopeful with the inexorable force of life that will not be lost. It is a double birthday not only of the two Alberts but of a new period of relationships as Margaret Parmenter plans to continue meeting with the Engelhardts. When Uncle Albert is reminded that Margaret is to see him tomorrow, he replies in the pride of sheer manhood: "Even in our ashes." He is quoting from Gray's "Elegy" on those obscure lives who even in death do not want to be forgotten: "Ev'n from the tomb the voice of nature cries, / Ev'n in our ashes live their wonted fires."

"Double Birthday" more than any other story in this group of seven would fit with the tone of the Nebraska stories which followed it— "Neighbour Rosicky," "Old Mrs. Harris," and "Two Friends," collected

27. Letter loaned to me by Helen Cather Southwick.
28. I am indebted to the late Dr. L. V. Jacks for this information about Miss Cather's financial assistance.

in *Obscure Destinies* (1932). It also has the mystery, the symbolic strain, that infuses Willa Cather's best work. One element here—the doubleness—is also present enough in other works to demonstrate something characteristic and meaningful in her handling of material. The two Alberts with the same birthday (alike and different) suggest other divisions and unions: Valentine and Charlotte, in "Uncle Valentine"; the two faces of Eden Bower, dead in life and alive in art; Paul Wanning and his young self recalled as he writes his autobiography; in "Consequences" a trio—Kier Cavenaugh, his future self, and his dead twin brother, the athlete who died young but remains, in his picture, "lying on the air." One of the notable contrasts in the group of stories is between the earliest and the latest: in "Consequences" Kier Cavenaugh who would not face the future and therefore cancelled his life; in "Double Birthday" old Albert Engelhardt in whom the fires of life still burn. Perhaps this is the main story: the power of art, yes, but even more the power of human life and the mystery of human personality. Paul Wanning once mused on the frailty of man contrasted by the permanence of the materials with which he worked: "All this material rubbish lasted. The linen clothing and cosmetics of the Egyptians had lasted. It was only the human flame that certainly, certainly went out." And yet this short-lived race of beings, who had not even "a fighting chance" to survive, were those who began enterprises, built towers and ships, and moved and created. This strange power in man was Willa Cather's central theme.

BERNICE SLOTE

University of Nebraska–Lincoln

Pittsburgh Stories

Uncle Valentine

(Adagio non troppo)

✶ ✶ ✶

One morning not long ago I heard Louise Ireland give a singing lesson to a young countrywoman of mine, in her studio in Paris. Ireland must be quite sixty now, but there is not a break in the proud profile; she is still beautiful, still the joy of men, young and old. To hear her give a lesson is to hear a fine performance. The pupil was a girl of exceptional talent, handsome and intelligent, but she had the characteristic deficiency of her generation—she found nothing remarkable. She realized that she was fortunate to get in a few lessons with Ireland, but good fortune was what she expected, and she probably thought Ireland didn't every day find such good material to work with.

When the vocal lesson was over the girl said, "May I try that song you told me to look at?"

"If you wish. Have you done anything with it?"

"I've worked on it a little." The young woman unstrapped a roll of music. "I've tried over most of the songs in this book. I'm crazy about them. I never heard of Valentine Ramsay before."

"Sad for him," murmured the teacher.

"Was he English?"

"No, American, like you," sarcastically.

"I went back to the shop for more of his things, but they had only this one collection. Didn't he do any others?"

"A few. But these are the best."

"But I don't understand. If he could do things like these, why didn't he keep it up? What prevented him?"

"Oh, the things that always prevent one: marriage, money, friends, the general social order. Finally a motor truck prevented him, one of the first in Paris. He was struck and killed one night, just out of the window there, as he was going on to the Pont Royal. He was barely thirty."

The girl said "Oh!" in a subdued voice, and actually crossed the room to look out of the window.

"If you wish to know anything further about him, this American lady can tell you. She knew him in his own country. Now I'll see what you've done with that." Ireland shook her loose sleeves back from her white arms and began to play the song:

I know a wall where red roses grow . . . .

I

Yes, I had known Valentine Ramsay. I knew him in a lovely place, at a lovely time, in a bygone period of American life; just at the incoming of this century which has made all the world so different.

I was a girl of sixteen, living with my aunt and uncle at Fox Hill, in Greenacre. My mother and father had died young, leaving me and my little sister, Betty Jane, with scant provision for our future. Aunt Charlotte and Uncle Harry Waterford took us to live with them, and brought us up with their own four little daughters. Harriet, their oldest girl, was two years younger than I, and Elizabeth, the youngest, was just the age of Betty Jane. When cousins agree at all, they agree better than sisters, and we were all extraordinarily happy. The Ramsays were our nearest neighbors; their place, Bonnie Brae, sat on the same hilltop as ours—a houseful of lonely men (and such strange ones!) tyrannized over by a Swedish woman who was housekeeper.

Greenacre was a little railway station where every evening dogcarts and carriages drew up and waited for the express that brought the business men down from the City, and then rolled them along smooth roads to their dwellings, scattered about on the fine line of hills, clad with forest, that rose above a historic American river.

The City up the river it is scarcely necessary to name; a big inland American manufacturing city, older and richer and gloomier than most, also more powerful and important. Greenacre was not a suburb in the modern sense. It was as old as the City, and there were no small holdings. The people who lived there had been born there, and inherited their land from fathers and grandfathers. Every householder had his own stables and pasture land, and hay meadows and orchard. There were plenty of servants in those days.

My Aunt Charlotte lived in the house where she was born, and ever since her marriage she had been playing with it and enlarging it, as if she had foreseen that she was one day to have a large family on her hands. She loved that house and she loved to work on it, making it always more and more just as she wanted it to be, and yet keeping it what it always had been—a big, rambling, hospitable old country house. As one drove up the hill from the station, Fox Hill, under its tall oaks and sycamores, looked like several old farmhouses pieced together; uneven roofs with odd gables and dormer windows sticking out, porches on different levels connected by sagging steps. It was all in the dull tone of scaling brown paint and old brown wood—though often, as we came up the hill in the late afternoon, the sunset flamed wonderfully on the diamond-paned windows that were so gray and inconspicuous by day.

The house kept its rusty outer shell, like an old turtle's, all the while that it was growing richer in color and deeper in comfort within. These changes were made very cautiously, very delicately. Though my aunt was constantly making changes, she was terribly afraid of them. When she brought things back from Spain or Italy for her house, they used to stay in the barn, in their packing cases, for months before she would even try them. Then some day, when we children were all at school and she was alone, they would be smuggled in one at a time—sometimes to vanish forever after a day or two. There was something she wanted to get, in this corner or that, but there was something she was even more afraid of losing. The boldest enterprise she ever undertook was the construction of the new music-room, on the north side of the house, toward the Ramsays'. Even that was done very quietly, by the village workmen. The piano was moved out into the big square hall, and the door between the hall and the scene of the carpenters' activities was closed up. When, after a month or so, it was opened again, there was the new music-room, a proper room for chamber music, such as the petty kings and grand dukes of old Germany had in their castles; finished and empty, as it was to remain; nothing to be seen but a long room of satisfying proportions, with many wax candles flickering in the polish of the dark wooden walls and floor.

It was into this music-room that Aunt Charlotte called Harriet and me one November afternoon to tell us that Valentine Ramsay was coming home. She was sitting at the piano with a book of Debussy's piano pieces open before her. His music was little known in America then, but when she was alone she played it a great deal. She took a letter from between the leaves of the book. There was a flutter of excitement in her voice and in her features as she told us: "He says he will take the next fast steamer after his letter. He must be on the water now."

"Oh, aren't you happy, Aunt Charlotte!" I cried, knowing well how fond she was of him.

"Very, Marjorie. And a little troubled too. I'm not quite sure that people will be nice to him. The Oglethorpes are very influential, and now that Janet is living here—"

"But she's married again."

"Nevertheless, people feel that Valentine behaved very badly. He'll be here for Christmas, and I've been thinking what we can do for him. We must work very hard on our part songs. Good singing pleases him more than anything. I've been hoping he may fall into the way of composing again while he's with us. His life has been so distracted for the last few years that he's almost given up writing songs. Go to the playroom,

Harriet, and tell the little girls to get their school work done early. We'll have a long rehearsal tonight. I suppose they scarcely remember him."

Three years before Valentine Ramsay had been at home for several weeks before his brother Horace died. Even at that sad time his being there was like a holiday for us children, and all the Greenacre people seemed glad to have him back again. But much had happened since then. Valentine had deserted his wife for a singer, notorious for her beauty and misconduct; had, as my friends at school often told me, utterly disgraced himself. His wife, Janet Oglethorpe, was now living in her house in the City. I had seen her twice at Saturday matinées, and I didn't wonder that Valentine had run away with a beautiful woman. The second time I saw her very well—it was a charity performance, and she was sitting in a box with her new husband, a young man who was the perfection of good tailoring, who was reputed handsome, who appeared so, indeed, until you looked closely into his vain, apprehensive face. He was immensely conceited, but not sure of himself, and kept arranging his features as he talked to the women in the box. As for Janet, I thought her an unattractive, red-faced woman, very ordinary, as we said. Aunt Charlotte murmured in my ear that she had once been better looking, but that after her marriage with Valentine she had grown stouter and "coarsened"—my aunt hurried over the word.

Aunt Charlotte had never, I knew, approved of the marriage. When he was a little boy Valentine had been her squire and had loved her devotedly. After his mother died, leaving him in a houseful of grown men, she had looked out for him and tried to direct his studies. She was ten years older than Valentine, and, in the years when Uncle Harry came a-courting, the spoiled neighbor boy was always hanging about and demanding attention. He had a pretty talent for the piano, and for composition; but he wouldn't work regularly at anything, and there was no one to make him. He drifted along until he was a young fellow of twenty, and then he met Janet Oglethorpe.

Valentine had a habit of running up to the City to dawdle about the Steinerts' music store and practice on their pianos. The two young Steinert lads were musical and were great friends of his. It was there, when she went in to buy tickets for a concert, that Janet Oglethorpe first saw Valentine and heard him play. He was a strikingly handsome boy, and picturesque—certainly very different from the canny Oglethorpe men and their friends. Janet took to him at once, began inviting him to the house and asking musicians there to meet him. The Ramsays were greatly pleased; the Oglethorpes were the richest family in a whole cityful of rich people. They owned mines and mills and oil wells and gas works and farms and banks. Unlike some of our great Scotch families, they didn't become idlers and coupon-clippers in the third generation. They held their edge—kept their keenness for money as if they were just beginning, must sink or swim, and hadn't millions behind them. Janet was one of the third generation, and it was well known that she was as shrewd in business as old Duncan himself, the founder of the Oglethorpe fortune, who was still living, having buried three wives, and spry enough to attend directors' meetings and make plenty of trouble for the young men.

Janet was older than Valentine in years, and much older in experience and judgment. Even after she had announced her engagement to him, Aunt Charlotte prevailed upon him to go abroad to study for a little. He was happily settled in Paris, under Saint-Saëns, but before the year was out Janet followed him up and married him. They lived abroad. Aunt Charlotte had visited them in Rome, but she never said much about them.

Later, when the scandal came, and everyone in the City, and in Greenacre as well, fell upon Valentine for a worthless scamp, Uncle Harry and Aunt Charlotte always stood up for him, and said that when Janet married a flighty student she took the chance with her eyes open. Some of our friends insisted that he had shattered himself with drink, like so many of the Ramsay men; others hinted that he must "take something," meaning drugs. No one could believe that a man entirely in his right mind would run away from so much money—toss it overboard, mills and mines, stocks and bonds; and that when he had none himself, and Bonnie Brae was plastered with mortgages, and old Uncle Jonathan had already two helpless men to take care of.

II

For ten days after his letter came we waited and waited for Valentine. Everyone was restless—except Uncle Jonathan, who often told us that he enjoyed anticipation as much as realization. Uncle Morton, Valentine's much older brother, used to stumble in of an evening, when we were all gathered in the big hall after dinner, to announce the same news about boats that he had given us the evening before, wave his long thin hands a little, and boast in a husky voice about his gifted brother. Aunt Charlotte put her impatience to some account by rehearsing us industriously in the part songs we were working up for Valentine. She called us her sextette, and she trained us very well. Several of us were said to have good voices. My aunt used to declare that she liked us better when we were singing than at any other time, and that drilling us was the chief pleasure she got out of having such a large family.

Aunt Charlotte was the person who felt all that went on about her—and all that did not go on—and understood it. I find that I did not know her very well then. It was not until years afterward, not until after her death, indeed, that I began really to know her. Recalling her quickly, I see a dark, full-figured woman, dressed in dark, rich materials; I remember certain velvet dresses, brown, claret-colored, deep violet, which especially became her, and certain fur hats and capes and coats. Though she was a little overweight, she seemed often to be withdrawing into her clothes, not shrinking, but retiring behind the folds of her heavy cloaks and gowns and soft barricades of fur. She had to do with people constantly, and her house was often overflowing with guests, but she was by nature very shy. I now believe that she suffered all her life from a really painful timidity, and had to keep taking herself in hand. I have said that she was dark; her skin and hair and eyes were all brown. Even when she was out in the garden her face seemed always in shadow.

As a child I understood that my aunt had what we call a strong nature; still, deep and, on the whole, happy. Whatever it is that enables us to make our peace with life, she had found it. She cared more for music than for anything else in the world, and after that for her family and her house and her friends. She was very intelligent, but she had entirely too much respect for the opinions of others. Even in music she was often dominated by people who were much less discerning than she, but more aggressive. If her preference was disputed or challenged, she easily gave up. She knew what she liked, but she was apt to be apologetic about it. When she mentioned a composition or an artist she admired, or spoke the name of a person or place she loved, I remember a dark, rich color used to come into her voice, and sometimes she uttered the name with a curious little intake of the breath.

Aunt Charlotte's real life went on very deep within her, I suspect, though she seemed so open and cordial, and not especially profound. No one ever thought of her as intellectual, though people often spoke of her wonderful taste; of how, without effort, she was able to make her garden and house exactly right. Our old friends considered taste as something quite apart from intelligence, instead of the flower of it. She read little, it is true; what other people learned from books she learned from music, —all she needed to give her a rich enjoyment of art and life. She played the piano extremely well; it was not an accomplishment with her, but a way of living. The rearing of six little girls did not seem to strain her patience much. She allowed us a great deal of liberty and demanded her own in return. We were permitted to have our own thoughts and feelings, and even Elizabeth and Betty Jane understood that it is a great happiness to be permitted to be glad or sorry in one's own way.

III

On the night of Valentine's return, our household went in a body over to Bonnie Brae to make a short call. It was delightful to see the old house looking so festive, with lights streaming from all the windows. We found the family in the long, pale parlor; the men of the house, and half a dozen Ramsay cousins with their wives and children.

Valentine was standing near the fireplace when we entered, beside his father's armchair. The little girls at once tripped down the long room toward him, Uncle Harry following. But Aunt Charlotte stopped short in the doorway and stood there in the shadow of the curtains, watching Valentine across the heads of the company, as if she wished to remain an outsider. Through the buzz and flutter of greetings, his eyes found her there. He left the others, crossed the room in a flash, and, giving her a quick, sidewise look, put down his head to be kissed, like a little boy. As he stood there for a moment, so close to us, he struck me at once as altogether too young to have had so much history, as very hardy and high-colored and unsubdued. His thick, seal-brown hair grew on his head exactly like fur, there was no part in it anywhere. His short mustache and eyebrows had the same furry look. His red lips and white teeth gave him a striking freshness—there was something very roguish and wayward, very individual about his mouth. He seldom looked at one when he talked to one—he had a habit of frowning at the floor or looking fixedly at some object when he was speaking, but one felt his eyes through the lowered lids—felt his pleasure or his annoyance, his affection or impatience.

Since gay Uncle Horace died the Ramsay men did not often give parties, and that night they roamed about somewhat uneasily, all but Uncle Jonathan, who was always superbly at his ease. He kept his armchair, with a cape about his shoulders to protect him from drafts. The old man's hair and beard were just the color of dirty white snow, and he was averse to having them trimmed. He was a gracious host, having the air of one to whom many congratulations are due. Roland had put on a frock coat and was doing his duty, making himself quietly agreeable to everyone. His handsome silver-gray head and fine physique would have added to the distinction of any company. Uncle Morton was wandering about from group to group, jerking his hands this way and that—a curiously individual gesture from the wrist, as if he were making signals from a world too remote for speech. He fastened himself upon me, as he was very likely to do (finding me out in the little corner sofa to which I had retreated), sat down beside me and began talking about his brother in disconnected sentences, trying to focus his almost insensible eyes upon me.

"My brother is very devoted to your aunt. She must help me with his studio. We are going to make a studio for him off in the wing, for the quiet. Something very nice. I think I shall have the walls upholstered, like cushions, to keep the noise out. It will be handsome, you understand. We can give parties there—receptions. My brother is a fine musician. Could play anything when he was eleven—classical music—the most difficult compositions." In the same expansive spirit Uncle Morton had once planned a sunken garden for my aunt, and a ballroom for Harriet and me.

Molla Carlsen brought in cake and port and sherry. She had been at the door to admit us, and had since been intermittently in the background, disappearing and reappearing as if she were much occupied. She had always this air of moving quietly and efficiently in her own province. Molla was very correct in her deportment, was there and not too much there. She was fair, and good looking, very. The only fault Aunt Charlotte had to find with her appearance was the way she wore her hair. It was yellow enough to be showy in any case, and she made it more so by parting it very low on one side, just over her left ear, indeed, so that it lay across her head in a long curly wave, making her low forehead lower still and giving her an air that, as some of our neighbors declared, was little short of "tough."

After we had sipped our wine the cousins began to gather up their babies for departure, and we younger ones had all to go up to Uncle Jonathan and kiss him good night. It was a rite we shrank from, he was always so strong of tobacco and snuff, but he liked to kiss us, and there was no escape.

When we left, Uncle Valentine put his arm through Aunt Charlotte's and walked with us as far as the summerhouse, looking about him and up overhead through the trees. I heard him say suddenly, as if it had just struck him:

"Isn't it funny, Charlotte; no matter how much things or people ought to be different, what we love them for is for being just the same!"

IV

The next afternoon when Harriet and I got home from Miss Demming's school, we heard two pianos going, and knew that Uncle Valentine was there. The door between the big hall and the music-room was open, and Aunt Charlotte called to us:

"Harriet and Marjorie? Run upstairs and make yourselves neat. You may have tea with us presently."

When we came down, the music had ceased, and the hall was empty. Black John, coming through with a plate of toast, told us he had taken tea into the study.

My uncle's study was my favorite spot in that house full of lovely places. It was a little room just off the library, very quiet, like a little pond off the main currents of the house. There was but one door, and no one ever passed through it on the way to another room. As it had formerly been a conservatory for winter flowers, it was all glass on two sides, with heavy curtains one could draw at night to shut out the chill. There was always a little coal fire in the grate, Uncle Harry's favorite books on the shelves, and the new ones he was reading arranged on the table, along with his pipes and tobacco jars. Sitting beside the red coals one could look out into the great forking sycamore limbs, with their mottled bark of white and olive green, and off across the bare tops of the winter trees that grew down the hill slopes—until finally one looked into nothingness, into the great stretch of open sky above the river, where the early sunsets burned or brooded over our valley. It was with delight I heard we were to have our tea there.

We found my aunt and Valentine before the grate, the steaming samovar between them, the glass room full of gray light, a little warmed by the glowing coals.

"Aren't you surprised to find us here?" There was just a shade of embarrassment in my aunt's voice. "This was Uncle Valentine's choice." Curious; though she always looked so at ease, so calm in her matronly figure, a little thing like having tea in an unusual room could make her a trifle self-conscious and apologetic.

Valentine, in brown corduroys with a soft shirt and a Chinese-red necktie, was sitting in Uncle Harry's big chair, one foot tucked under him. He told us he had been all over the hills that morning, clear up to Flint Ridge. "I came home by the near side of Blinker's Hill, past the Wakeley place. I wish Belle wouldn't stay abroad so long; it's a shame to keep that jolly old house shut up." He said he liked having tea in the study because the outlook was the same as from his upstairs room at home. "I was always supposed to be doing lessons there as evening came on. I'm sure I don't know what I was doing—writing serenades for you, probably, Charlotte."

Aunt Charlotte was nursing the samovar along—it never worked very well. "I've been hoping," she murmured, "that you would bring me home some new serenades—or songs of some kind."

"Songs? Oh, hell, Charlotte!" He jerked his foot from under him and sat up straight. "Sorry I swore, but you evidently don't know what I've been up against these last four years. You'll have to know, and so will your maidens fair. Anyhow, if you're to have a rake next door to a house-ful of daughters, you'd better look into it."

Aunt Charlotte caught her breath painfully, glanced at Harriet and me and then at the door. Valentine sprang up, went to the door and closed it. "Oh, don't look so frightened!" he exclaimed irritably, "and don't send the girls away. Do you suppose they've heard nothing? What do you think girls whisper about at school, anyway? You'd better let me explain a little."

"I think it unnecessary," she murmured entreatingly.

"It isn't unnecessary!" he stamped his foot down upon the rug. "You mean they'll think what you tell them to—stay where you put them, like china shepherdesses. Well, they won't!"

We were almost as much frightened as Aunt Charlotte. He was standing before us, his brow wrinkled in a heavy frown, his shoulders lowered, his red lips thrust out petulantly. I am sure I was hoping that he wouldn't quite explain away the legend of his awful wickedness. As he addressed us he looked not at us but at the floor.

"You've heard, haven't you, Harriet and Marjorie, that I deserted a noble wife and ran away with a wicked woman? Well, she wasn't a wicked woman. She is kind and generous, and she ran away with me out of charity, to get me out of the awful mess I was in. The mess, you understand, was just being married to this noble wife. Janey is all right for her own kind, for Oglethorpes in general, but she was all wrong for me."

Here he stopped and made a wry face, as if his pedagogical tone put a bad taste in his mouth. He glanced at my aunt for help, but she was looking steadfastly at the samovar.

"Hang it, Charlotte," he broke out, "these girls are not in the nursery! They must hear what they hear and think what they think. It's got to come out. You know well enough what dear Janey is; you've known ever since you stayed with us in Rome. She's a common, energetic, close-fisted little tradeswoman, who ought to be keeping a shop and doing people out of their eyeteeth. She thinks, day and night, about common, trivial, worthless things. And what's worse, she talks about them day and night. She bargains in her sleep. It's what she can get out of this dressmaker or that porter; it's getting the royal suite in a hotel for the price of some other suite. We left you in Rome and dashed off to Venice that fall because she could get a palazzo at a bargain. Some English people had to go home on account of a grandmother dying and had to sub-let in a hurry. That was her only reason for going to Venice. And when we got there she did nothing but beat the house servants down to lower wages, and get herself burned red as a lobster staying out in boats all day to get her money's worth. I was dragged about the world for five years in an atmosphere of commonness and meanness and coarseness. I tell you I was paralyzed by the flood of trivial, vulgar nagging that poured over me and never stopped. Even Dickie—I might have had some fun with the little chap, but she never let me. She never let me have any but the most painful relations with him. With two nurses sitting idle, she'd make me chase off in a cab to demand his linen from special laundresses, or scurry around a whole day to find some silly kind of milk—all utter nonsense. The child was never sick and could take any decent milk. But she likes to make a fuss; calls it 'managing.'

"Sometimes I used to try to get off by myself long enough to return to consciousness, to find whether I had any consciousness left to return to —but she always came pelting after. I got off for Bayreuth one time. Thought I'd covered my tracks so well. She arrived in the middle of the Ring. My God, the agony of having to sit through music with that woman!" Valentine sat down and wiped his forehead. It glistened with perspiration; the roots of his furry hair were quite wet.

After a moment he said doggedly, "I give you my word, Charlotte, there was nothing for it but to make a scandal; to hurt her pride so openly that she'd have to take action. I don't know that she'd have done it then, if Seymour Towne hadn't turned up to sympathize with her. You can't hurt anybody as beefy as that without being a butcher!" He shuddered.

"Louise Ireland offered to be the sacrifice. She hadn't much to lose in the way of—well, of the proprieties, of course. But she's a glorious creature. I couldn't have done it with a horrid woman. Don't think anything nasty of her, any of you, I won't have it. Everything she does is lovely, somehow or other, just as every song she sings is more beautiful than it ever was before. She's been more or less irregular in behavior—as you've doubtless heard with augmentation. She had certainly run away with desperate men before. But behavior, I find, is more or less accidental, Charlotte. Oh, don't look so scared! Your dovelets will have to face facts some day. Æsthetics come back to predestination, if theology doesn't. A woman's behavior may be irreproachable and she herself may be gross —just gross. She may do her duty, and defile everything she touches. And another woman may be erratic, imprudent, self-indulgent if you like, and all the while be—what is it the Bible says? Pure in heart. People are as they are, and that's all there is to life. And now—" Valentine got up and went toward the door to open it.

Aunt Charlotte came out of her lethargy and held up her finger. "Valentine," she said with a deep breath, "I wasn't afraid of letting the girls hear what you had to say—not exactly afraid. But I thought it unnecessary. I understood everything as soon as I looked at you last night. One hasn't watched people from their childhood for nothing."

He wheeled round to her. "Of course *you* would know! But these girls aren't you, my dear! I doubt if they ever will be, even with luck!" The tone in which he said this, the proud, sidelong glance he flashed upon her, made this a rich and beautiful compliment—so violent a one that it seemed almost to hurt that timid woman. Slowly, slowly, the red burned up in her dark cheeks, and it was a long while dying down.

"Now we've finished with this—what a relief!" Valentine knelt down on the window seat between Harriet and me and put an arm lightly around each of us. "There's a fine sunset coming on, come and look at it, Charlotte."

We huddled together, looking out over the descending knolls of bare tree tops into the open space over the river, where the smoky gray atmosphere was taking on a purple tinge, like some thick liquid changing color. The sun, which had all day been a shallow white ring, emerged and swelled into an orange-red globe. It hung there without changing, as if the density of the atmosphere supported it and would not let it sink. We sat hushed and still, living in some strong wave of feeling or memory that came up in our visitor. Valentine had that power of throwing a mood over people. There was nothing imaginary about it; it was as real as any form of pain or pleasure. One had only to look at Aunt Charlotte's face, which had become beautiful, to know that.

It was Uncle Harry who brought us back into the present again. He had caught an early train down from the City, hoping to come upon us just like this, he said. He was almost pathetically eager for anything of this sort he could get, and was glad to come in for cold toast and tea.

"Awfully happy I got here before Valentine got away," he said, as he turned on the light. "And, Charlotte, how rosy you are! It takes you to do that to her, Val." She still had the dusky color which had been her unwilling response to Valentine's compliment.

V

Within a few days Uncle Valentine ran over to beg my aunt to go shopping with him. Something had reminded him that Christmas was very near.

"It's awfully embarrassing," he said. "Nobody in Paris was saying anything about Christmas before I sailed. Here I've come home with empty trunks, and Paris full of things that everybody wants."

Aunt Charlotte laughed at him and said she thought they would find plenty of things from Paris up in the City.

The next morning Valentine appeared before we left for school. He was in a very businesslike mood, and his check book was sticking out from the breast pocket of his fur coat. They were to catch the eight-thirty train. The day was dark and gray, I remember, though our valley was white, for there had been a snowfall the day before. Standing on the porch with my school satchel, I watched them get into the carriage and go down the hill as the train whistled for the station below ours—they would just have time to catch it. Aunt Charlotte looked so happy. She didn't often have Valentine to herself for a whole day. Well, she deserved it.

I could follow them in my mind: Valentine with his brilliant necktie and foreign-cut clothes, hurrying about the shops, so lightning-quick, when all the men they passed in the street were so slow and ponderous or, when they weren't ponderous, stiff—stiff because they were wooden, or because they weren't wooden and were in constant dread of betraying it. Everybody would be trying not to look at bright-colored, foreign-living, disgracefully divorced Valentine Ramsay; some in contempt—some in secret envy, because everything about him told how free he was. And up there, nobody was free. They were imprisoned in their harsh Calvinism, or in their merciless business grind, or in mere apathy—a mortal dullness.

Oh, I could see those two, walking about the narrow streets of the grim, raw, dark gray old city, cold with its river damp, and severe by reason of the brooding frown of huge stone churches that loomed up even in the most congested part of the shopping district. There were old grave-yards round those churches, with gravestones sunken and tilted and blackened—covered this morning with dirty snow—and jangling car lines all about them. The street lamps would be burning all day, on account of the fog, full of black smoke from the furnace chimneys. Hidden away in the grime and damp and noise were the half dozen special shops which imported splendors for the owners of those mills that made the city so dark and so powerful.

Their shopping over, Valentine was going to take Aunt Charlotte to lunch at a hotel where they could get a very fine French wine she loved. What a day they would have! There was only one thing to be feared. They might easily chance to meet one of the Oglethorpe men, there were so many of them, or Janet herself, face to face, or her new husband, Seymour Towne, who had been the idle son of an industrious family, and by idling abroad had stepped into such a good thing that now his hard-working brothers found life bitter in their mouths.

But they didn't meet with anything disagreeable. They came home on the four-thirty train, before the rush, bringing their spoils with them (no motor truck deliveries down the valley in those days), and their faces shone like the righteous in his Heavenly Father's house. Aunt Charlotte admitted that she was tired and went upstairs to lie down directly after tea. Valentine took me down into the music-room to show me where to put the blossoming mimosa tree he had found for Aunt Charlotte, when it came down on the express tomorrow. The little girls followed us, and when he told them to be still they crept into the corners.

Valentine sat down at the piano and began to play very softly; some-thing dark and rich and shadowy, but not somber, with a silvery air flowing through its mysteriousness. It might, I thought, be something of Debussy's that I had never heard . . . but no, I was sure it was not.

Presently he rose abruptly to go without taking leave, but one of the little girls ran up to him—Helen, probably, she was the most musical—and asked him what he had been playing, please.

"Oh, some old thing, I guess. I wasn't thinking," he muttered vaguely, and escaped through the glass doors that led directly into the garden between our house and his. I felt very sure that it was nothing old, but something new—just beginning, indeed. That would be a pleasant thing to tell Aunt Charlotte. I ran upstairs; the door of her room was ajar, but all was dark within. I entered on tiptoe and listened; she was sound asleep. What a day she had had!

VI

Aunt Charlotte planned a musical party for Christmas eve and invited a dozen or more of her old friends. They were coming home with her after the evening church service; we were to sing carols, and Uncle Valentine was to play. She telephoned the invitations, and made it very clear that Valentine Ramsay was going to be there. Whoever didn't want to meet him could decline. Nobody declined; some even said it would be a pleasure to hear him play again.

On Christmas eve, after dinner, Uncle Harry and I were left alone in the house. All the children went to the church with Aunt Charlotte; she left me to help Black John arrange the table for a late supper after the music. After I had seen to everything, I had an hour or so alone upstairs in my own room.

I well remember how beautiful our valley looked from my window that winter night. Through the creaking, shaggy limbs of the great sycamores I could look off at the white, white landscape; the deep folds of the snow-covered hills, the high drifts over the bushes, the gleaming ice on the broken road, and the thin, gauzy clouds driving across the crystal-clear, star-spangled sky.

Across the garden was Bonnie Brae, with so many windows lighted; the parlor, the library, Uncle Jonathan's room, Morton's room, a yellow patch on the snow from Roland's window, which I could not see; off there, at the end of the long, dark, sagging wing, Valentine's study, lit up like a lantern. I often looked over at our neighbors' house and thought about how much life had gone on in it, and about the muted, mysterious lives that still went on there. In the garret were chests full of old letters; all the highly descriptive letters that Uncle Jonathan had written his wife when he was traveling abroad; family letters, love letters, every letter the boys had written home when they were away at school. And in all these letters were tender references to the garden, the old trees, the house itself. And now so many of those who had loved the old place and danced in the long parlor were dead. I wondered, as young people often do, how my elders had managed to bear life at all, either its killing happiness or its despair.

I heard wheels on the drive, and laughter. Looking out I saw guests alighting on one side of the house, and on the other side Uncle Valentine running across the garden, bareheaded in the snow. I started downstairs with a little faintness at heart—I knew how much my aunt had counted on bringing Valentine again into the circle of her friends, under her own roof. I found him in the big hall, surrounded by the ladies—they hadn't yet taken off their wraps—and I surveyed them from the second landing where the stairway turned. They were doing their best, I thought. Some of the younger women kept timidly at the outer edge of the group, but all the ones who counted most were emphatic in their cordiality. Deaf old Mrs. Hungerford, who rather directed public opinion in Greenacre, patted him on the back, shouted that now the naughty boy had come home to be good, and thrust out her ear trumpet at him. Julia Knewstubb, who for some reason, I never discovered why, was an important person, stood beside him in a brassy, patronizing way, and Ida Milholland, the intellectual light of the valley, began speaking slow, crusty French at him. In short, all was well.

Salutations over, Aunt Charlotte led the way to the music-room and signaled to her six girls. We sang one carol after another, and a fragment of John Bennett's we had especially practiced for Uncle Valentine—a song about a bluebird flying over a gray landscape and making it all blue; a pretty thing for high voices. But when we finished this and looked about to see whether it had pleased him, Valentine was nowhere to be found. Aunt Charlotte drew me aside while the others went out to supper and told me I must search all through the house, go to Bonnie Brae if necessary, and fetch him. It would never do for him to behave thus, when they had unbent so far as to come and greet him.

I looked out of the window and saw a light in his study at the end of the wing. The rooms between his study and the main house were unused, filled with old furniture. He avoided that chain of dusty, echoing chambers and came and went by a back door that opened into the old apple orchard. I dashed across the garden and ran in upon him without knocking.

There he was, lounging before the fire in his slippers and wine-colored velvet jacket, a pipe in his mouth and a yellow French book on his knee. I gasped and explained to him that he must come at once; the company was waiting for him.

He shrugged and waved his pipe. "I'm not going back at all. Pouf, what's the use? I'd only behave badly if I did. I don't want to lose my temper on Christmas eve."

"But you promised Aunt Charlotte, and she's told them you'd play," I pleaded.

He flung down his book wrathfully. "Oh, I can't stand them! I didn't know who Charlotte was going to ask . . . seems to me she's got together all the most objectionable old birds in the valley. There's Julia Knewstubb, with her nippers hanging on her nose, looking more like a horse than ever. Old Mrs. Hungerford, poking her ear trumpet at me and stroking me on the back—I can't talk into an ear trumpet—can't think of anything important enough to say! And that bump of intellect, Ida Milholland, creaking at every joint and practicing her French grammar on me. Charlotte knows I hate ugly women—what did she get such a bunch together for? Not much, I'm not going back. Sit down and I'll read you something. I've got a new collection of all the legends about Tristan and Iseult. You can understand French?"

I said I would be dreadfully scolded if I did such a thing. "And you will hurt Aunt Charlotte's feelings, terribly!"

He laughed and poked out his red lower lip at me. "Shall I? Oh, but I can mend them again! Listen, I've got a new song for her, a good one. You sit down, and we'll work a spell on her; we'll wish and wish, and she'll come running over. While we wait I'll play it for you."

He put his pipe on the mantel, went to the piano, and commenced to play the Ballad of the Young Knight, which begins:

"From the Ancient Kingdoms,
Through the wood of dreaming, . . ."

It was the same thing I had heard him trying out the afternoon he and Aunt Charlotte got home from the City.

"Now, you try it over with me, Margie. It's meant for high voice, you see. By the time she comes, we can give her a good performance."

"But she won't come, Uncle Valentine! She can't leave her guests."

"Oh, they'll soon be gone! Old tabbies always get sleepy after supper —you said they were at supper. She'll come."

I was so excited, so distressed and delighted, that I made a poor showing at reading the manuscript, and was well scolded. Valentine always wrote the words of his songs, as well as the music, like the old troubadours, and the words of this one were beautiful. "And what wood do you suppose it is?" He played the dark music with his left hand.

I said it made me think of the wood on the other side of Blinker's Hill.

"I guess so," he muttered. "But of course it will be different woods to different people. Don't tell Charlotte, but I'm doing a lot of songs. I think of a new one almost every morning, when I waken up. Our woods are full of them, but they're terribly, terribly coy. You can't trap them, they're too wild. . . . No, you can't catch them . . . sometimes one comes and lights on your shoulder; I always wonder why."

It did not seem very long until Aunt Charlotte entered, bareheaded, her long black cape over her shoulders, a look of distress and anxiety on her face. Valentine sprang up and caught her hand.

"Not a word, Charlotte, don't scold, look before you leap! I kept Margie because I knew you'd come to hunt her, and I didn't just know any other way of getting you here. Now don't be angry, because when you get angry your face puffs up just a little, and I have reason to hate women whose faces swell. Sit down by the fire. We've had a rehearsal, and now we'll sing my new song for you. Don't glare at the child, or she can't sing. Why haven't you taught her to follow manuscript better?"

Aunt Charlotte didn't have a chance to speak until we had gone through with the song. But though my eyes were glued to the page, I knew her face was going through many changes.

"Now," he said exultantly as we finished, "with a song like that under my shirt, did I have to sit over there and let old Ida wise-bump practice her French on me—period of Bossuet, I guess!"

Aunt Charlotte laughed softly and asked us to sing it again. The second time we did better; Valentine hadn't much voice, but of course he knew how. As we finished we heard a queer sound, something like a snore and something like a groan, in the wall behind us. Valentine held up his finger sharply, tiptoed to the door behind the fireplace that led into the old wing, put down his head and listened for a moment. Then he wrenched open the door.

There stood Roland, holding himself steady by an old chest of drawers, his eyes looking blind, tears shining on his white face. He did not say a word; put his hands to his forehead as if to collect himself, and went away through the dark rooms, swaying slightly and groping along the floor with his feet.

"Poor old chap, perfectly soaked! I thought it was Molla Carlsen, spooking round." Valentine threw himself into a chair. "Do you suppose that's the way I'll be keeping Christmas ten years from now, Charlotte?

What else is there for us to do, I ask you? Sons of an easy-going, self-satisfied American family, never taught anything until we are too old to learn. What could Roland do when he came home from Germany fifteen years ago? . . . Lord, it's more than that now . . . it's nineteen! Nineteen years!" Valentine dropped his head into his hands and rumpled his hair as if he were washing it, which was a sign with him that a situation was too hopeless for discussion. "Well, what could he have done, Charlotte? What could he do now? Teach piano, take the bread out of somebody's mouth? My son Dickie, he'll be an Oglethorpe! He'll get on, and won't carry this damned business any farther."

On Christmes morning Molla Carlsen came over and reported with evident satisfaction that Roland and Valentine had made a night of it, and were both keeping their rooms in consequence. Aunt Charlotte was sad and downcast all day long.

VII

Molla Carlsen loved to give my aunt the worst possible account of the men she kept house for, though in talking to outsiders I think she was discreet and loyal. She was a strange woman, then about forty years old, and she had been in the Ramsay household for more than twelve years. She managed everything over there, and was paid very high wages. She was grasping, but as honest as she was heartless. The house was well conducted, though it was managed, as Valentine said, somewhat like an institution. No matter how many thousand roses were blooming in the garden, it never occurred to Molla to cut any and put them in the bare, faded parlor. The men who lived there got no coddling; they were terribly afraid of her. When a wave of red went over Molla's white skin, poor Uncle Morton's shaky hands trembled more than ever, and his faraway eyes shrank to mere pin-points. He was the one who most often angered her, because he dropped things. Once when Aunt Charlotte remonstrated with her about her severity, she replied that a woman who managed a houseful of alcoholics must be a tyrant, or the place would be a sty.

This made us all indignant. Morton, we thought, was the only one who could justly be thus defined. He was the oldest of Uncle Jonathan's sons; tall, narrow, utterly spare, with a long, thin face, a shriveled scalp with a little dry hair on it, parted in the middle, eyes that never looked at you because the pupils were always shrunk so small. Morton was awfully proud of the fact that he was a business man; he alone of that household went up on the business men's train in the morning. He went to an office in the City, climbed upon a high stool, and fastened his distant eyes upon a ledger. (It was a coal business, in which his father owned a good deal of stock, and every night an accountant went over Morton's books and corrected his mistakes.) On his way to the office, he stopped at the bar of a most respectable hotel. He stopped there again before lunch at noon, and on his way to the station in the late afternoon. He often told Uncle Harry that he never took anything during business hours. Nobody ever saw Morton thoroughly intoxicated, but nobody ever saw him quite himself. He had good manners, a kind voice, though husky, and he was usually very quiet.

Uncle Jonathan, to be sure, took a good deal of whisky during the day—but then he ate almost nothing. Whisky and tobacco were his nourishment. He was frail, but he had been so even as a young man, and he outlived all his sons except Morton—lived on until the six little girls at Fox Hill were all grown women. No, I don't think it was alcohol that preserved him; I think it was his fortunate nature, his happy form of self-esteem. He was perfectly satisfied with himself and his family—with whatever they had done and whatever they had not done. He was glad that Roland had declined the nervous strain of an artistic career, and that Morton was in business; in each generation some of the Ramsays had been business men. Uncle Jonathan had loved his wife dearly and he must have missed her, but he was pleased with the verses he had written about her since her death, verses in the manner of Tom Moore, whom he considered an absolutely satisfactory poet. He had, of course, been proud of Valentine's brilliant marriage. The divorce he certainly regretted. But whatever pill life handed out to him he managed to swallow with equanimity.

Uncle Jonathan spent his days in the library, across the hall from the parlor, where he was writing a romance of the French and Indian wars. The room was lined with his father's old brown theological books, and everything one touched there felt dusty. There was always a scattering of tobacco crumbs over the hearth, the floor, the desk, and over Uncle Jonathan's waistcoat and whiskers. It wasn't in Molla Carlsen's contract to keep the tobacco dust off her master.

Roland Ramsay was Uncle Jonathan's much younger brother. When he was a boy of twelve and fourteen, he had been a musical prodigy, had played to large and astonished audiences in New York and

Boston and Philadelphia. Later he was sent to Germany to study under Liszt and D'Albert. At twenty-eight he returned to Bonnie Brae—and he had been there ever since. He was a big, handsome man, never ill, but something had happened to his nervous system. He could not play in public, not even in his own city. Ever since Valentine was a little boy, Uncle Roland and his piano had lived upstairs at Bonnie Brae. There were several stories: that he had been broken by a love affair with a German singer; that Wagner had hurt his feelings so cruelly he could never get over it; that at his début in Paris he had forgotten in the middle of his sonata in what key the next movement was written, and had labored through the rest of his program like a man stupefied by drugs.

At any rate, Roland had broken nerves, just as some people have a weak heart, and he lived in solitude and silence. Occasionally when some fine orchestra or a new artist played in the City up the river, Roland's waxy, frozen face was to be seen in the audience; but not often. Five or six times a year he went on a long spree. Then he would shut himself up in his room and play the piano—it couldn't be called practicing—for eight or ten hours a day. Sometimes in the evening Aunt Charlotte would put on a cloak and go out into the garden to listen to him. "Harry," she said once when she came back into the house, "I was walking under Roland's window. Really, he is playing like a god tonight."

Inert and inactive as he was, Roland kept his good physique. He used to sit all afternoon beside his window with a book; as we came up the hill we could see his fine head and shoulders there, motionless as if in a frame. I never liked to look at his face, for his strong, well-cut features never moved. His eyes were large and uncomfortable-looking, under heavy lids with deep hollows beneath—curiously like the eyes of the tired American business men whose pictures appear in the papers when they are getting a divorce.

I had heard it whispered at school that Uncle Jonathan was "in Molla Carlsen's power," because Horace, the wild son, had made vehement advances to her long ago when she first came into the house, and that his bad behavior had hastened his mother's end. However it came about, in her power the lonely men at Bonnie Brae certainly were. When Molla was dressed to go up to the City, she walked down the front steps and got into the carriage with the air of mistress of the place. And her furs, we knew, had cost more than Aunt Charlotte's.

VIII

All that winter Valentine was tremendously busy. He was not only writing ever so many new songs, but was hunting up beautiful old ones for our sextette, and he trained us so industriously that the little girls fell behind in their lessons, and Aunt Charlotte had to limit rehearsals to three nights a week. I remember he made us an arrangement for voices of the minuet in the third movement of Brahms' second symphony, and wrote words to it.

We were not allowed to sing any of Valentine's songs in company, not even for Aunt Charlotte's old friends. He was rather proud and sulky with most of the neighbors, and wouldn't have it. When we tried out his new songs for the home circle, as he said, Uncle Morton was allowed to come over, and Uncle Jonathan in his black cape. Roland came too, and sat off in a corner by himself. Uncle Jonathan thought very well of his own judgment in music. He liked all Valentine's songs, but warned him against writing things without a sufficient "climax," mildly bidding him beware of a too modern manner.

I remember he used to repeat for his son's guidance two lines from one of his favorite poets, accenting the measure with the stogie he held in his fingers—a particularly noxious kind of cigar which he not only smoked but, on occasion, ate!

"Avoid eccentricity, Val," he would say, beaming softly at his son. "Remember this admirable rule for poets and composers:

Be not the first by whom the new is tried,
Nor yet the last to lay the old aside."

That year the spring began early. I remember March and April as a succession of long walks and climbs with Valentine. Sometimes Aunt Charlotte went with us, but she was not a nimble walker, and Valentine liked climb and dash and short-cut. We would plunge into the wooded course of Blue Run or Powhatan Creek, and get to the top of Flint Ridge by a quicker route than any path. That long, windy ridge lay behind Blinker's Hill and Fox Hill; the top was a bare expanse, except for a few bleached boulders and twisted oaks. From there we could look off over all the great wrinkles of hills, catch glimpses of the river, and see the black pillar of cloud to the north where the City lay. This dark cloud, as evening came on, took deep rich colors from the sunset; and after the sun was gone it sent out all night an orange glow from the furnace fires that burned there. But that smoke did not come down to us; our evenings were pure and silvery—soft blue skies seen through the budding trees above us, or over the folds and folds of lavender forest below us.

One Saturday afternoon we took Aunt Charlotte along and got to the top of Flint Ridge by the winding roadway. As we were walking upon the crest, curtains of mist began to rise from the river and from between the lines of hills. Soon the darkening sky was full of fleecy clouds, and the countryside below us disappeared into nothingness.

Suddenly, in the low cut between the hills across the river, we saw a luminousness, throbbing and phosphorescent, a ghostly brightness with mists streaming about it and enfolding it, struggling to quench it. We knew it was the moon, but we could see no form, no solid image; it was a flowing, surging, liquid gleaming; now stronger, now softer.

"The Rhinegold!" murmured Valentine and Aunt Charlotte in one breath. The little girls were silent; Betty Jane felt for my hand. They were awed, not so much by the light, as by something in the two voices that had spoken together. Presently we dropped into the dark winding road along Blue Run and got home late for dinner.

While we were at dessert, Uncle Valentine went into the music-room and began to play the Rhine music. He played on as if he would never stop; Siegmund's love song and the Valhalla music and back to the Rhine journey and the Rhine maidens. The cycle was like a plaything in his hands. Presently a shadow fell in the patch of moonlight on the floor, and looking out I saw Roland, without a hat, standing just outside the open window. He often appeared at the window or the doorway when we were singing with Valentine, but if we noticed him, or addressed him, he faded quickly away.

As Valentine stopped for a moment, his uncle tapped on the window glass.

"Going over now, Valentine? It's getting late."

"Yes, I suppose it is. I say, Charlotte, do you remember how we used to play the Ring to each other hours on end, long ago, when Damrosch first brought the German opera over? Why can't people stay young forever?"

"Maybe you will, Val," said Aunt Charlotte, musing. "What a difference Wagner made in the world, after all!"

"It's not a good thing to play Wagner at night," said the gray voice outside the window. "It brings on sleeplessness."

"I'll come along presently, Roland," the nephew called. "I'm warm now; I'll take cold if I go out."

The large figure went slowly away.

"Poor old Roland, isn't he just a coffin of a man!" Valentine got up and lit the fagots in the fireplace. "I feel shivery. I've had him on my hands a good deal this winter. He'll come drifting in through the wing and settle himself in my study and sit there half the night without opening his head."

"Doesn't he talk to you, even?" I asked.

"Hardly, though I get fidgety and talk to him. Sometimes he plays. He's always interesting at the piano. It's remarkable that he plays as well as he does, when he's so irregular."

"Does he really read? We so often see him sitting by his upstairs window with a book."

"He reads too much, German philosophy and things that aren't good for him. Did you know, Charlotte, that he keeps a diary. At least he writes often in a big ledger Morton brought him from town. Sometimes he's at it for hours. Lord, I'd like to know what he puts down in it!" Valentine plunged his head in his hands and began rumpling his hair. "Can you remember him much before he went abroad, Charlotte?"

"When I was little I was taken to hear him play in Steinway Hall, just before he went to Germany. From what I can remember, it was very brilliant. He had splendid hands, and a wonderful memory. When he came back he was much more musical, but he couldn't play in public."

"Queer! How he supports the years as they come and go. . . . Of course, he loves the place, just as I do; that's something. By the way, when I was home three years ago I was let into a family secret; it was Roland who was Molla Carlsen's suitor and made all the row, not poor Horace at all! Oh, shouldn't I have said that before the sextette? They'll forget it. They forget most things. What haunts me about Roland is the feeling of kinship. So often it flashes into my mind: 'Yes, I might be struck dumb some day, just like that.' Oh, don't laugh! It *was* like that, for months and months, while I was trying to live with Janet. My skin would get yellow, and I'd feel a perfect loathing of speech. My jaws would set together so that I couldn't open them. I'd walk along the quais in Paris and go without a newspaper because I couldn't bring myself to say good-morning to the old woman and buy one. I'd wander about awfully hungry because I couldn't bear the sound of talk in a restaurant. I dodged everybody I knew, or cut them."

There was something funny about his self-commiseration, and I wanted to hear more; but just at this point we were told that we must go instantly to bed.

"And I?" Valentine asked, "must I go too?"

"No. You may stay a little longer."

Aunt Charlotte must have thought he needed a serious talking-to, for she almost never saw him alone. Her life was hedged about by very subtle but sure conventionalities, and that was only one of many things she did not permit herself.

IX

Fox Hill was soon besieged on all sides by spring. The first attack came by way of the old apple orchard that ran irregularly behind our carriage house and Uncle Valentine's studio. The foaming, flowery trees were a beautiful sight from his doorstep. Aunt Charlotte and Morton were carrying on a hot rivalry in tulips. Uncle Jonathan now came out to sun himself on the front porch, in a broad-rimmed felt hat and a green plaid shawl which his father used to wear on horseback trips over the hills.

Though spring first attacked us through the orchard, the great assault, for which we children waited, came on the side of the hill next the river; it was violent, blood-red, long drawn-out, and when it was over, our hill belonged to summer. The vivid event of our year was the blooming of the wall.

Along the front of Fox Hill, where the lawn ended in a steep descent, Uncle Harry had put in a stone retaining wall to keep the ground from washing out. This wall, he said, he intended to manage himself, and when he first announced that he was going to cover it with red rambler roses, his wife laughed at him and told him he would spoil the whole hill. But in the event she was converted. Nowhere in the valley did ramblers thrive so well and bloom so gorgeously. From the railway station our home-coming business men could see that crimson wall, running along high on the green hillside.

One Sunday morning when the ramblers were at their height, we all went with Uncle Harry and Valentine down the driveway to admire them. Aunt Charlotte admitted that they were very showy, very decorative, but she added under her breath that she couldn't feel much enthusiasm for scentless roses.

"But they are quite another sort of thing," Uncle Harry expostulated.

"They go right about their business and bloom. I like their being without an odor; it gives them a kind of frankness and innocence."

In the bright sunlight I could see her dark skin flush a little. "Innocence?" she murmured, "I shouldn't call it just that."

I was wondering what she would call it, when our stableman Bill came up from the post office with his leather bag and emptied the contents on the grass. He always brought the Ramsays' mail with ours, and we often teased Uncle Valentine about certain bright purple letters from Paris, addressed to him in a woman's hand. Because of the curious ways of mail steamers they sometimes came in pairs, and that morning there were actually five of these purple punctuations in the pile of white letters. The children laughed immoderately. Betty Jane and Elizabeth shouted for joy as they fished them out. "Poor Uncle Val! When will you ever get time to answer them all?"

"Ah, that's it!" he said as he began stuffing them away in his pockets.

The next afternoon Aunt Charlotte and I were sewing, seated in the little covered balcony out of her room, with honeysuckle vines all about us. We saw Valentine, hatless, in his striped blazer, come around the corner of the house and seat himself at the tea-table under one of the big sycamores, just below us. We were about to call to him, when he took out those five purple envelopes and spread them on the table before him as if he were going to play a game with them. My aunt looked at me with a sparkle in her eye and put her finger to her lips to keep me quiet. Elizabeth came running across from the summerhouse with her kitten. He called to her.

"Just a moment, Elizabeth. I want you to choose one of these."

"But how? What for?" she asked, much astonished.

"Oh, just choose one, any one," he said carelessly. "Put your finger down." He took out a lead pencil. "Now, we'll mark that 1. Choose again; very well, that's number 2; another, another. Thank you. Now the one that's left will necessarily be 5, won't it?"

"But, Uncle Val, aren't these the ones that came yesterday? And you haven't read them yet?"

"Hush, not so loud, dear." He took up his half-burned cigarette. "You see, when so many come at once, it's not easy to know which should be read first. But you've settled that difficulty for me." He swept them lightly into the two side pockets of his blazer and sprang up. "Where are the others? Can't we go off for a tramp somewhere? Up Blue Run, to see the wild azaleas?"

Elizabeth came into the house calling for us, and Aunt Charlotte and I went down to him.

"We're going up Blue Run to see the azaleas, Charlotte, won't you come?"

She looked wistful. "It's very hot. I'm afraid I ought not to climb, and you'll want to go the steep way."

She waited, hoping to be urged, but he said no more about it. He was sometimes quite heartless.

That evening we came home tired, and the little girls were sent to bed soon after dinner. It was the most glorious of summer nights; I couldn't think of giving it up and going to sleep. Our valley was still, breathlessly still, and full of white moonlight. The garden gave off a heavy perfume, the lawn and house were mottled with intense black and intense white, a mosaic so perplexing that I could hardly find my way along the familiar paths. There was a languorous spirit of beauty abroad—warm, sensuous, oppressive, like the pressure of a warm, clinging body. I felt vaguely afraid to be alone.

I looked for Aunt Charlotte, and found her in the little balcony off her bedroom, where we had been sitting that morning. She spoke to me impatiently, in a way that quite hurt my feelings.

"You must go to bed, Marjorie. I have a headache and I can't be with anyone tonight."

I could feel that she did not want me near her, that my intrusion was most unwelcome. I went downstairs. Uncle Harry was in his study, doing accounts.

"Fine night, isn't it?" he said cheerfully. "I'm going out to see a little of it presently. Almost done my figures." His accounts must have troubled him sometimes; his household cost a great deal of money.

I retreated to the apple orchard. Seeing that the door of Valentine's study was open, I approached cautiously and looked in. He was on his divan, which he had pulled up into the moonlight, lying on his back with his arms under his head.

"Run away, Margie, I'm busy," he muttered, not looking at me but staring past me.

I walked alone about the garden, smelling the stocks until I could smell them no more. I noticed how many moonflowers had come out on the Japanese summerhouse that stood on the line between our ground and the Ramsays'. As I drew near it I heard a groan, not loud, but long, long, as if the unhappiness of a whole lifetime were coming out in one despairing breath. I looked in through the vines. There sat Roland, his head in his hands, the moonlight on his silver hair. I stole softly away through the grass. It seemed that tonight everyone wanted to be alone with his ghost.

Going home through the garden I heard a low call; "Wait, wait a minute!" Uncle Morton came out of the darkness of the vine-covered side porch and beckoned me to follow him. He led me to the plot where his finest roses were in bloom and stopped before a bush that had a great many buds on it, but only one open flower—a great white rose, almost as big as a moonflower, its petals beautifully curled.

"Wait a minute," he whispered again. He took out his pocket knife, and with great care and considerable difficulty managed to cut the rose with a long stem. He held it out to me in his shaking hand. "There," he said proudly. "That's my best one, the Queen of Savoy. I've been waiting for someone to give it to!"

This was a bold adventure for Morton. I saw that he meant it as a high compliment, and that he was greatly pleased with himself as he wavered back along the white path and disappeared into the darkness under the honeysuckle vines.

X

The next morning Valentine went up to town with Morton on the early train, and at six o'clock that evening Morton came back without him. Aunt Charlotte, who was watching in the garden, went quickly across the Ramsays' lawn.

"Morton, where is Valentine?"

Morton stood holding his straw hat before him in both hands, telling her vaguely that Valentine was going to spend the night in town, at a hotel. "He has to be near the cable office—been sending messages all day—something very important."

Valentine remained in the City for several days. We did not see him again until he joined us one afternoon when we were having tea in the garden. He looked fresh and happy, in new white flannels and one of his gayest neckties.

"Oh, it's delightful to be back, Charlotte!" he exclaimed as he sank into a chair near her.

"We've missed you, Valentine." She, too, looked radiantly happy.

"I should hope so! Because you're probably going to have a great deal of me. Likely I'm here forever, like Roland and the oak trees. I've been staying up in the City, on neutral ground for a few days, to find out what I really want. Do you know, Betty Jane and Elizabeth, that's a sure test; the place you wish for the first moment you're awake in the morning, is the place where you most want to be. I often want to do two things at once, be in two places at once, but this time I don't think I had a moment's indecision." He did not say about what, but presently he drew off a seal ring he wore on his little finger and began playing with it. I knew it was Louise Ireland's ring, he had told me so once. It was an intaglio, a three-masted ship under full sail, and over it, in old English letters, *Telle est la Vie*.

He sat playing with the ring, tossing it up into the sunlight and catching it in his palm, while he addressed my aunt.

"Ireland's leaving Paris. Off for a long tour in South Africa and Australia. She's like a sea gull or a swallow, that woman, forever crossing water. I'm sorry I can't be with her. She's the best friend I've ever had—except you, Charlotte." He did not look at my aunt, but the drop in his voice was a look. "I do seem to be tied to you."

"It's the valley you're tied to. The place is necessary to you, Valentine."

"Yes, it's the place, and it's you and the children—it's even Morton and Roland, God knows why!"

Aunt Charlotte was right. It was the place. The people were secondary. Indeed, I have often wondered, had he been left to his own will, how long he would have been content there. A man under thirty does not settle down to live with old men and children. But the place was vocal to him. During the year that he was with us he wrote all of the thirty-odd songs by which he lives. Some artists profit by exile. He was one of those who do not. And his country was not a continent, but a few wooded hills in a river valley, a few old houses and gardens that were home.

XI

The summer passed joyously. Valentine went on making new songs for us and we went on singing them. I expected life to be like that forever. The golden year, Aunt Charlotte called it, when I visited her at Fox Hill years afterward. September came and went, and then a cold wind blew down upon us.

Uncle Harry and Morton came home one night with disturbing news. It was said in the City that the old Wakeley estate had been sold. Miss Belle Wakeley, the sole heir, had lived in Italy for several years; her big house on the unwooded side of Blinker's Hill had been shut up, her many acres rented out or lying idle.

Very soon after Uncle Harry startled us with this news, Valentine came over to ask whether such a thing were possible. No large tract of land had changed hands in Greenacre for many years.

"I rather think it's true," said Uncle Harry. "I'm going to the agent tomorrow to find out any particulars I can. It seems to be a very guarded transaction. I suppose this means that Belle has decided to live abroad for good. I'm sorry."

"It's very wrong of her," said Aunt Charlotte, "and I think she'll regret it. If she hasn't any feeling for her property now, she will have some day. Why, her grandfather was born there!"

"Yes, I'm disappointed. I thought Belle had a great deal of sentiment underneath." Uncle Harry had always been Miss Wakeley's champion, liked her independent ways, and was amused by her brusque manners.

Valentine was standing by the fireplace, abstracted and deeply concerned.

"Just how much does the Wakeley property take in, Harry? I've never known exactly."

"A great deal. It covers the courses of both creeks, Blue Run and Powhatan Creek, and runs clear back to the top of Flint Ridge. It's our biggest estate, by long odds."

Valentine began pacing the floor. "Did you know she wanted to sell? Couldn't the neighbors have clubbed together and bought it, rather than let strangers in?"

Uncle Harry laughed and shook his head. "I'm afraid we're not rich enough, Val. It's worth a tremendous lot of money. Most of us have all the land we can take care of."

"I suppose so," he muttered. "Father's pretty well mortgaged up, isn't he?"

"Pretty well," Uncle Harry admitted. "Don't worry. I'll see what I can find out tomorrow. I can't think Belle would sell to a speculator, and let her estate be parceled out. She'd have too much consideration for the rest of us. She was the finest kind of neighbor. I wish we had her back."

"It never occurred to me, Harry, that the actual countryside could be sold; the creeks and woods and hills. That shouldn't be permitted. They ought to be kept just as they are, since they give the place its character."

Uncle Harry said he was afraid the only way of keeping a place the same, in this country, was to own it.

"But there are some things one doesn't think of in terms of money," Valentine persisted. "If I'd had bushels of money when I came home last winter, it would never have occurred to me to try to buy Blinker's Hill, any more than the sky over it. I didn't know that the Wakeleys or anybody else owned the creeks, and the forest up toward the Ridge."

Aunt Charlotte rose and went up to Uncle Harry's chair. "Is it really too late to do anything? Too late to cable Belle and ask her to give her neighbors a chance to buy it in first?"

"My dear, you never do realize much about the cost of things. But remember, Belle is a shrewd business woman. She knows well enough that no dozen of her neighbors could raise so much ready money. I understand it's a cash transaction."

Aunt Charlotte looked hurt. "Well, I can only say it was faithless of her. People have some responsibility toward the place where they were born, and toward their old friends."

Dinner was announced, and Valentine was urged to stay, but he refused.

"I don't want any dinner, I'm too nervous. I'm awfully fussed by this affair, Charlotte." He stood beside my aunt at the door for a moment, hanging his head despondently, and went away.

That evening my aunt and uncle could talk of nothing but the sale of the Wakeley property. Uncle Harry said sadly that he had never before so wished that he were a rich man. "Though even if I were, I don't know that I'd have thought of making Belle an offer. I'm as impractical as Valentine. But if I'd had money, I do believe Belle would have given me the first chance. We're her nearest neighbors, and whoever buys Blinker's Hill has to be a part of our landscape, and to come into our life more or less."

"Have you any suspicion who it may be?" She spoke very low.

Uncle Harry was standing beside her, his back to the hall fire, smoking his church-warden pipe. "The purchaser? Not the slightest. Have you?"

"Yes." She spoke lower still. "A suspicion that tortures me. It flashed into my mind the moment you told us. I don't know why."

"Then keep it to yourself, my dear," he said resolutely, as if he had all he cared to shoulder. I heard a snap, and saw that he had broken the long stem of his pipe. "There," he said, throwing it into the fire, "you and Valentine have got me worked up with your fussing. I'm as shaky as poor Morton tonight."

XII

The next day Uncle Harry telephoned my aunt from his office in town; Miss Wakeley's agent was not at liberty to disclose the purchaser's name, but assured him that the estate was not sold to a speculator, but an old resident of the City who would preserve the property very much as it was and would respect the feelings of the community.

I was sent over to Bonnie Brae with the good tidings. We all felt so much encouraged that we decided to spend the afternoon in the woods that had been restored to us. It was a yellow October day, and our country had never looked more beautiful. We had tea beside Powhatan Creek, where it curved wide and shallow through green bottom land. A plantation of sycamores grew there, their old white roots bursting out of the low banks and forking into the stream itself. The bark of those sycamores was always peculiarly white, and the sunlight played on the silvery interlacing of the great boughs. Dry ledges of slate rock stood out of the cold green water here and there, and on the up-stream side of each ledge lay a little trembling island of yellow leaves, unable to pass the barrier. The meadow in which we lingered was smooth turf, of that intense green of autumn grass that has been already a little touched by frost.

As we sat on the warm slate rocks, we looked up at the wooded side of Blinker's Hill—like a mellow old tapestry. The fiercest autumn colors had burned themselves out; the gold on the smoke-colored beeches was thin and pale, so that through their horizontal branches one could see the colored carpet of leaves on the ground. Only the young oaks held all their ruby leaves, the deepest tone in the whole scale of reds—and they would still be there, a little duller, when the snow was flying.

I remember my aunt's voice, a tone not quite natural, when she said suddenly, "Valentine, how beautiful the Tuileries gardens are on an afternoon like this—down about the second fountain. The color lasts in the sky so long after dusk comes on,—behind the Eiffel tower."

He was lying on his back. He sat up and looked at her sharply. "Oh, yes!"

"Aren't you beginning to be a little homesick for it?" she asked bashfully.

"A little. But it's rather nice to sit safe and lazy on Fox Hill and be a trifle homesick for far-away places. Even Roland gets homesick for Bavaria in the spring, he tells me. He takes a drink or two and recovers. Are you trying to shove me off somewhere?"

She sighed. "Oh, no! No, indeed, I'm not."

But she had, in some way, broken the magical contentment of the afternoon. The little girls began to seem restless, so we gathered them up and started home.

We followed the road round the foot of Blinker's Hill, to the cleared side on which stood the old Wakeley house. There we saw a man and woman coming down the driveway from the house itself. The man stopped and hesitated, but the woman quickened her pace and came toward us. Aunt Charlotte became very pale. She had recognized them at a distance, and so had I; Janet Oglethorpe and her second husband. I remember exactly how she looked. She was wearing a black and white check out-of-door coat and a hard black turban. Her face, always high-colored, was red and shiny from exercise. She waved to us cordially as she came up, but did not offer to shake hands. Her husband took off his hat and smiled scornfully. He stood well behind her, looking very ill at ease, with his elbows out and his chin high, and as the conversation went on his haughty smile became a nervous grin.

"How do you do, Mrs. Waterford, and how do you do, Valentine," Mrs. Towne began effusively. She spoke very fast, and her lips seemed not to keep up with her enunciation; they were heavy and soft, and made her speech slushy. Her mouth was her bad feature—her teeth were too far apart, there was something crude and inelegant about them. "We are going to be neighbors, Mrs. Waterford. I don't want it noised abroad yet, but I've just bought the Wakeley place. I'm going to do the house over and live down here. I hope you won't mind our coming."

Aunt Charlotte made some reply. Valentine did not utter a sound. He took off his hat, replaced it, and stood with his hands in his jacket pockets, looking at the ground.

"I've always had my eye on this property," Mrs. Towne went on, "but it took Belle a long while to make up her mind. It's too fine a place to be left going to waste. It will be nice for Valentine's boy to grow up here where he did, and to be near his Grandfather Ramsay. I want him to know his Ramsay kin."

Valentine behaved very badly. He addressed her without lifting his eyes from the ground or taking his hands out of his pockets; merely kicked a dead leaf out of the road and said: "He's not my boy, and the less he sees of the Ramsays, the better. You've got him, it's your affair to make an Oglethorpe of him and see that he stays one. What do you want to make the kid miserable for?"

Mrs. Towne grew as much redder as it was possible to be, but she spoke indulgently. "Now, Valentine, why can't you be sensible? Certainly, on Mrs. Waterford's account—"

"Oh, yes!" he muttered. "That's the Oglethorpe notion of good manners, before people!"

"I'm sorry, Mrs. Waterford. I had no idea he would be so naughty, or I wouldn't have stopped you. But I did want you to be the first person to know." Mrs. Towne turned to my aunt with great self-command and a ready flow of speech. Her alarmingly high color and a slight swelling of the face, a puffing-up about her eyes and nose, betrayed her state of feeling.

The women talked politely for a few moments, while the two men stood sulking, each in his own way. When the conference was over, Mrs. Towne crossed the road resolutely and took the path to the station. Towne again took off his hat, looking nowhere, and followed her. Valentine did not return the salute.

As our meek band went on around the foot of the hill, he merely pulled his hat lower over his eyes and said, "She's Scotch; she couldn't let anything get away—not even me. All damned bunk about wanting to get Dickie down here. Everything about her's bunk, except her damned money. That's a fact, and it's got me—it's got me."

Aunt Charlotte's breathing was so irregular that she could scarcely speak. "Valentine, I've had a presentiment of that, from the beginning. I scarcely slept at all last night. I can't have it so. Harry must find some way out."

"No way out, Charlotte," he went along swinging his shoulders and speaking in a dull sing-song voice. "That was her creek we were playing along this afternoon; Blue Run, Powhatan Creek, the big woods, Flint Ridge, Blinker's Hill. I can't get in or out. What does it say on the rat-bane bottle; *put the poison along all his runways.* That's the right idea!"

He did not stop with us, but cut back through the orchard to his study. After dinner we waited for him, sitting solemnly about the fire. At last Aunt Charlotte started up as if she could bear it no longer.

"Come on, Harry," she said firmly. "We must see about Valentine."

He looked up at her pathetically. "Take Marjorie, won't you? I really don't want to see the poor chap tonight, Charlotte."

We hurried across the garden. The studio was dark, the fire had gone out. He was lying on the couch, but he did not answer us. I found a box of matches and lit a candle.

One of Uncle Jonathan's rye bottles stood half empty on the mantel-piece. He had had no dinner, had drunk off nearly a pint of whisky and dropped on the couch. He was deathly white, and his eyes were rolled up in his head.

Aunt Charlotte knelt down beside him and covered him with her cloak. "Run for your Uncle Harry, as fast as you can," she said.

XIII

The end? That was the end for us. Within the week workmen were pulling down the wing of the Wakeley house, in order to get as much work as possible done before the cold weather came on. The sound of the stone masons' tools rang out clear across the cut between the two hills; even in Valentine's study one could not escape it. We wished that Morton had carried out his happy idea of making a padded cell of it!

Valentine lingered on at Bonnie Brae for a month, though he never went off his father's place again. He did not sail until the end of November, stayed out his year with us, but he had become a different man. All of us, except Aunt Charlotte, were eager to have him go. He had tonsillitis, I remember, and lay on the couch in his study ill and feverish for two weeks. He seemed not to be working, yet he must have been, for when he went away he left between the leaves of one of my aunt's music books the manuscript of the most beautiful and heart-breaking of all his songs:

I know a wall where red roses grow . . .

He deferred his departure from date to date, changed his passage several times. The night before he went we were sitting by the hall fire, and he said he wished that all the trains and all the boats in the world would stop moving, stop forever.

When his trunks had gone, and his bags were piled up ready to be put into the carriage, he took a latchkey from his pocket and gave it to Aunt Charlotte.

"That's the key to my study. Keep it for me. I don't know that I'll ever need it again, but I'd like to think that you have it."

Less than two years afterward, Valentine was accidentally killed, struck by a motor truck one night at the Pont Royal, just as he was leaving Louise Ireland's apartment on the quai.

Aunt Charlotte survived him by eleven years, but after her death we found his latchkey in her jewel box. I have it still. There is now no door for it to open. Bonnie Brae was pulled down during the war. The wave of industrial expansion swept down that valley, and roaring mills belch their black smoke up to the heights where those lovely houses used to stand. Fox Hill is gone, and our wall is gone. *I know a wall where red roses grow*; youngsters sing it still. The roses of song and the roses of memory, they are the only ones that last.

Woman's Home Companion 52 (February, March 1925): 7–9, 86, 89–90; 15–16, 75–76, 79–80

Double Birthday

✣ ✣ ✣

I

Even in American cities, which seem so much alike, where people seem all to be living the same lives, striving for the same things, thinking the same thoughts, there are still individuals a little out of tune with the times —there are still survivals of a past more loosely woven, there are disconcerting beginnings of a future yet unforeseen.

Coming out of the gray stone Court House in Pittsburgh on a dark November afternoon, Judge Hammersley encountered one of these men whom one does not readily place, whom one is, indeed, a little embarrassed to meet, because they have not got on as they should. The Judge saw him mounting the steps outside, leaning against the wind, holding his soft felt hat on with his hand, his head thrust forward—hurrying with a light, quick step, and so intent upon his own purposes that the Judge could have gone out by a side door and avoided the meeting. But that was against his principles.

"Good day, Albert," he muttered, seeming to feel, himself, all the embarrassment of the encounter, for the other snatched off his hat with a smile of very evident pleasure, and something like pride. His gesture bared an attractive head—small, well-set, definite and smooth, one of those heads that look as if they had been turned out of some hard, rich wood by a workman deft with the lathe. His smooth-shaven face was dark—a warm coffee color—and his hazel eyes were warm and lively. He was not young, but his features had a kind of quick-silver mobility. His manner toward the stiff, frowning Judge was respectful and admiring— not in the least self-conscious.

The Judge inquired after his health and that of his uncle.

"Uncle Albert is splendidly preserved for his age. Frail, and can't stand any strain, but perfectly all right if he keeps to his routine. He's going to have a birthday soon. He will be eighty on the first day of December, and I shall be fifty-five on the same day. I was named after him because I was born on his twenty-fifth birthday."

"Umph." The Judge glanced from left to right as if this announcement were in bad taste, but he put a good face on it and said with a kind of testy heartiness, "That will be an—occasion. I'd like to remember it in some way. Is there anything your uncle would like, any—recognition?" He stammered and coughed.

Young Albert Engelhardt, as he was called, laughed apologetically, but with confidence. "I think there is, Judge Hammersley. Indeed, I'd thought of coming to you to ask a favor. I am going to have a little supper for him, and you know he likes good wine. In these dirty bootlegging times, it's hard to get."

"Certainly, certainly." The Judge spoke up quickly and for the first time looked Albert squarely in the eye. "Don't give him any of that bootleg stuff. I can find something in my cellar. Come out tomorrow night after eight, with a gripsack of some sort. Very glad to help you out, Albert. Glad the old fellow holds up so well. Thank'ee, Albert," as Engelhardt swung the heavy door open and held it for him to pass.

Judge Hammersley's car was waiting for him, and on the ride home to Squirrel Hill he thought with vexation about the Engelhardts. He was really a sympathetic man, and though so stern of manner, he had deep affections; was fiercely loyal to old friends, old families, and old ideals. He didn't think highly of what is called success in the world today, but such as it was he wanted his friends to have it, and was vexed with them when they missed it. He was vexed with Albert for unblushingly, almost proudly, declaring that he was fifty-five years old, when he had nothing whatever to show for it. He was the last of the Engelhardt boys, and they had none of them had anything to show. They all died much worse off in the world than they began. They began with a flourishing glass factory up the river, a comfortable fortune, a fine old house on the park in Allegheny, a good standing in the community; and it was all gone, melted away.

Old August Engelhardt was a thrifty, energetic man, though pig-headed—Judge Hammersley's friend and one of his first clients. August's five sons had sold the factory and wasted the money in fantastic individual enterprises, lost the big house, and now they were all dead except Albert. They ought all to be alive, with estates and factories and families. To be sure, they had that queer German streak in them; but so had old August, and it hadn't prevented his amounting to something. Their bringing-up was wrong; August had too free a hand, he was too proud of his five handsome boys, and too conceited. Too much tennis, Rhine wine punch, music, and silliness. They were always running over to New York, like this Albert. Somebody, when asked what in the world young Albert had ever done with his inheritance, had laughingly replied that he had spent it on the Pennsylvania Railroad.

Judge Hammersley didn't see how Albert could hold his head up. He had some small job in the County Clerk's office, was dependent upon it, had nothing else but the poor little house on the South Side where he lived with his old uncle. The county took care of him for the sake of his father, who had been a gallant officer in the Civil War, and afterward a public-spirited citizen and a generous employer of labor. But, as Judge Hammersley had bitterly remarked· to Judge Merriman when Albert's name happened to come up, "If it weren't for his father's old friends seeing that he got something, that fellow wouldn't be able to make a living." Next to a charge of dishonesty, this was the worst that could be said of any man.

Judge Hammersley's house out on Squirrel Hill sat under a grove of very old oak trees. He lived alone, with his daughter, Margaret Parmenter, who was a widow. She had a great many engagements, but she usually managed to dine at home with her father, and that was about as much society as he cared for. His house was comfortable in an old-fashioned way, well appointed—especially the library, the room in which he lived when he was not in bed or at the Court House. Tonight, when he came down to dinner, Mrs. Parmenter was already at the table, dressed for an evening party. She was tall, handsome, with a fine, easy carriage, and her face was both hard and sympathetic, like her father's. She had not, however, his stiffness of manner, that contraction of the muscles which was his unconscious protest at any irregularity in the machinery of life. She accepted blunders and accidents smoothly if not indifferently.

As the old colored man pulled back the Judge's chair for him, he glanced at his daughter from under his eyebrows.

"I saw that son of old Gus Engelhardt's this afternoon," he said in an angry, challenging tone.

As a young girl his daughter had used to take up the challenge and hotly defend the person who had displeased or disappointed her father. But as she grew older she was conscious of that same feeling in herself when people fell short of what she expected; and she understood now that when her father spoke as if he were savagely attacking someone, it merely meant that he was disappointed or sorry for them; he never spoke thus of persons for whom he had no feeling. So she said calmly:

"Oh, did you really? I haven't seen him for years, not since the war. How was he looking? Shabby?"

"Not so shabby as he ought to. That fellow's likely to be in want one of these days."

"I'm afraid so," Mrs. Parmenter sighed. "But I believe he would be rather plucky about it."

The Judge shrugged. "He's coming out here tomorrow night, on some business for his uncle."

"Then I'll have a chance to see for myself. He must look much older. I can't imagine his ever looking really old and settled, though."

"See that you don't ask him to stay. I don't want the fellow hanging around. He'll transact his business and get it over. He had the face to admit to me that he'll be fifty-five years old on the first of December. He's giving some sort of birthday party for old Albert, a-hem." The Judge coughed formally but was unable to check a smile; his lips sarcastic, but his eyes full of sly humor.

"Can he be as old as that? Yes, I suppose so. When we were both at Mrs. Sterrett's, in Rome, I was fifteen, and he must have been about thirty."

Her father coughed. "He'd better have been in Homestead!"

Mrs. Parmenter looked up; that was rather commonplace, for her father. "Oh, I don't know. Albert would never have been much use in Homestead, and he was very useful to Mrs. Sterrett in Rome."

"What did she want the fellow hanging round for? All the men of her family amounted to something."

"To too much! There must be some butterflies if one is going to give house parties, and the Sterretts and Dents were all heavyweights. He was in Rome a long while; three years, I think. He had a gorgeous time. Anyway, he learned to speak Italian very well, and that helps him out now, doesn't it? You still send for him at the Court House when you need an interpreter?"

"That's not often. He picks up a few dollars. Nice business for his father's son."

After dinner the Judge retired to his library, where the gas fire was lit, and his book at hand, with a paper-knife inserted to mark the place where he had left off reading last night at exactly ten-thirty. On his way he went to the front door, opened it, turned on the porch light, and looked at the thermometer, making an entry in a little notebook. In a few moments his daughter, in an evening cloak, stopped at the library door to wish him good night and went down the hall. He listened for the closing of the front door; it was a reassuring sound to him. He liked the feeling of an orderly house, empty for himself and his books all evening. He was deeply read in divinity, philosophy, and in the early history of North America.

II

While Judge Hammersley was settling down to his book, Albert Engelhardt was sitting at home in a garnet velvet smoking-jacket, at an upright piano, playing Schumann's *Kreisleriana* for his old uncle. They lived, certainly, in a queer part of the city, on one of the dingy streets that run uphill off noisy Carson Street, in a little two-story brick house, a workingman's house, that Albert's father had taken over long ago in satisfaction of a bad debt. When his father had acquired this building, it was a mere nothing—the Engelhardts were then living in their big, many-gabled, so-German house on the Park, in Allegheny; and they owned many other buildings, besides the glass factory up the river. After the father's death, when the sons converted houses and lands into cash, this forgotten little house on the South Side had somehow never been sold or mortgaged. A day came when Albert, the last surviving son, found this piece of property the only thing he owned in the world besides his personal effects. His uncle, having had a crushing disappointment, wanted at that time to retire from the practice of medicine, so Albert settled in the South Side house and took his uncle with him.

He had not gone there in any mood of despair. His impoverishment had come about gradually, and before he took possession of these quarters he had been living in a boarding house; the change seemed going up instead of going down in the world. He was delighted to have a home again, to unpack his own furniture and his books and pictures—the most valuable in the world to him, because they were full of his own history and that of his family, were like part of his own personality. All the years and the youth which had slipped away from him still clung to these things.

At his piano, under his Degas drawing in black and red—three ballet girls at the bar—or seated at his beautiful inlaid writing table, he was still the elegant young man who sat there long ago. His rugs were fine ones, his collection of books was large and very personal. It was full of works which, though so recent, were already immensely far away and diminished. The glad, rebellious excitement they had once caused in the world he could recapture only in memory. Their power to seduce and stimulate the young, the living, was utterly gone. There was a complete file of the *Yellow Book*, for instance; who could extract sweet poison from those volumes now? A portfolio of the drawings of Aubrey Beardsley—decadent, had they been called? A slender, padded volume—the complete

works of a great new poet, Ernest Dowson. Oscar Wilde, whose wickedness was now so outdone that he looked like the poor old hat of some
Victorian belle, wired and feathered and garlanded and faded.

Albert and his uncle occupied only the upper floor of their house.
The ground floor was let to an old German glass engraver who had once
been a workman in August Engelhardt's factory. His wife was a good
cook, and every night sent their dinner up hot on the dumb-waiter.
The house opened directly upon the street, and to reach Albert's apartment
one went down a narrow paved alley at the side of the building and
mounted an outside flight of wooden stairs at the back. They had only
four rooms—two bedrooms, a snug sitting room in which they dined,
and a small kitchen where Albert got breakfast every morning. After he
had gone to work, Mrs. Rudder came up from downstairs to wash the
dishes and do the cleaning, and to cheer up old Doctor Engelhardt.

At dinner this evening Albert had told his uncle about meeting Judge
Hammersley, and of his particular inquiries after his health. The old man
was very proud and received this intelligence as his due, but could not
conceal a certain gratification.

"The daughter, she still lives with him? A damned fine-looking
woman!" he muttered between his teeth. Uncle Albert, a bachelor, had
been a professed connoisseur of ladies in his day.

Immediately after dinner, unless he were going somewhere, Albert
always played for his uncle for an hour. He played extremely well. Doctor
Albert sat by the fire smoking his cigar. While he listened, the look of
wisdom and professional authority faded, and many changes went over
his face, as if he were playing a little drama to himself; moods of scorn
and contempt, of rakish vanity, sentimental melancholy . . . and something remote and lonely. The Doctor had always flattered himself that he
resembled a satyr, because the tops of his ears were slightly pointed; and he
used to hint to his nephews that his large pendulous nose was the index of
an excessively amorous disposition. His mouth was full of long, yellowish
teeth, all crowded irregularly, which he snapped and ground together
when he uttered denunciations of modern art or the Eighteenth Amend-
ment. He wore his mustache short and twisted up at the corners. His
thick gray hair was cut close and upright, in the bristling French fashion.
His hands were small and fastidious, high-knuckled, quite elegant in shape.

Across the Doctor's throat ran a long, jagged scar. He used to mutter
to his young nephews that it had been justly inflicted by an outraged
husband—a pistol shot in the dark. But his brother August always said

that he had been cut by glass, when, wandering about in the garden one night after drinking too much punch, he had fallen into the cold-frames.

After playing Schumann for some time, Albert, without stopping, went into Stravinsky.

Doctor Engelhardt by the gas fire stirred uneasily, turned his important head toward his nephew, and snapped his teeth. "Br-r-r, that stuff! Poverty of imagination, poverty of musical invention; *fin-de-siècle!*"

Albert laughed. "I thought you were asleep. Why will you use that phrase? It shows your vintage. Like this any better?" He began the second act of *Pélleas et Mélisande*.

The Doctor nodded. "Yes, that is better, though I'm not fooled by it." He wrinkled his nose as if he were smelling out something, and squinted with superior discernment. "To this *canaille* that is all very new; but to me it goes back to Bach."

"Yes, if you like."

Albert, like Judge Hammersley, was jealous of his solitude—liked a few hours with his books. It was time for Uncle Doctor to be turning in. He ended the music by playing half a dozen old German songs which the old fellow always wanted but never asked for. The Doctor's chin sank into his shirt front. His face took on a look of deep, resigned sadness; his features, losing their conscious importance, seemed to shrink a good deal. His nephew knew that this was the mood in which he would most patiently turn to rest and darkness. Doctor Engelhardt had had a heavy loss late in life. Indeed, he had suffered the same loss twice.

As Albert left the piano, the Doctor rose and walked a little stiffly across the room. At the door of his chamber he paused, brought his hand up in a kind of military salute and gravely bowed, so low that one saw only the square up-standing gray brush on the top of his head and the long pear-shaped nose. After this he closed the door behind him. Albert sat down to his book. Very soon he heard the bath water running. Having taken his bath, the Doctor would get into bed immediately to avoid catching cold. Luckily, he usually slept well. Perhaps he dreamed of that unfortunate young singer whom he sometimes called, to his nephew and himself, "the lost Lenore."

III

Long years ago, when the Engelhardt boys were still living in the old house in Allegheny with their mother, after their father's death, Doctor Engelhardt was practising medicine, and had an office on the Park, five minutes' walk from his sister-in-law. He usually lunched with the family, after his morning office hours were over. They always had a good cook, and the Allegheny market was one of the best in the world. Mrs. Engelhardt went to market every morning of her life; such vegetables and poultry, such cheeses and sausages and smoked and pickled fish as one could buy there! Soon after she had made her rounds, boys in white aprons would come running across the Park with her purchases. Everyone knew the Engelhardt house, built of many-colored bricks, with gables and turrets, and on the west a large stained-glass window representing a scene on the Grand Canal in Venice, the Church of Santa Maria della Salute in the background, in the foreground a gondola with a slender gondolier. People said August and Mrs. Engelhardt should be solidly seated in the prow to make the picture complete.

Doctor Engelhardt's especial interest was the throat, preferably the singing throat. He had studied every scrap of manuscript that Manuel Garcia had left behind him, every reported conversation with him. He had doctored many singers, and imagined he had saved many voices. Pittsburgh air is not good for the throat, and traveling artists often had need of medical assistance. Conductors of orchestras and singing societies recommended Doctor Engelhardt because he was very lax about collecting fees from professionals, especially if they sent him a photograph floridly inscribed. He had been a medical student in New York while Patti was still singing; his biography fell into chapters of great voices as a turfman's falls into chapters of fast horses. This passion for the voice had given him the feeling of distinction, of being unique in his profession, which had made him all his life a well-satisfied and happy man, and had left him a poor one.

One morning when the Doctor was taking his customary walk about the Park before office hours, he stopped in front of the Allegheny High School building because he heard singing—a chorus of young voices. It was June, and the chapel windows were open. The Doctor listened for a few moments, then tilted his head on one side and laid his forefinger on his pear-shaped nose with an anxious, inquiring squint. Among the voices he certainly heard one Voice. The final bang of the piano was followed by laughter and buzzing. A boy ran down the steps. The Doctor stopped him and learned that this was a rehearsal for Class Day exercises. Just then the piano began again, and in a moment he heard the same voice, alone:

"*Still wie die Nacht, tief wie das Meer.*"

No, he was not mistaken; a full, rich soprano voice, so easy, so sure; a golden warmth, even in the high notes. Before the second verse was over he went softly into the building, into the chapel, and for the first time laid eyes on Marguerite Thiesinger. He saw a sturdy, blooming German girl standing beside the piano; good-natured one knew at a glance, glowing with health. She looked like a big peony just burst into bloom and full of sunshine—sunshine in her auburn hair, in her rather small hazel eyes. When she finished the song, she began waltzing on the platform with one of the boys.

Doctor Albert waited by the door, and accosted her as she came out carrying her coat and schoolbooks. He introduced himself and asked her if she would go over to Mrs. Engelhardt's for lunch and sing for him.

Oh, yes! she knew one of the Engelhardt boys, and she'd always wanted to see that beautiful window from the inside.

She went over at noon and sang for them before lunch, and the family took stock of her. She spoke a very ordinary German and her English was still worse; her people were very ordinary. Her flat, slangy speech was somehow not vulgar because it was so naïve—she knew no other way. The boys were delighted with her because she was jolly and interested in everything. She told them about the glorious good times she had going to dances in suburban Turner halls, and to picnics in the damp, smoke-smeared woods up the Allegheny. The boys roared with laughter at the unpromising places she mentioned. But she had the warm bubble in her blood that makes everything fair; even being a junior in the Allegheny High School was "glorious," she told them!

She came to lunch with them again and again, because she liked the boys, and she thought the house magnificent. The Doctor observed her narrowly all the while. Clearly she had no ambition, no purpose; she sang to be agreeable. She was not very intelligent, but she had a kind of personal warmth that, to his way of thinking, was much better than brains. He took her over to his office and poked and pounded her. When he had finished his examination, he stood before the foolish, happy young thing and inclined his head in his peculiar fashion.

"Miss Thiesinger, I have the honor to announce to you that you are on the threshold of a brilliant, possibly a great career."

She laughed her fresh, ringing laugh. "Aren't you nice, though, to take so much trouble about me!"

The Doctor lifted a forefinger. "But for that you must turn your back on this childishness, these sniveling sapheads you play marbles with.

[49]

You must uproot this triviality." He made a gesture as if he were wringing a chicken's neck, and Marguerite was thankful she was able to keep back a giggle.

Doctor Engelhardt wanted her to go to New York with him at once, and begin her studies. He was quite ready to finance her. He had made up his mind to stake everything upon this voice.

But not at all. She thought it was lovely of him, but she was very fond of her classmates, and she wanted to graduate with her class next year. Moreover, she had just been given a choir position in one of the biggest churches in Pittsburgh, though she was still a schoolgirl; she was going to have money and pretty clothes for the first time in her life and wouldn't miss it all for anything.

All through the next school year Doctor Albert went regularly to the church where she sang, watched and cherished her, expostulated and lectured, trying to awaken fierce ambition in his big peony flower. She was very much interested in other things just then, but she was patient with him; accepted his devotion with good nature, respected his wisdom, and bore with his "stagey" manners as she called them. She graduated in June, and immediately after Commencement, when she was not quite nineteen, she eloped with an insurance agent and went to Chicago to live. She wrote Doctor Albert: "I do appreciate all your kindness to me, but I guess I will let my voice rest for the present."

He took it hard. He burned her photographs and the foolish little scrawls she had written to thank him for presents. His life would have been dull and empty if he hadn't had so many reproaches to heap upon her in his solitude. How often and how bitterly he arraigned her for the betrayal of so beautiful a gift. Where did she keep it hidden now, that jewel, in the sordid life she had chosen?

Three years after her elopement, suddenly, without warning, Marguerite Thiesinger walked into his office on Arch Street one morning and told him she had come back to study! Her husband's "affairs were involved"; he was now quite willing that she should make as much as possible of her voice—and out of it.

"My voice is better than it was," she said, looking at him out of her rather small eyes—greenish yellow, with a glint of gold in them. He believed her. He suddenly realized how uncommonly truthful she had always been. Rather stupid, unimaginative, but carried joyously along on a flood of warm vitality, and truthful to a degree he had hardly known in any woman or in any man. And now she was a woman.

He took her over to his sister-in-law's. Albert, who chanced to be at home, was sent to the piano. She was not mistaken. The Doctor kept averting his head to conceal his delight, to conceal, once or twice, a tear— the moisture that excitement and pleasure brought to his eyes. The voice, after all, he told himself, is a physical thing. She had been growing and ripening like fruit in the sun, and the voice with the body. Doctor Engelhardt stepped softly out of the music room into the conservatory and addressed a potted palm, his lips curling back from his teeth: "So we get that out of you, *Monsieur le commis voyageur*, and now we throw you away like a squeezed lemon."

When he returned to his singer, she addressed him very earnestly from under her spring hat covered with lilacs: "Before my marriage, Doctor Engelhardt, you offered to take me to New York to a teacher, and lend me money to start on. If you still feel like doing it, I'm sure I could repay you before very long. I'll follow your instructions. What was it you used to tell me I must have—application and ambition?"

He glared at her; "Take note, Gretchen, that I change the prescription. There is something vulgar about ambition. Now we will play for higher stakes; for ambition read aspiration!" His index finger shot upward.

In New York he had no trouble in awakening the interest of his friends and acquaintances. Within a week he had got his protégée to a very fine artist, just then retiring from the Opera, a woman who had been a pupil of Pauline Garcia Viardot. In short, Doctor Engelhardt had realized the dream of a lifetime: he had discovered a glorious voice, backed by a rich vitality. Within a year Marguerite had one of the best church positions in New York; she insisted upon repaying her benefactor before she went abroad to complete her studies. Doctor Engelhardt went often to New York to counsel and advise, to gloat over his treasure. He often shivered as he crossed the Jersey ferry; he was afraid of Fate. He would tell over her assets on his fingers to reassure himself. You might have seen a small, self-important man of about fifty, standing by the rail of the ferry boat, his head impressively inclined as if he were addressing an amphi- theatre full of students, gravely counting upon his fingers.

But Fate struck, and from the quarter least under suspicion—through that blooming, rounded, generously molded young body, from that abundant, glowing health which the Doctor proudly called peasant vigor. Marguerite's success had brought to his office many mothers of singing daughters. He was not insensible to the compliment, but he usually dis- missed them by dusting his fingers delicately in the air and growling;

"Yes, she can sing a little, she has a voice; *aber kleine, kleine!*" He exulted in the opulence of his cabbage rose. To his nephews he used to match her possibilities with the singers of that period. Emma Eames he called *die Puritan*, Geraldine Farrar *la voix blanche*, another was *trop raffinée*.

Marguerite had been in New York two years, her path one of uninterrupted progress, when she wrote the Doctor about a swelling of some sort; the surgeons wanted to operate. Doctor Albert took the next train for New York. An operation revealed that things were very bad indeed; a malignant growth, so far advanced that the knife could not check it. Her mother and grandmother had died of the same disease.

Poor Marguerite lived a year in a hospital for incurables. Every weekend when Doctor Albert went over to see her he found great changes—it was rapid and terrible. That winter and spring he lived like a man lost in a dark morass, the Slave in the Dismal Swamp. He suffered more than his Gretchen, for she was singularly calm and hopeful to the very end, never doubting that she would get well.

The last time he saw her she had given up. But she was noble and sweet in mood, and so piteously apologetic for disappointing him—like a child who has broken something precious and is sorry. She was wasted, indeed, until she was scarcely larger than a child, her beautiful hair cut short, her hands like shadows, but still a stain of color in her cheeks.

"I'm so sorry I didn't do as you wanted instead of running off with Phil," she said. "I see now how little he cared about me—and you've just done everything. If I had my twenty-six years to live over, I'd live them very differently."

Doctor Albert dropped her hand and walked to the window, the tears running down his face. "*Pourquoi, pourquoi?*" he muttered, staring blindly at that brutal square of glass. When he could control himself and came back to the chair at her bedside, she put her poor little sheared head out on his knee and lay smiling and breathing softly.

"I expect you don't believe in the hereafter," she murmured. "Scientific people hardly ever do. But if there is one, I'll not forget you. I'll love to remember you."

When the nurse came to give her her hypodermic, Doctor Albert went out into Central Park and wandered about without knowing where or why, until he smelled something sweet which suddenly stopped his breath, and he sat down under a flowering linden tree. He dropped his face in his hands and cried like a woman. Youth, art, love, dreams, true-heartedness—why must they go out of the summer world into darkness?

Warum, warum? He thought he had already suffered all that man could, but never had it come down on him like this. He sat on that bench like a drunken man or like a dying man, muttering Heine's words, "God is a grimmer humorist than I. Nobody but God could have perpetrated anything so cruel." She was ashamed, he remembered it afresh and struck his bony head with his clenched fist—ashamed at having been used like this; she was apologetic for the power, whatever it was, that had tricked her. "Yes, by God, she apologized for God!"

The tortured man looked up through the linden branches at the blue arch that never answers. As he looked, his face relaxed, his breathing grew regular. His eyes were caught by puffy white clouds like the cherub-heads in Raphael's pictures, and something within him seemed to rise and travel with those clouds. The moment had come when he could bear no more. . . . When he went back to the hospital that evening, he learned that she had died very quietly between eleven and twelve, the hour when he was sitting on the bench in the park.

Uncle Doctor now sometimes spoke to Albert out of a long silence: "Anyway, I died for her; that was given to me. She never knew a death-struggle—she went to sleep. That struggle took place in my body. Her dissolution occurred within me."

IV

Old Doctor Engelhardt walked abroad very little now. Sometimes on a fine Sunday, his nephew would put him aboard a street car that climbs the hills beyond Mount Oliver and take him to visit an old German graveyard and a monastery. Every afternoon, in good weather, he walked along the pavement which ran past the front door, as far as the first corner, where he bought his paper and cigarettes. If Elsa, the pretty little grand-daughter of his housekeeper, ran out to join him and see him over the crossings, he would go a little farther. In the morning, while Mrs. Rudder did the sweeping and dusting, the Doctor took the air on an upstairs back porch, overhanging the court.

The court was bricked, and had an old-fashioned cistern and hydrant, and three ailanthus trees—the last growing things left to the Engelhardts, whose flowering shrubs and greenhouses had once been so well known in Allegheny. In these trees, which he called *les Chinoises*, the Doctor took a great interest. The clothes line ran about their trunks in a triangle, and on Mondays he looked down upon the washing. He was too near-sighted to be distressed by the sooty flakes descending from neighboring chimneys upon the white sheets. He enjoyed the dull green leaves of his *Chinoises* in summer, scarcely moving on breathless, sticky nights, when the moon came up red over roofs and smokestacks. In autumn he watched the yellow fronds drop down upon the brick pavement like great ferns. Now, when his birthday was approaching, the trees were bare; and he thought he liked them best so, especially when all the knotty, curly twigs were outlined by a scurf of snow.

As he sat there, wrapped up in rugs, a stiff felt hat on his head—he would never hear to a cap—and woolen gloves on his hands, Elsa, the granddaughter, would bring her cross-stitch and chatter to him. Of late she had been sewing on her trousseau, and that amused the Doctor highly—though it meant she would soon go to live in lower Allegheny, and he would lose her. Her young man, Carl Abberbock, had now a half-interest in a butcher stall in the Allegheny market, and was in a hurry to marry.

When Mrs. Rudder had quite finished her work and made the place neat, she would come and lift the rug from his knees and say, "Time to go in, Herr Doctor."

V

The next evening after dinner Albert left the house with a suitcase, the bag that used to make so many trips to New York in the opera season. He stopped downstairs to ask Elsa to carry her sewing up and sit with his uncle for a while, then he took the street car across the Twenty-second Street Bridge by the blazing steel mills. As he waited on Soho Hill to catch a Fifth Avenue car, the heavy, frosty air suddenly began to descend in snow flakes. He wished he had worn his old overcoat; didn't like to get this one wet. He had to consider such things now. He was hesitating about a taxi when his car came, bound for the East End.

He got off at the foot of one of the streets running up Squirrel Hill, and slowly mounted. Everything was white with the softly-falling snow. Albert knew all the places; old school friends lived in many of them. Big, turreted stone houses, set in ample grounds with fine trees and shrubbery and driveways. He stepped aside now and then to avoid a car, rolling from the gravel drives on to the stone-block pavement. If the occupants had recognized Albert, they would have felt sorry for him. But he did not feel sorry for himself. He looked up at the lighted windows, the red gleam on the snowy rhododendron bushes, and shrugged. His old schoolfellows went to New York now as often as he had done in his youth; but they went to consult doctors, to put children in school, or to pay the bills of incorrigible sons.

He thought he had had the best of it; he had gone a-Maying while it was May. This solid comfort, this iron-bound security, didn't appeal to him much. These massive houses, after all, held nothing but the heavy domestic routine; all the frictions and jealousies and discontents of family life. Albert felt light and free, going up the hill in his thin overcoat. He believed he had had a more interesting life than most of his friends who owned real estate. He could still amuse himself, and he had lived to the full all the revolutions in art and music that his period covered. He wouldn't at this moment exchange his life and his memories—his memories of his teacher, Rafael Joseffy, for instance—for any one of these massive houses and the life of the man who paid the upkeep. If Mephistopheles were to emerge from the rhododendrons and stand behind his shoulder with such an offer, he wouldn't hesitate. Money? Oh, yes, he would like to have some, but not what went with it.

He turned in under Judge Hammersley's fine oak trees. A car was waiting in the driveway, near the steps by which he mounted to the door. The colored man admitted him, and just as he entered the hall Mrs. Parmenter came down the stairs.

"Ah, it's you, Albert! Father said you were coming in this evening, and I've kept the car waiting, to have a glimpse of you."

Albert had dropped his hat and bag, and stood holding her hand with the special grace and appreciation she remembered in him.

"What a pleasure to see you!" he exclaimed, and she knew from his eyes it was. "It doesn't happen often, but it's always such a surprise and pleasure." He held her hand as if he wanted to keep her there. "It's a long while since the Villa Scipione, isn't it?"

They stood for a moment in the shrouded hall light. Mrs. Parmenter was looking very handsome, and Albert was thinking that she had all her father's authority, with much more sweep and freedom. She was impulsive and careless, where he was strong and shrinking—a powerful man terribly afraid of little annoyances. His daughter, Albert believed, was not afraid of anything. She had proved more than once that if you aren't afraid of gossip, it is harmless. She did as she pleased. People took it. Even Parmenter had taken it, and he was rather a stiff sort.

Mrs. Parmenter laughed at his allusion to their summer at Mrs. Sterrett's, in Rome, and gave him her coat to hold.

"You remember, Albert, how you and I used to get up early on fête days, and go down to the garden gate to see the young king come riding in from the country at the head of the horse guards? How the sun flashed on his helmet! Heavens, I saw him last summer! So grizzled and battered."

"And we were always going to run away to Russia together, and now there is no Russia. Everything has changed but you, Mrs. Parmenter."

"Wish I could think so. But you don't know any Mrs. Parmenter. I'm Marjorie, please. How often I think of those gay afternoons I had with you and your brothers in the garden behind your old Allegheny house. There's such a lot I want to talk to you about. And this birthday—when is it? May I send your uncle some flowers? I always remember his goodness to poor Marguerite Thiesinger. He never got over that, did he? But I'm late, and father is waiting. Good-night, you'll have a message from me."

Albert bent and kissed her hand in the old-fashioned way, keeping it a moment and breathing in softly the fragrance of her clothes, her furs, her person, the fragrance of that other world to which he had once belonged and out of which he had slipped so gradually that he scarcely realized it, unless suddenly brought face to face with something in it that was charming. Releasing her, he caught up his hat and opened the door to follow her, but she pushed him back with her arm and smiled over her shoulder. "No, no, father is waiting for you in the library. Good-night."

Judge Hammersley stood in the doorway, fingering a bunch of keys and blinking with impatience to render his service and have done with it. The library opened directly into the hall; he couldn't help overhearing his daughter, and he disliked her free and unreproachful tone with this man who was young when he should be old, single when he should be married, and penniless when he should be well-fixed.

Later, as Albert came down the hill with two bottles of the Judge's best champagne in his bag, he was thinking that the greatest disadvantage of being poor and dropping out of the world was that he didn't meet attractive women any more. The men he could do without, Heaven knew! But the women, the ones like Marjorie Hammersley, were always grouped where the big fires burned—money and success and big houses and fast boats and French cars; it was natural.

Mrs. Parmenter, as she drove off, resolved that she would see more of Albert and his uncle—wondered why she had let an old friendship lapse for so long. When she was a little girl, she used often to spend a week with her aunt in Allegheny. She was fond of the aunt, but not of her

cousins, and she used to escape whenever she could to the Engelhardts'
garden only a few doors away. No grass in that garden—in Allegheny
grass was always dirty—but glittering gravel, and lilac hedges beautiful in
spring, and barberry hedges red in the fall, and flowers and bird cages and
striped awnings, boys lying about in tennis clothes, making mint juleps
before lunch, having coffee under the sycamore trees after dinner. The
Engelhardt boys were different, like people in a book or a play. All the
young men in her set were scornful of girls until they wanted one; then
they grabbed her rather brutally, and it was over. She had felt that the
Engelhardt boys admired her without in the least wanting to grab her,
that they enjoyed her æsthetically, so to speak, and it pleased her to be
liked in that way.

VI

On the afternoon of the first of December, Albert left his desk in the
County Clerk's office at four o'clock, feeling very much as he used to when
school was dismissed in the middle of the afternoon just before the
Christmas holidays. It was his uncle's birthday that was in his mind; his
own, of course, gave him no particular pleasure. If one stopped to think
of that, there was a shiver waiting round the corner. He walked over the
Smithfield Street Bridge. A thick brown fog made everything dark, and
there was a feeling of snow in the air. The lights along the sheer cliffs of
Mount Washington, high above the river, were already lighted. When
Albert was a boy, those cliffs, with the row of lights far up against the sky,
always made him think of some far-away, cloud-set city in Asia; the for-
bidden city, he used to call it. Well, that was a long time ago; a lot of
water had run under this bridge since then, and kingdoms and empires
had fallen. Meanwhile, Uncle Doctor was still hanging on, and things
were not so bad with them as they might be. Better not reflect too much.
He hopped on board a street car, and old women with market baskets
shifted to make room for him.

When he reached home, the table was already set in the living room.
Beautiful table linen had been one of his mother's extravagances (he had
boxes of it, meant to give some to Elsa on her marriage), and Mrs.
Rudder laundered it with pious care. She had put out the best silver. He
had forgotten to order flowers, but the old woman had brought up one
of her blooming geraniums for a centerpiece. Uncle Albert was dozing by
the fire in his old smoking jacket, a volume of Schiller on his knee.

"I'll put the studs in your shirt for you. Time to dress, Uncle Doctor."
The old man blinked and smiled drolly. "So? *Die* claw-hammer?"

"Of course *die* claw-hammer! Elsa is going to a masquerade with
Carl, and they are coming up to see us before they go. I promised her you
would dress."

"Albert," the Doctor called him back, beckoned with a mysterious
smile; "where did you get that wine now?"

"Oh, you found it when she put it on ice, did you? That's Judge
Hammersley's, the best he had. He insisted on sending it to you, with his
compliments and good wishes."

Uncle Albert rose and drew up his shoulders somewhat pompously.
"From my own kind I still command recognition." Then dropping into
homely vulgarity he added, with a sidelong squint at his nephew, "By
God, some of that will feel good, running down the gullet."

"You'll have all you want for once. It's a great occasion. Did you
shave carefully? I'll take my bath, and then you must be ready for
me."

In half an hour Albert came out in his dress clothes and found his
uncle still reading his favorite poet. "The trousers are too big," the
Doctor complained. "Why not *die* claw-hammer and my old trousers?
Elsa wouldn't notice."

"Oh yes, she would! She's seen these every day for five years. Quick
change!"

Doctor Engelhardt submitted, and when he was dressed, surveyed
himself in his mirror with satisfaction, though he slyly slipped a cotton
handkerchief into his pocket instead of the linen one Albert had laid out.
When they came back to the sitting room, Mrs. Rudder had been up
again and had put on the wine glasses. There was still half an hour before
dinner, and Albert sat down to play for his uncle. He was beginning to
feel that it was all much ado about nothing, after all.

A gentle tap at the door, and Elsa came in with her young man. She
was dressed as a Polish maiden, and Carl Abberbock was in a Highlander's
kilt.

"Congratulations on your birthday, Herr Doctor, and I've brought
you some flowers." She went to his chair and bent down to be kissed,
putting a bunch of violets in his hand.

The Doctor rose and stood looking down at the violets. "Hey, you
take me for a Bonapartist? What is Mussolini's flower, Albert? Advise
your friends in Rome that a Supreme Dictator should always have a

flower." He turned the young girl around in the light and teased her about her thin arms—such an old joke, but she laughed for him.

"But that's the style now, Herr Doctor. Everybody wants to be as thin as possible."

"Bah, there are no styles in such things! A man will always want something to take hold of, till Hell freezes over! Is dat so, Carl?"

Carl, a very broad-faced, smiling young man with outstanding ears, was suddenly frightened into silence by the entrance of a fine lady, and made for the door to get his knotty knees into the shadow. Elsa, too, caught her breath and shrank away.

Without knocking, Mrs. Parmenter, her arms full of roses, appeared in the doorway, and just behind her was her chauffeur, carrying a package. "Put it down there and wait for me," she said to him, then swept into the room and lightly embraced Doctor Engelhardt without waiting to drop the flowers or take off her furs. "I wanted to congratulate you in person. They told me below that you were receiving. Please take these flowers, Albert. I want a moment's chat with Doctor Engelhardt."

The Doctor stood with singular gravity, like someone in a play, the violets still in his hand. "To what," he muttered with his best bow, "to what am I indebted for such distinguished consideration?"

"To your own distinction, my dear sir—always one of the most distinguished men I ever knew."

The Doctor, to whom flattery was thrice dearer than to ordinary men, flushed deeply. But he was not so exalted that he did not notice his little friend of many lonely hours slipping out of the entry-way—the bare-kneed Highland chief had already got down the wooden stairs. "Elsa," he called commandingly, "come here and kiss me good-night." He pulled her forward. "This is Elsa Rudder, Mrs. Parmenter, and my very particular friend. You should have seen her beautiful hair before she cut it off." Elsa reddened and glanced up to see whether the lady understood. Uncle Doctor kissed her on the forehead and ran his hand over her shingled head. "Nineteen years," he said softly. "If the next nineteen are as happy, we won't bother about the rest. *Behüt' dich, Gott!*"

"Thank you, Uncle Doctor. Good-night."

After she fluttered out, he turned to Mrs. Parmenter. "That little girl," he said impressively, "is the rose in winter. She is my heir. Everything I have, I leave to her."

"Everything but my birthday present, please! You must drink that. I've brought you a bottle of champagne."

Both Alberts began to laugh. "But your father has already given us two!"

Mrs. Parmenter looked from one to the other. "My father? Well, that is a compliment! It's unheard of. Of course he and I have different lockers. We could never agree when to open them. I don't think he's opened his since the Chief Justice dined with him. Now I must leave you. Be as jolly as the night is long; with three bottles you ought to do very well! The good woman downstairs said your dinner would be served in half an hour."

Both men started toward her. "Don't go. Please, please, stay and dine with us! It's the one thing we needed." Albert began to entreat her in Italian, a language his uncle did not understand. He confessed that he had been freezing up for the last hour, couldn't go on with it alone. "One can't do such things without a woman—a beautiful woman."

"Thank you, Albert. But I've a dinner engagement; I ought to be at the far end of Ellsworth Avenue this minute."

"But this is once in a lifetime—for him! Still, if your friends are waiting for you, you can't. Certainly not." He took up her coat and held it for her. But how the light had gone out of his face; he looked so different, so worn, as he stood holding her coat at just the right height. She slipped her arms into it, then pulled them out. "I can't, but I just will! Let me write a note, please. I'll send Henry on with it and tell them I'll drop in after dinner." Albert pressed her hand gratefully and took her to his desk. "Oh, Albert, your Italian writing table, and all the lovely things on it, just as it stood in your room at the Villa Scipione! You used to let me write letters at it. You had the nicest way with young girls. If I had a daughter, I'd want you to do it all over again."

She scratched a note, and Albert put a third place at the table. He noticed Uncle Doctor slip away, and come back with his necktie set straight, attended by a wave of *eau de cologne*. While he was lighting the candles and bringing in the wine cooler, Mrs. Parmenter sat down beside the Doctor, accepted one of his cigarettes, and began to talk to him simply and naturally about Marguerite Thiesinger. Nothing could have been more tactful, Albert knew; nothing could give the old man more pleasure on his birthday. Albert himself couldn't do it any more; he had worn out his power of going over that sad story. He tried to make up for it by playing the songs she had sung.

"Albert," said Mrs. Parmenter when they sat down to dinner, "this is the only spot I know in the world that is before-the-war. You've got a period shut up in here; the last ten years of one century, and the first ten of another. Sitting here, I don't believe in aeroplanes, or jazz, or Cubists. My father is nearly as old as Doctor Engelhardt, and we never buy anything new; yet we haven't kept it out. How do you manage?"

Albert smiled a little ruefully. "I suppose it's because we never have any young people about. They bring it in."

"Elsa," murmured the Doctor. "But I see; she is only a child."

"I'm sorry for the young people now," Mrs. Parmenter went on. "They seem to me coarse and bitter. There's nothing wonderful left for them, poor things; the war destroyed it all. Where could any girl find such a place to escape to as your mother's house, full of chests of linen like this? All houses now are like hotels; nothing left to cherish. Your house was wonderful! And what music we used to have. Do you remember the time you took me to hear Joseffy play the second Brahms, with Gericke? It was the last time I ever heard him. What did happen to him, Albert? Went to pieces in some way, didn't he?"

Albert sighed and shook his head; wine was apt to plunge him into pleasant, poetic melancholy. "I don't know if anyone knows. I stayed in Rome too long to know, myself. Before I went abroad, I'd been taking lessons with him right along—I saw no change in him, though he gave fewer and fewer concerts. When I got back, I wrote him the day I landed in New York—he was living up the Hudson then. I got a reply from his housekeeper, saying that he was not giving lessons, was ill and was seeing nobody. I went out to his place at once. I wasn't asked to come into the house. I was told to wait in the garden. I waited a long while. At last he came out, wearing white clothes, as he often did, a panama hat, carrying a little cane. He shook hands with me, asked me about Mrs. Sterrett—but he was another man, that's all. He was gone; he wasn't there. I was talking to his picture."

"Drugs!" muttered the Doctor out of one corner of his mouth.

"Nonsense!" Albert shrugged in derision. "Or if he did, that was secondary; a result, not a cause. He'd seen the other side of things; he'd let go. Something had happened in his brain that was not paresis."

Mrs. Parmenter leaned forward. "Did he *look* the same? Surely, he had the handsomest head in the world. Remember his forehead? Was he gray? His hair was a reddish chestnut, as I remember."

"A little gray; not much. There was no change in his face, except his eyes. The bright spark had gone out, and his body had a sort of trailing languor when he moved."

"Would he give you a lesson?"

"No. Said he wasn't giving any. Said he was sorry, but he wasn't seeing people at all any more. I remember he sat making patterns in the gravel with his cane. He frowned and said he simply couldn't see people; said the human face had become hateful to him—and the human voice! 'I am sorry,' he said, 'but that is the truth.' I looked at his left hand, lying on his knee. I wonder, Marjorie, that I had the strength to get up and go away. I felt as if everything had been drawn out of me. He got up and took my hand. I understood that I must leave. In desperation I asked him whether music didn't mean anything to him still. 'Music,' he said slowly, with just a ghost of his old smile, 'yes—some music.' He went back into the house. Those were the last words I ever heard him speak."

"Oh dear! And he had everything that is beautiful—and the name of an angel! But we're making the Doctor melancholy. Open another bottle, Albert—father did very well by you. We've not drunk a single toast. Many returns, we take for granted. Why not each drink a toast of our own, to something we care for." She glanced at Doctor Engelhardt, who lifted the bunch of violets by his plate and smelled them absently. "Now, Doctor Engelhardt, a toast!"

The Doctor put down his flowers, delicately took up his glass and held it directly in front of him; everything he did with his hands was deft and sure. A beautiful, a wonderful look came over his face as she watched him.

"I drink," he said slowly, "to a memory; to the lost Lenore."

"And I," said young Albert softly, "to my youth, to my beautiful youth!"

Tears flashed into Mrs. Parmenter's eyes. "Ah," she thought, "that's what liking people amounts to; it's liking their silliness and absurdities. That's what it really is."

"And I," she said aloud, "will drink to the future; to our renewed friendship, and many dinners together. I like you two better than anyone I know."

When Albert came back from seeing Mrs. Parmenter down to her car, he found his uncle standing by the fire, his elbow on the mantle, thoughtfully rolling a cigarette. "Albert," he said in a deeply confidential tone, "good wine, good music, beautiful women; that is all there is worth turning over the hand for."

Albert began to laugh. The old man wasn't often banal. "Why Uncle, you and Martin Luther—"

The Doctor lifted a hand imperiously to stop him, and flushed darkly. He evidently hadn't been aware that he was quoting—it came from the heart. "Martin Luther," he snapped, "was a vulgarian of the first water; cabbage soup!" He paused a moment to light his cigarette. "But don't fool yourself; one like her always knows when a man has had success with women!"

Albert poured a last glass from the bottle and sipped it critically. "Well, you had success tonight, certainly. I could see that Marjorie was impressed. She's coming to take you for a ride tomorrow, after your nap, so you must be ready."

The Doctor passed his flexible, nervous hand lightly over the thick bristles of his French hair-cut. *"Even in our ashes,"* he muttered haughtily.

Forum 81 (February 1929): 78–82, 124–28

New York Stories

Consequences

�֍ ✖ ✖

Henry Eastman, a lawyer, aged forty, was standing beside the Flatiron Building in a driving November rainstorm, signaling frantically for a taxi. It was six-thirty, and everything on wheels was engaged. The streets were in confusion about him, the sky was in turmoil above him, and the Flatiron Building, which seemed about to blow down, threw water like a mill-shoot. Suddenly, out of the brutal struggle of men and cars and machines and people tilting at each other with umbrellas, a quiet, well-mannered limousine paused before him, at the curb, and an agreeable, ruddy countenance confronted him through the open window of the car.

"Don't you want me to pick you up, Mr. Eastman? I'm running directly home now."

Eastman recognized Kier Cavenaugh, a young man of pleasure, who lived in the house on Central Park South, where he himself had an apartment.

"Don't I?" he exclaimed, bolting into the car. "I'll risk getting your cushions wet without compunction. I came up in a taxi, but I didn't hold it. Bad economy. I thought I saw your car down on Fourteenth Street about half an hour ago."

The owner of the car smiled. He had a pleasant, round face and round eyes, and a fringe of smooth, yellow hair showed under the brim of his soft felt hat. "With a lot of little broilers fluttering into it? You did. I know some girls who work in the cheap shops down there. I happened to be downtown and I stopped and took a load of them home. I do sometimes. Saves their poor little clothes, you know. Their shoes are never any good."

Eastman looked at his rescuer. "Aren't they notoriously afraid of cars and smooth young men?" he inquired.

Cavenaugh shook his head. "They know which cars are safe and which are chancy. They put each other wise. You have to take a bunch at a time, of course. The Italian girls can never come along; their men shoot. The girls understand, all right; but their fathers don't. One gets to see queer places, sometimes, taking them home."

Eastman laughed drily. "Every time I touch the circle of your acquaintance, Cavenaugh, it's a little wider. You must know New York pretty well by this time."

"Yes, but I'm on my good behavior below Twenty-third Street," the young man replied with simplicity. "My little friends down there would give me a good character. They're wise little girls. They have grand ways with each other, a romantic code of loyalty. You can find a good many of the lost virtues among them."

The car was standing still in a traffic block at Fortieth Street, when Cavenaugh suddenly drew his face away from the window and touched Eastman's arm. "Look, please. You see that hansom with the bony gray horse—driver has a broken hat and red flannel around his throat. Can you see who is inside?"

Eastman peered out. The hansom was just cutting across the line, and the driver was making a great fuss about it, bobbing his head and waving his whip. He jerked his dripping old horse into Fortieth Street and clattered off past the Public Library grounds toward Sixth Avenue. "No, I couldn't see the passenger. Someone you know?"

"Could you see whether there was a passenger?" Cavenaugh asked.

"Why, yes. A man, I think. I saw his elbow on the apron. No driver ever behaves like that unless he has a passenger."

"Yes, I may have been mistaken," Cavenaugh murmured absent-mindedly. Ten minutes or so later, after Cavenaugh's car had turned off Fifth Avenue into Fifty-eighth Street, Eastman exclaimed, "There's your same cabby, and his cart's empty. He's headed for a drink now, I suppose." The driver in the broken hat and the red flannel neck cloth was still brandishing the whip over his old gray. He was coming from the west now, and turned down Sixth Avenue, under the elevated.

Cavenaugh's car stopped at the bachelor apartment house between Sixth and Seventh Avenues where he and Eastman lived, and they went up in the elevator together. They were still talking when the lift stopped at Cavenaugh's floor, and Eastman stepped out with him and walked down the hall, finishing his sentence while Cavenaugh found his latch-key. When he opened the door, a wave of fresh cigarette smoke greeted them. Cavenaugh stopped short and stared into his hallway. "Now how in the devil—!" he exclaimed angrily.

"Someone waiting for you? Oh, no, thanks. I wasn't coming in. I have to work tonight. Thank you, but I couldn't." Eastman nodded and went up the two flights to his own rooms.

Though Eastman did not customarily keep a servant he had this winter a man who had been lent to him by a friend who was abroad. Rollins met him at the door and took his coat and hat.

"Put out my dinner clothes, Rollins, and then get out of here until ten o'clock. I've promised to go to a supper tonight. I shan't be dining.

I've had a late tea and I'm going to work until ten. You may put out some kumiss and biscuit for me."

Rollins took himself off, and Eastman settled down at the big table in his sitting-room. He had to read a lot of letters submitted as evidence in a breach of contract case, and before he got very far he found that long paragraphs in some of the letters were written in German. He had a German dictionary at his office, but none here. Rollins had gone, and anyhow, the bookstores would be closed. He remembered having seen a row of dictionaries on the lower shelf of one of Cavenaugh's bookcases. Cavenaugh had a lot of books, though he never read anything but new stuff. Eastman prudently turned down his student's lamp very low—the thing had an evil habit of smoking—and went down two flights to Cavenaugh's door.

The young man himself answered Eastman's ring. He was freshly dressed for the evening, except for a brown smoking jacket, and his yellow hair had been brushed until it shone. He hesitated as he confronted his caller, still holding the door knob, and his round eyes and smooth forehead made their best imitation of a frown. When Eastman began to apologize, Cavenaugh's manner suddenly changed. He caught his arm and jerked him into the narrow hall. "Come in, come in. Right along!" he said excitedly. "Right along," he repeated as he pushed Eastman before him into his sitting-room. "Well I'll—" he stopped short at the door and looked about his own room with an air of complete mystification. The back window was wide open and a strong wind was blowing in. Cavenaugh walked over to the window and stuck out his head, looking up and down the fire escape. When he pulled his head in, he drew down the sash.

"I had a visitor I wanted you to see," he explained with a nervous smile. "At least I thought I had. He must have gone out that way," nodding toward the window.

"Call him back. I only came to borrow a German dictionary, if you have one. Can't stay. Call him back."

Cavenaugh shook his head despondently. "No use. He's beat it. Nowhere in sight."

"He must be active. Has he left something?" Eastman pointed to a very dirty white glove that lay on the floor under the window.

"Yes, that's his." Cavenaugh reached for his tongs, picked up the glove, and tossed it into the grate, where it quickly shriveled on the coals. Eastman felt that he had happened in upon something disagreeable, possibly something shady, and he wanted to get away at once. Cavenaugh stood staring at the fire and seemed stupid and dazed; so he repeated his request rather sternly, "I think I've seen a German dictionary down there among your books. May I have it?"

Cavenaugh blinked at him. "A German dictionary? Oh, possibly! Those were my father's. I scarcely know what there is." He put down the tongs and began to wipe his hands nervously with his handkerchief.

Eastman went over to the bookcase behind the Chesterfield, opened the door, swooped upon the book he wanted and stuck it under his arm. He felt perfectly certain now that something shady had been going on in Cavenaugh's rooms, and he saw no reason why he should come in for any hang-over. "Thanks. I'll send it back tomorrow," he said curtly as he made for the door.

Cavenaugh followed him. "Wait a moment. I wanted you to see him. You did see his glove," glancing at the grate.

Eastman laughed disagreeably. "I saw a glove. That's not evidence. Do your friends often use that means of exit? Somewhat inconvenient."

Cavenaugh gave him a startled glance. "Wouldn't you think so? For an old man, a very rickety old party? The ladders are steep, you know, and rusty." He approached the window again and put it up softly. In a moment he drew his head back with a jerk. He caught Eastman's arm and shoved him toward the window. "Hurry, please. Look! Down there." He pointed to the little patch of paved court four flights down.

The square of pavement was so small and the walls about it were so high, that it was a good deal like looking down a well. Four tall buildings backed upon the same court and made a kind of shaft, with flagstones at the bottom, and at the top a square of dark blue with some stars in it. At the bottom of the shaft Eastman saw a black figure, a man in a caped coat and a tall hat stealing cautiously around, not across the square of pavement, keeping close to the dark wall and avoiding the streak of light that fell on the flagstones from a window in the opposite house. Seen from that height he was of course fore-shortened and probably looked more shambling and decrepit than he was. He picked his way along with exaggerated care and looked like a silly old cat crossing a wet street. When he reached the gate that led into an alley way between two buildings, he felt about for the latch, opened the door a mere crack, and then shot out under the feeble lamp that burned in the brick arch over the gateway. The door closed after him.

"He'll get run in," Eastman remarked curtly, turning away from the window. "That door shouldn't be left unlocked. Any crook could come in. I'll speak to the janitor about it, if you don't mind," he added sarcastically.

"Wish you would." Cavenaugh stood brushing down the front of his jacket, first with his right hand and then with his left. "You saw him, didn't you?"

"Enough of him. Seems eccentric. I have to see a lot of buggy people. They don't take me in any more. But I'm keeping you and I'm in a hurry myself. Good night."

Cavenaugh put out his hand detainingly and started to say something; but Eastman rudely turned his back and went down the hall and out of the door. He had never felt anything shady about Cavenaugh before, and he was sorry he had gone down for the dictionary. In five minutes he was deep in his papers; but in the half hour when he was loafing before he dressed to go out, the young man's curious behavior came into his mind again.

Eastman had merely a neighborly acquaintance with Cavenaugh. He had been to a supper at the young man's rooms once, but he didn't particularly like Cavenaugh's friends; so the next time he was asked, he had another engagement. He liked Cavenaugh himself, if for nothing else than because he was so cheerful and trim and ruddy. A good complexion is always at a premium in New York, especially when it shines reassuringly on a man who does everything in the world to lose it. It encourages fellow mortals as to the inherent vigor of the human organism and the amount of bad treatment it will stand for. "Footprints that perhaps another," etc.

Cavenaugh, he knew, had plenty of money. He was the son of a Pennsylvania preacher, who died soon after he discovered that his ancestral acres were full of petroleum, and Kier had come to New York to burn some of the oil. He was thirty-two and was still at it; spent his life, literally, among the breakers. His motor hit the Park every morning as if it were the first time ever. He took people out to supper every night. He went from restaurant to restaurant, sometimes to half-a-dozen in an evening. The head waiters were his hosts and their cordiality made him happy. They made a life-line for him up Broadway and down Fifth Avenue. Cavenaugh was still fresh and smooth, round and plump, with a lustre to his hair and white teeth and a clear look in his round eyes. He seemed absolutely unwearied and unimpaired; never bored and never carried away.

Eastman always smiled when he met Cavenaugh in the entrance hall, serenely going forth to or returning from gladiatorial combats with joy, or when he saw him rolling smoothly up to the door in his car in the morning after a restful night in one of the remarkable new roadhouses he was always finding. Eastman had seen a good many young men disappear on Cavenaugh's route, and he admired this young man's endurance.

Tonight, for the first time, he had got a whiff of something unwholesome about the fellow—bad nerves, bad company, something on hand that he was ashamed of, a visitor old and vicious, who must have had a key to Cavenaugh's apartment, for he was evidently there when Cavenaugh returned at seven o'clock. Probably it was the same man Cavenaugh had seen in the hansom. He must have been able to let himself in, for Cavenaugh kept no man but his chauffeur; or perhaps the janitor had been instructed to let him in. In either case, and whoever he was, it was clear enough that Cavenaugh was ashamed of him and was mixing up in questionable business of some kind.

Eastman sent Cavenaugh's book back by Rollins, and for the next few weeks he had no word with him beyond a casual greeting when they happened to meet in the hall or the elevator. One Sunday morning Cavenaugh telephoned up to him to ask if he could motor out to a roadhouse in Connecticut that afternoon and have supper; but when Eastman found there were to be other guests he declined.

On New Year's eve Eastman dined at the University Club at six o'clock and hurried home before the usual manifestations of insanity had begun in the streets. When Rollins brought his smoking coat, he asked him whether he wouldn't like to get off early.

"Yes, sir. But won't you be dressing, Mr. Eastman?" he inquired.

"Not tonight." Eastman handed him a bill. "Bring some change in the morning. There'll be fees."

Rollins lost no time in putting everything to rights for the night, and Eastman couldn't help wishing that he were in such a hurry to be off somewhere himself. When he heard the hall door close softly, he wondered if there were any place, after all, that he wanted to go. From his window he looked down at the long lines of motors and taxis waiting for a signal to cross Broadway. He thought of some of their probable destinations and decided that none of those places pulled him very hard. The night was warm and wet, the air was drizzly. Vapor hung in clouds about the *Times* Building, half hid the top of it, and made a luminous haze along Broadway.

While he was looking down at the army of wet, black carriage-tops and their reflected headlights and tail-lights, Eastman heard a ring at his door. He deliberated. If it were a caller, the hall porter would have telephoned up. It must be the janitor. When he opened the door, there stood a rosy young man in a tuxedo, without a coat or hat.

"Pardon. Should I have telephoned? I half thought you wouldn't be in."

Eastman laughed. "Come in, Cavenaugh. You weren't sure whether you wanted company or not, eh, and you were trying to let chance decide it? That was exactly my state of mind. Let's accept the verdict." When they emerged from the narrow hall into his sitting-room, he pointed out a seat by the fire to his guest. He brought a tray of decanters and soda bottles and placed it on his writing table.

Cavenaugh hesitated, standing by the fire. "Sure you weren't starting for somewhere?"

"Do I look it? No, I was just making up my mind to stick it out alone when you rang. Have one?" he picked up a tall tumbler.

"Yes, thank you. I always do."

Eastman chuckled. "Lucky boy! So will I. I had a very early dinner. New York is the most arid place on holidays," he continued as he rattled the ice in the glasses. "When one gets too old to hit the rapids down there, and tired of gobbling food to heathenish dance music, there is absolutely no place where you can get a chop and some milk toast in peace, unless you have strong ties of blood brotherhood on upper Fifth Avenue. But you, why aren't you starting for somewhere?"

The young man sipped his soda and shook his head as he replied:

"Oh, I couldn't get a chop, either. I know only flashy people, of course." He looked up at his host with such a grave and candid expression that Eastman decided there couldn't be anything very crooked about the fellow. His smooth cheeks were positively cherubic.

"Well, what's the matter with them? Aren't they flashing tonight?"

"Only the very new ones seem to flash on New Year's eve. The older ones fade away. Maybe they are hunting a chop, too."

"Well"—Eastman sat down—"holidays do dash one. I was just about to write a letter to a pair of maiden aunts in my old home town, up-state; old coasting hill, snow-covered pines, lights in the church windows. That's what you've saved me from."

Cavenaugh shook himself. "Oh, I'm sure that wouldn't have been good for you. Pardon me," he rose and took a photograph from the bookcase, a handsome man in shooting clothes. "Dudley, isn't it? Did you know him well?"

"Yes. An old friend. Terrible thing, wasn't it? I haven't got over the jolt yet."

"His suicide? Yes, terrible! Did you know his wife?"

"Slightly. Well enough to admire her very much. She must be terribly broken up. I wonder Dudley didn't think of that."

Cavenaugh replaced the photograph carefully, lit a cigarette, and standing before the fire began to smoke. "Would you mind telling me about him? I never met him, but of course I'd read a lot about him, and I can't help feeling interested. It was a queer thing."

Eastman took out his cigar case and leaned back in his deep chair. "In the days when I knew him best he hadn't any story, like the happy nations. Everything was properly arranged for him before he was born. He came into the world happy, healthy, clever, straight, with the right sort of connections and the right kind of fortune, neither too large nor too small. He helped to make the world an agreeable place to live in until he was twenty-six. Then he married as he should have married. His wife was a Californian, educated abroad. Beautiful. You have seen her picture?"

Cavenaugh nodded. "Oh, many of them."

"She was interesting, too. Though she was distinctly a person of the world, she had retained something, just enough of the large Western manner. She had the habit of authority, of calling out a special train if she needed it, of using all our ingenious mechanical contrivances lightly and easily, without over-rating them. She and Dudley knew how to live better than most people. Their house was the most charming one I have ever known in New York. You felt freedom there, and a zest of life, and safety—absolute sanctuary—from everything sordid or petty. A whole society like that would justify the creation of man and would make our planet shine with a soft, peculiar radiance among the constellations. You think I'm putting it on thick?"

The young man sighed gently. "Oh, no! One has always felt there must be people like that. I've never known any."

"They had two children, beautiful ones. After they had been married for eight years, Rosina met this Spaniard. He must have amounted to something. She wasn't a flighty woman. She came home and told Dudley how matters stood. He persuaded her to stay at home for six months and try to pull up. They were both fair-minded people, and I'm as sure as if I were the Almighty, that she did try. But at the end of the time, Rosina went quietly off to Spain, and Dudley went to hunt in the Canadian Rockies. I met his party out there. I didn't know his wife had left him and talked about her a good deal. I noticed that he never drank anything, and his light used to shine through the log chinks of his room until all hours, even after a hard day's hunting. When I got back to New York, rumors were creeping about. Dudley did not come back. He bought a ranch in Wyoming, built a big log house and kept splendid dogs and horses. One of his sisters went out to keep house for him, and the children were there when they were not in school. He had a great many visitors, and everyone who came back talked about how well Dudley kept things going.

"He put in two years out there. Then, last month, he had to come back on business. A trust fund had to be settled up, and he was administrator. I saw him at the club; same light, quick step, same gracious handshake. He was getting gray, and there was something softer in his manner; but he had a fine red tan on his face and said he found it delightful to be here in the season when everything is going hard. The Madison Avenue house had been closed since Rosina left it. He went there to get some things his sister wanted. That, of course, was the mistake. He went alone, in the afternoon, and didn't go out for dinner—found some sherry and tins of biscuit in the sideboard. He shot himself sometime that night. There were pistols in his smoking-room. They found burnt out candles beside him in the morning. The gas and electricity were shut off. I suppose there, in his own house, among his own things, it was too much for him. He left no letters."

Cavenaugh blinked and brushed the lapel of his coat. "I suppose," he said slowly, "that every suicide is logical and reasonable, if one knew all the facts."

Eastman roused himself. "No, I don't think so. I've known too many fellows who went off like that—more than I deserve, I think—and some of them were absolutely inexplicable. I can understand Dudley; but I can't see why healthy bachelors, with money enough, like ourselves, need such a device. It reminds me of what Dr. Johnson said, that the most discouraging thing about life is the number of fads and hobbies and fake religions it takes to put people through a few years of it."

"Dr. Johnson? The specialist? Oh, the old fellow!" said Cavenaugh imperturbably. "Yes, that's interesting. Still, I fancy if one knew the facts— Did you know about Wyatt?"

"I don't think so."

"You wouldn't, probably. He was just a fellow about town who spent money. He wasn't one of the *forestieri*, though. Had connections here and owned a fine old place over on Staten Island. He went in for botany, and had been all over, hunting things; rusts, I believe. He had a yacht and used to take a gay crowd down about the South Seas, botanizing. He really did botanize, I believe. I never knew such a spender—only not flashy. He helped a lot of fellows and he was awfully good to girls, the kind who come down here to get a little fun, who don't like to work and still aren't really tough, the kind you see talking hard for their dinner. Nobody knows what becomes of them, or what they get out of it, and there are hundreds of new ones every year. He helped dozens of 'em; it was he who got me curious about the little shop girls. Well, one afternoon when his tea was brought, he took prussic acid instead. He didn't leave any letters, either; people of any taste don't. They wouldn't leave any material reminder if they could help it. His lawyers found that he had just $314.72 above his debts when he died. He had planned to spend all his money, and then take his tea; he had worked it out carefully."

Eastman reached for his pipe and pushed his chair away from the fire. "That looks like a considered case, but I don't think philosophical suicides like that are common. I think they usually come from stress of feeling and are really, as the newspapers call them, desperate acts; done without a motive. You remember when Anna Karenina was under the wheels, she kept saying, 'Why am I here?'"

Cavenaugh rubbed his upper lip with his pink finger and made an effort to wrinkle his brows. "May I, please?" reaching for the whiskey. "But have you," he asked, blinking as the soda flew at him, "have you ever known, yourself, cases that were really inexplicable?"

"A few too many. I was in Washington just before Captain Jack Purden was married and I saw a good deal of him. Popular army man, fine record in the Philippines, married a charming girl with lots of money; mutual devotion. It was the gayest wedding of the winter, and they started for Japan. They stopped in San Francisco for a week and missed their boat because, as the bride wrote back to Washington, they were too happy to move. They took the next boat, were both good sailors, had exceptional weather. After they had been out for two weeks, Jack got up from his deck chair one afternoon, yawned, put down his book, and stood before his wife. 'Stop reading for a moment and look at me.' She laughed and asked him why. 'Because you happen to be good to look at.' He nodded to her, went back to the stern and was never seen again. Must have gone down to the lower deck and slipped overboard, behind the machinery. It was the luncheon hour, not many people about; steamer cutting through a soft green sea. That's one of the most baffling cases I know. His friends raked up his past, and it was as trim as a cottage garden. If he'd so much as dropped an ink spot on his fatigue uniform, they'd have found it. He wasn't emotional or moody; wasn't, indeed, very interesting; simply a good soldier, fond of all the pompous little formalities that make up a military man's life. What do you make of that, my boy?"

Cavenaugh stroked his chin. "It's very puzzling, I admit. Still, if one knew everything—"

"But we do know everything. His friends wanted to find something to help them out, to help the girl out, to help the case of the human creature."

"Oh, I don't mean things that people could unearth," said Cavenaugh uneasily. "But possibly there were things that couldn't be found out."

Eastman shrugged his shoulders. "It's my experience that when there are 'things' as you call them, they're very apt to be found. There is no such thing as a secret. To make any move at all one has to employ human agencies, employ at least one human agent. Even when the pirates killed the men who buried their gold for them, the bones told the story."

Cavenaugh rubbed his hands together and smiled his sunny smile.

"I like that idea. It's reassuring. If we can have no secrets, it means that we can't, after all, go so far afield as we might," he hesitated, "yes, as we might."

Eastman looked at him sourly. "Cavenaugh, when you've practised law in New York for twelve years, you find that people can't go far in any direction, except—" He thrust his forefinger sharply at the floor. "Even in that direction, few people can do anything out of the ordinary. Our range is limited. Skip a few baths, and we become personally objectionable. The slightest carelessness can rot a man's integrity or give him ptomaine poisoning. We keep up only by incessant cleansing operations, of mind and body. What we call character, is held together by all sorts of tacks and strings and glue."

Cavenaugh looked startled. "Come now, it's not so bad as that, is it? I've always thought that a serious man, like you, must know a lot of Launcelots." When Eastman only laughed, the younger man squirmed about in his chair. He spoke again hastily, as if he were embarrassed. "Your military friend may have had personal experiences, however, that his friends couldn't possibly get a line on. He may accidentally have come to a place where he saw himself in too unpleasant a light. I believe people can be chilled by a draft from outside, somewhere."

"Outside?" Eastman echoed. "Ah, you mean the far outside! Ghosts, delusions, eh?"

Cavenaugh winced. "That's putting it strong. Why not say tips from the outside? Delusions belong to a diseased mind, don't they? There are some of us who have no minds to speak of, who yet have had experiences. I've had a little something in that line myself and I don't look it, do I?"

Eastman looked at the bland countenance turned toward him. "Not exactly. What's your delusion?"

"It's not a delusion. It's a haunt."

The lawyer chuckled. "Soul of a lost Casino girl?"

"No; an old gentleman. A most unattractive old gentleman, who follows me about."

"Does he want money?"

Cavenaugh sat up straight. "No. I wish to God he wanted anything—but the pleasure of my society! I'd let him clean me out to be rid of him. He's a real article. You saw him yourself that night when you came to my rooms to borrow a dictionary, and he went down the fire escape. You saw him down in the court."

"Well, I saw somebody down in the court, but I'm too cautious to take it for granted that I saw what you saw. Why, anyhow, should I see your haunt? If it was your friend I saw, he impressed me disagreeably. How did you pick him up?"

Cavenaugh looked gloomy. "That was queer, too. Charley Burke and I had motored out to Long Beach, about a year ago, sometime in October, I think. We had supper and stayed until late. When we were coming home, my car broke down. We had a lot of girls along who had to get back for morning rehearsals and things; so I sent them all into town in Charley's car, and he was to send a man back to tow me home. I was driving myself, and didn't want to leave my machine. We had not taken a direct road back; so I was stuck in a lonesome, woody place, no houses about. I got chilly and made a fire, and was putting in the time comfortably enough, when this old party steps up. He was in shabby evening clothes and a top hat, and had on his usual white gloves. How he got there, at three o'clock in the morning, miles from any town or railway, I'll leave it to you to figure out. *He* surely had no car. When I saw him coming up to the fire, I disliked him. He had a silly, apologetic walk. His teeth were chattering, and I asked him to sit down. He got down like a clothes-horse folding up. I offered him a cigarette, and when he took off his gloves I couldn't help noticing how knotted and spotty his hands were. He was asthmatic, and took his breath with a wheeze. 'Haven't you got anything—refreshing in there?' he asked, nodding at the car. When I told him I hadn't, he sighed. 'Ah, you young fellows are greedy. You drink it all up. You drink it all up, all up—up!' he kept chewing it over."

Cavenaugh paused and looked embarrassed again. "The thing that was most unpleasant is difficult to explain. The old man sat there by the fire and leered at me with a silly sort of admiration that was—well, more than humiliating. 'Gay boy, gay dog!' he would mutter, and when he grinned he showed his teeth, worn and yellow—shells. I remembered that it was better to talk casually to insane people; so I remarked carelessly that I had been out with a party and got stuck.

"'Oh yes, I remember,' he said, 'Flora and Lottie and Maybelle and Marcelline, and poor Kate.'

"He had named them correctly; so I began to think I had been hitting the bright waters too hard.

"Things I drank never had seemed to make me woody; but you can never tell when trouble is going to hit you. I pulled my hat down and tried to look as uncommunicative as possible; but he kept croaking on from time to time, like this: 'Poor Katie! Splendid arms, but dope got her. She took up with Eastern religions after she had her hair dyed. Got to going to a Swami's joint, and smoking opium. Temple of the Lotus, it was called, and the police raided it.'

"This was nonsense, of course; the young woman was in the pink of condition. I let him rave, but I decided that if something didn't come out for me pretty soon, I'd foot it across Long Island. There wasn't room enough for the two of us. I got up and took another try at my car. He hopped right after me.

"'Good car,' he wheezed, 'better than the little Ford.'

"I'd had a Ford before, but so has everybody; that was a safe guess.

"'Still,' he went on, 'that run in from Huntington Bay in the rain wasn't bad. Arrested for speeding, he-he.'

"It was true I had made such a run, under rather unusual circumstances, and had been arrested. When at last I heard my life-boat snorting up the road, my visitor got up, sighed, and stepped back into the shadow of the trees. I didn't wait to see what became of him, you may believe. That was visitation number one. What do you think of it?"

Cavenaugh looked at his host defiantly. Eastman smiled.

"I think you'd better change your mode of life, Cavenaugh. Had many returns?" he inquired.

"Too many, by far." The young man took a turn about the room and came back to the fire. Standing by the mantel he lit another cigarette before going on with his story:

"The second visitation happened in the street, early in the evening, about eight o'clock. I was held up in a traffic block before the Plaza. My chauffeur was driving. Old Nibbs steps up out of the crowd, opens the door of my car, gets in and sits down beside me. He had on wilted evening clothes, same as before, and there was some sort of heavy scent about him. Such an unpleasant old party! A thorough-going rotter; you knew it at once. This time he wasn't talkative, as he had been when I first saw him. He leaned back in the car as if he owned it, crossed his hands on his stick and looked out at the crowd—sort of hungrily.

"I own I really felt a loathing compassion for him. We got down the avenue slowly. I kept looking out at the mounted police. But what could I do? Have him pulled? I was afraid to. I was awfully afraid of getting him into the papers.

"'I'm going to the New Astor,' I said at last. 'Can I take you any-where?'

"'No, thank you,' says he. 'I get out when you do. I'm due on West Forty-fourth. I'm dining tonight with Marcelline—all that is left of her!'

"He put his hand to his hat brim with a grewsome salute. Such a scandalous, foolish old face as he had! When we pulled up at the Astor, I stuck my hand in my pocket and asked him if he'd like a little loan.

"'No, thank you, but'—he leaned over and whispered, ugh!—'but save a little, save a little. Forty years from now—a little—comes in handy. Save a little.'

"His eyes fairly glittered as he made his remark. I jumped out. I'd have jumped into the North River. When he tripped off, I asked my chauffeur if he'd noticed the man who got into the car with me. He said he knew someone was with me, but he hadn't noticed just when he got in. Want to hear any more?"

Cavenaugh dropped into his chair again. His plump cheeks were a trifle more flushed than usual, but he was perfectly calm. Eastman felt that the young man believed what he was telling him.

"Of course I do. It's very interesting. I don't see quite where you are coming out though."

Cavenaugh sniffed. "No more do I. I really feel that I've been put upon. I haven't deserved it any more than any other fellow of my kind. Doesn't it impress you disagreeably?"

"Well, rather so. Has anyone else seen your friend?"

"You saw him."

"We won't count that. As I said, there's no certainty that you and I saw the same person in the court that night. Has anyone else had a look in?"

"People sense him rather than see him. He usually crops up when I'm alone or in a crowd on the street. He never approaches me when I'm with people I know, though I've seen him hanging about the doors of theatres when I come out with a party; loafing around the stage exit, under a wall; or across the street, in a doorway. To be frank, I'm not anxious to introduce him. The third time, it was I who came upon him. In November my driver, Harry, had a sudden attack of appendicitis. I took him to the Presbyterian Hospital in the car, early in the evening. When I came home, I found the old villain in my rooms. I offered him a drink, and he sat down. It was the first time I had seen him in a steady light, with his hat off.

"His face is lined like a railway map, and as to color—Lord, what a liver! His scalp grows tight to his skull, and his hair is dyed until it's perfectly dead, like a piece of black cloth."

Cavenaugh ran his fingers through his own neatly trimmed thatch, and seemed to forget where he was for a moment.

"I had a twin brother, Brian, who died when we were sixteen. I have a photograph of him on my wall, an enlargement from a kodak of him, doing a high jump, rather good thing, full of action. It seemed to annoy the old gentleman. He kept looking at it and lifting his eyebrows, and finally he got up, tip-toed across the room, and turned the picture to the wall.

" 'Poor Brian! Fine fellow, but died young,' says he.

"Next morning, there was the picture, still reversed."

"Did he stay long?" Eastman asked interestedly.

"Half an hour, by the clock."

"Did he talk?"

"Well, he rambled."

"What about?"

Cavenaugh rubbed his pale eyebrows before answering.

"About things that an old man ought to want to forget. His conversation is highly objectionable. Of course he knows me like a book; everything I've ever done or thought. But when he recalls them, he throws a bad light on them, somehow. Things that weren't much off color, look rotten. He doesn't leave one a shred of self-respect, he really doesn't. That's the amount of it." The young man whipped out his handkerchief and wiped his face.

"You mean he really talks about things that none of your friends know?"

"Oh, dear, yes! Recalls things that happened in school. Anything disagreeable. Funny thing, he always turns Brian's picture to the wall."

"Does he come often?"

"Yes, oftener, now. Of course I don't know how he gets in downstairs. The hall boys never see him. But he has a key to my door. I don't know how he got it, but I can hear him turn it in the lock."

"Why don't you keep your driver with you, or telephone for me to come down?"

"He'd only grin and go down the fire escape as he did before. He's often done it when Harry's come in suddenly. Everybody has to be alone sometimes, you know. Besides, I don't want anybody to see him. He has me there."

"But why not? Why do you feel responsible for him?"

Cavenaugh smiled wearily. "That's rather the point, isn't it? Why do I? But I absolutely do. That identifies him, more than his knowing all about my life and my affairs."

Eastman looked at Cavenaugh thoughtfully. "Well, I should advise you to go in for something altogether different and new, and go in for it hard; business, engineering, metallurgy, something this old fellow wouldn't be interested in. See if you can make him remember logarithms."

Cavenaugh sighed. "No, he has me there, too. People never really change; they go on being themselves. But I would never make much trouble. Why can't they let me alone, damn it! I'd never hurt anybody, except, perhaps—"

"Except your old gentleman, eh?" Eastman laughed. "Seriously, Cavenaugh, if you want to shake him, I think a year on a ranch would do it. He would never be coaxed far from his favorite haunts. He would dread Montana."

Cavenaugh pursed up his lips. "So do I!"

"Oh, you think you do. Try it, and you'll find out. A gun and a horse beats all this sort of thing. Besides losing your haunt, you'd be putting ten years in the bank for yourself. I know a good ranch where they take people, if you want to try it."

"Thank you. I'll consider. Do you think I'm batty?"

"No, but I think you've been doing one sort of thing too long. You need big horizons. Get out of this."

Cavenaugh smiled meekly. He rose lazily and yawned behind his hand. "It's late, and I've taken your whole evening." He strolled over to the window and looked out. "Queer place, New York; rough on the little fellows. Don't you feel sorry for them, the girls especially? I do. What a fight they put up for a little fun! Why, even that old goat is sorry for them, the only decent thing he kept."

Eastman followed him to the door and stood in the hall, while Cavenaugh waited for the elevator. When the car came up Cavenaugh extended his pink, warm hand. "Good night."

The cage sank and his rosy countenance disappeared, his round-eyed smile being the last thing to go.

Weeks passed before Eastman saw Cavenaugh again. One morning, just as he was starting for Washington to argue a case before the Supreme Court, Cavenaugh telephoned him at his office to ask him about the Montana ranch he had recommended; said he meant to take his advice and go out there for the spring and summer.

When Eastman got back from Washington, he saw dusty trunks, just up from the trunk room, before Cavenaugh's door. Next morning, when he stopped to see what the young man was about, he found Cavenaugh in his shirt sleeves, packing.

"I'm really going; off tomorrow night. You didn't think it of me, did you?" he asked gaily.

"Oh, I've always had hopes of you!" Eastman declared. "But you are in a hurry, it seems to me."

"Yes, I am in a hurry." Cavenaugh shot a pair of leggings into one of the open trunks. "I telegraphed your ranch people, used your name, and they said it would be all right. By the way, some of my crowd are giving a little dinner for me at Rector's tonight. Couldn't you be persuaded, as it's a farewell occasion?" Cavenaugh looked at him hopefully.

Eastman laughed and shook his head. "Sorry, Cavenaugh, but that's too gay a world for me. I've got too much work lined up before me. I wish I had time to stop and look at your guns, though. You seem to know something about guns. You've more than you'll need, but nobody can have too many good ones." He put down one of the revolvers regretfully. "I'll drop in to see you in the morning, if you're up."

"I shall be up, all right. I've warned my crowd that I'll cut away before midnight."

"You won't, though," Eastman called back over his shoulder as he hurried downstairs.

The next morning, while Eastman was dressing, Rollins came in greatly excited.

"I'm a little late, sir. I was stopped by Harry, Mr. Cavenaugh's driver. Mr. Cavenaugh shot himself last night, sir."

Eastman dropped his vest and sat down on his shoe-box. "You're drunk, Rollins," he shouted. "He's going away today!"

"Yes, sir. Harry found him this morning. Ah, he's quite dead, sir. Harry's telephoned for the coroner. Harry don't know what to do with the ticket."

Eastman pulled on his coat and ran down the stairway. Cavenaugh's trunks were strapped and piled before the door. Harry was walking up and down the hall with a long green railroad ticket in his hand and a look of complete stupidity on his face.

"What shall I do about this ticket, Mr. Eastman?" he whispered. "And what about his trunks? He had me tell the transfer people to come early. They may be here any minute. Yes, sir. I brought him home in the car last night, before twelve, as cheerful as could be."

"Be quiet, Harry. Where is he?"

"In his bed, sir."

Eastman went into Cavenaugh's sleeping-room. When he came back to the sitting-room, he looked over the writing table; railway folders, time-tables, receipted bills, nothing else. He looked up for the photograph of Cavenaugh's twin brother. There it was, turned to the wall. Eastman took it down and looked at it; a boy in track clothes, half lying in the air, going over the string shoulders first, above the heads of a crowd of lads who were running and cheering. The face was somewhat blurred by the motion and the bright sunlight. Eastman put the picture back, as he found it. Had Cavenaugh entertained his visitor last night, and had the old man been more convincing than usual? "Well, at any rate, he's seen to it that the old man can't establish identity. What a soft lot they are, fellows like poor Cavenaugh!" Eastman thought of his office as a delightful place.

McClure's 46 (November 1915): 30–32, 63–64

The Bookkeeper's Wife

✤ ✤ ✤

Nobody but the janitor was stirring about the offices of the Remsen Paper Company, and still Percy Bixby sat at his desk, crouched on his high stool and staring out at the tops of the tall buildings flushed with the winter sunset, at the hundreds of windows, so many rectangles of white electric light, flashing against the broad waves of violet that ebbed across the sky. His ledgers were all in their places, his desk was in order, his office coat on its peg, and yet Percy's smooth, thin face wore the look of anxiety and strain which usually meant that he was behind in his work. He was trying to persuade himself to accept a loan from the company without the company's knowledge. As a matter of fact, he had already accepted it. His books were fixed, the money, in a black-leather bill-book, was already inside his waistcoat pocket.

He had still time to change his mind, to rectify the false figures in his ledger, and to tell Stella Brown that they couldn't possibly get married next month. There he always halted in his reasoning, and went back to the beginning.

The Remsen Paper Company was a very wealthy concern, with easy, old-fashioned working methods. They did a long-time credit business with safe customers, who never thought of paying up very close on their large indebtedness. From the payments on these large accounts Percy had taken a hundred dollars here and two hundred there until he had made up the thousand he needed. So long as he stayed by the books himself and attended to the mail-orders he couldn't possibly be found out. He could move these little shortages about from account to account indefinitely. He could have all the time he needed to pay back the deficit, and more time than he needed.

Although he was so far along in one course of action, his mind still clung resolutely to the other. He did not believe he was going to do it. He was the least of a sharper in the world. Being scrupulously honest even in the most trifling matters was a pleasure to him. He was the sort of young man that Socialists hate more than they hate capitalists. He loved his desk, he loved his books, which had no handwriting in them but his own. He never thought of resenting the fact that he had written away in those books the good red years between twenty-one and twenty-seven. He would have hated to let any one else put so much as a pen-scratch in them. He liked all the boys about the office; his desk, worn smooth by the sleeves of his alpaca coat; his rulers and inks and pens and calendars. He had a great pride in working economics, and he always got so far ahead when supplies were distributed that he had drawers full of pencils and pens and rubber bands against a rainy day.

Percy liked regularity: to get his work done on time, to have his half-day off every Saturday, to go to the theater Saturday night, to buy a new necktie twice a month, to appear in a new straw hat on the right day in May, and to know what was going on in New York. He read the morning and evening papers coming and going on the elevated, and preferred journals of approximate reliability. He got excited about ball-games and elections and business failures, was not above an interest in murders and divorce scandals, and he checked the news off as neatly as he checked his mail-orders. In short, Percy Bixby was like the model pupil who is satisfied with his lessons and his teachers and his holidays, and who would gladly go to school all his life. He had never wanted anything outside his routine until he wanted Stella Brown to marry him, and that had upset everything.

It wasn't, he told himself for the hundredth time, that she was extravagant. Not a bit of it. She was like all girls. Moreover, she made good money, and why should she marry unless she could better herself? The trouble was that he had lied to her about his salary. There were a lot of fellows rushing Mrs. Brown's five daughters, and they all seemed to have fixed on Stella as first choice and this or that one of the sisters as second. Mrs. Brown thought it proper to drop an occasional hint in the presence of these young men to the effect that she expected Stella to "do well." It went without saying that hair and complexion like Stella's could scarcely be expected to do poorly. Most of the boys who went to the house and took the girls out in a bunch to dances and movies seemed to realize this. They merely wanted a whirl with Stella before they settled down to one of her sisters. It was tacitly understood that she came too high for them. Percy had sensed all this through those slumbering instincts which awake in us all to befriend us in love or in danger.

But there was one of his rivals, he knew, who was a man to be reckoned with. Charley Greengay was a young salesman who wore tailor-made clothes and spotted waistcoats, and had a necktie for every day in the month. His air was that of a young man who is out for things that come high and who is going to get them. Mrs. Brown was ever and again dropping a word before Percy about how the girl that took Charley would have her flat furnished by the best furniture people, and her china-closet stocked with the best ware, and would have nothing to worry about but nicks and scratches. It was because he felt himself pitted against this pulling power of Greengay's that Percy had brazenly lied to Mrs. Brown, and told her that his salary had been raised to fifty a week, and that now he wanted to get married.

When he threw out this challenge to Mother Brown, Percy was getting thirty-five dollars a week, and he knew well enough that there were several hundred thousand young men in New York who would do his work as well as he did for thirty.

These were the factors in Percy's present situation. He went over them again and again as he sat stooping on his tall stool. He had quite lost track of time when he heard the janitor call good night to the watchman. Without thinking what he was doing, he slid into his overcoat, caught his hat, and rushed out to the elevator, which was waiting for the janitor. The moment the car dropped, it occurred to him that the thing was decided without his having made up his mind at all. The familiar floors passed him, ten, nine, eight, seven. By the time he reached the fifth, there was no possibility of going back; the click of the drop-lever seemed to settle that. The money was in his pocket. Now, he told himself as he hurried out into the exciting clamor of the street, he was not going to worry about it any more.

When Percy reached the Browns' flat on 123d Street that evening he felt just the slightest chill in Stella's greeting. He could make that all right, he told himself, as he kissed her lightly in the dark three-by-four entrance-hall. Percy's courting had been prosecuted mainly in the Bronx or in winged pursuit of a Broadway car. When he entered the crowded sitting-room he greeted Mrs. Brown respectfully and the four girls playfully. They were all piled on one couch, reading the continued story in the evening paper, and they didn't think it necessary to assume more formal attitudes for Percy. They looked up over the smeary pink sheets of paper, and handed him, as Percy said, the same old jolly:

"Hullo, Perc'! Come to see me, ain't you? So flattered!"

"Any sweet goods on you, Perc'? Anything doing in the bong-bong line tonight?"

"Look at his new neckwear! Say, Perc', remember me. That tie would go lovely with my new tailored waist."

"Quit your kiddin', girls!" called Mrs. Brown, who was drying shirt-waists on the dining-room radiator. "And, Percy, mind the rugs when you're steppin' round among them gum-drops."

Percy fired his last shot at the recumbent figures, and followed Stella into the dining-room, where the table and two large easy-chairs formed, in Mrs. Brown's estimation, a proper background for a serious suitor.

"I say, Stell'," he began as he walked about the table with his hands in his pockets, "seems to me we ought to begin buying our stuff." She brightened perceptibly. "Ah," Percy thought, "so that *was* the trouble!" "Tomorrow's Saturday; why can't we make an afternoon of it?" he went on cheerfully. "Shop till we're tired, then go to Houtin's for dinner, and end up at the theater."

As they bent over the lists she had made of things needed, Percy glanced at her face. She was very much out of her sisters' class and out of his, and he kept congratulating himself on his nerve. He was going in for something much too handsome and expensive and distinguished for him, he felt, and it took courage to be a plunger. To begin with, Stella was the sort of girl who had to be well dressed. She had pale primrose hair, with bluish tones in it, very soft and fine, so that it lay smooth however she dressed it, and pale-blue eyes, with blond eyebrows and long, dark lashes. She would have been a little too remote and languid even for the fastidious Percy had it not been for her hard, practical mouth, with lips that always kept their pink even when the rest of her face was pale. Her employers, who at first might be struck by her indifference, understood that anybody with that sort of mouth would get through the work.

After the shopping-lists had been gone over, Percy took up the question of the honeymoon. Stella said she had been thinking of Atlantic City. Percy met her with firmness. Whatever happened, he couldn't leave his books now.

"I want to do my traveling right here on Forty-second Street, with a high-price show every night," he declared. He made out an itinerary, punctuated by theaters and restaurants, which Stella consented to accept as a substitute for Atlantic City.

"They give your fellows a week off when they're married, don't they?" she asked.

"Yes, but I'll want to drop into the office every morning to look after my mail. That's only businesslike."

"I'd like to have you treated as well as the others, though." Stella turned the rings about on her pale hand and looked at her polished finger-tips.

"I'll look out for that. What do you say to a little walk, Stell'?" Percy put the question coaxingly. When Stella was pleased with him she went to walk with him, since that was the only way in which Percy could ever see her alone. When she was displeased, she said she was too tired to go out. Tonight she smiled at him incredulously, and went to put on her hat and gray fur piece.

Once they were outside, Percy turned into a shadowy side street that was only partly built up, a dreary waste of derricks and foundation holes, but comparatively solitary. Stella liked Percy's steady, sympathetic silences; she was not a chatterbox herself. She often wondered why she was going to marry Bixby instead of Charley Greengay. She knew that Charley would go further in the world. Indeed, she had often coolly told herself that Percy would never go very far. But, as she admitted with a shrug, she was "weak to Percy." In the capable New York stenographer, who estimated values coldly and got the most for the least outlay, there was something left that belonged to another kind of woman—something that liked the very things in Percy that were not good business assets. However much she dwelt upon the effectiveness of Greengay's dash and color and assurance, her mind always came back to Percy's neat little head, his clean-cut face, and warm, clear, gray eyes, and she liked them better than Charley's fullness and blurred floridness. Having reckoned up their respective chances with no doubtful result, she opposed a mild obstinacy to her own good sense. "I guess I'll take Percy, *anyway*," she said simply, and that was all the good her clever business brain did her.

Percy spent a night of torment, lying tense on his bed in the dark, and figuring out how long it would take him to pay back the money he was advancing to himself. Any fool could do it in five years, he reasoned, but he was going to do it in three. The trouble was that his expensive courtship had taken every penny of his salary. With competitors like Charley Greengay, you had to spend money or drop out. Certain birds, he reflected ruefully, are supplied with more attractive plumage when they are courting, but nature hadn't been so thoughtful for men. When Percy reached the office in the morning he climbed on his tall stool and leaned his arms on his ledger. He was so glad to feel it there that he was faint and weak-kneed.

Oliver Remsen, Junior, had brought new blood into the Remsen Paper Company. He married shortly after Percy Bixby did, and in the five succeeding years he had considerably enlarged the company's business and profits. He had been particularly successful in encouraging efficiency and loyalty in the employees. From the time he came into the office he had stood for shorter hours, longer holidays, and a generous consideration of men's necessities. He came out of college on the wave of economic reform, and he continued to read and think a good deal about how the machinery of labor is operated. He knew more about the men who worked for him than their mere office records.

Young Remsen was troubled about Percy Bixby because he took no summer vacations—always asked for the two weeks' extra pay instead. Other men in the office had skipped a vacation now and then, but Percy had stuck to his desk for five years, had tottered to his stool through attacks of grippe and tonsillitis. He seemed to have grown fast to his ledger, and it was to this that Oliver objected. He liked his men to stay men, to look like men and live like men. He remembered how alert and wide-awake Bixby had seemed to him when he himself first came into the office. He had picked Bixby out as the most intelligent and interested of his father's employees, and since then had often wondered why he never seemed to see chances to forge ahead. Promotions, of course, went to the men who went after them. When Percy's baby died, he went to the funeral, and asked Percy to call on him if he needed money. Once when he chanced to sit down by Bixby on the elevated and found him reading Bryce's "American Commonwealth," he asked him to make use of his own large office library. Percy thanked him, but he never came for any books. Oliver wondered whether his bookkeeper really tried to avoid him.

One evening Oliver met the Bixbys in the lobby of a theater. He introduced Mrs. Remsen to them, and held them for some moments in conversation. When they got into their motor, Mrs. Remsen said:

"Is that little man afraid of you, Oliver? He looked like a scared rabbit."

Oliver snapped the door, and said with a shade of irritation:

"I don't know what's the matter with him. He's the fellow I've told you about who never takes a vacation. I half believe it's his wife. She looks pitiless enough for anything."

"She's very pretty of her kind," mused Mrs. Remsen, "but rather chilling. One can see that she has ideas about elegance."

"Rather unfortunate ones for a bookkeeper's wife. I surmise that Percy felt she was overdressed, and that made him awkward with me. I've always suspected that fellow of good taste."

After that, when Remsen passed the counting-room and saw Percy screwed up over his ledger, he often remembered Mrs. Bixby, with her cold, pale eyes and long lashes, and her expression that was something between indifference and discontent. She rose behind Percy's bent shoulders like an apparition.

One spring afternoon Remsen was closeted in his private office with his lawyer until a late hour. As he came down the long hall in the dusk he glanced through the glass partition into the counting-room, and saw Percy Bixby huddled up on his tall stool, though it was too dark to work. Indeed, Bixby's ledger was closed, and he sat with his two arms resting on the brown cover. He did not move a muscle when young Remsen entered.

"You are late, Bixby, and so am I," Oliver began genially as he crossed to the front of the room and looked out at the lighted windows of other tall buildings. "The fact is, I've been doing something that men have a foolish way of putting off. I've been making my will."

"Yes, sir." Percy brought it out with a deep breath.

"Glad to be through with it," Oliver went on. "Mr. Melton will bring the paper back tomorrow, and I'd like to ask you to be one of the witnesses."

"I'd be very proud, Mr. Remsen."

"Thank you, Bixby. Good night." Remsen took up his hat just as Percy slid down from his stool.

"Mr. Remsen, I'm told you're going to have the books gone over."

"Why, yes, Bixby. Don't let that trouble you. I'm taking in a new partner, you know, an old college friend. Just because he is a friend, I insist upon all the usual formalities. But it is a formality, and I'll guarantee the expert won't make a scratch on your books. Good night. You'd better be coming, too." Remsen had reached the door when he heard "Mr. Remsen!" in a desperate voice behind him. He turned, and saw Bixby standing uncertainly at one end of the desk, his hand still on his ledger, his uneven shoulders drooping forward and his head hanging as if he were seasick. Remsen came back and stood at the other end of the long desk. It was too dark to see Bixby's face clearly.

"What is it, Bixby?"

"Mr. Remsen, five years ago, just before I was married, I falsified the books a thousand dollars, and I used the money." Percy leaned forward against his desk, which took him just across the chest.

"What's that, Bixby?" Young Remsen spoke in a tone of polite surprise. He felt painfully embarrassed.

"Yes, sir. I thought I'd get it all paid back before this. I've put back three hundred, but the books are still seven hundred out of true. I've played the shortages about from account to account these five years, but an expert would find 'em in twenty-four hours."

"I don't just understand how—" Oliver stopped and shook his head.

"I held it out of the Western remittances, Mr. Remsen. They were coming in heavy just then. I was up against it. I hadn't saved anything to marry on, and my wife thought I was getting more money than I was. Since we've been married, I've never had the nerve to tell her. I could have paid it all back if it hadn't been for the unforeseen expenses."

Remsen sighed.

"Being married is largely unforeseen expenses, Percy. There's only one way to fix this up: I'll give you seven hundred dollars in cash to-morrow, and you can give me your personal note, with the understanding that I hold ten dollars a week out of your pay-check until it is paid. I think you ought to tell your wife exactly how you are fixed, though. You can't expect her to help you much when she doesn't know."

That night Mrs. Bixby was sitting in their flat, waiting for her husband. She was dressed for a bridge party, and often looked with impatience from her paper to the Mission clock, as big as a coffin and with nothing but two weights dangling in its hollow framework. Percy had been loath to buy the clock when they got their furniture, and he had hated it ever since. Stella had changed very little since she came into the flat a bride. Then she wore her hair in a Floradora pompadour; now she wore it hooded close about her head like a scarf, in a rather smeary manner, like an Impressionist's brush-work. She heard her husband come in and close the door softly. While he was taking off his hat in the narrow tunnel of a hall, she called to him:

"I hope you've had something to eat downtown. You'll have to dress right away." Percy came in and sat down. She looked up from the evening paper she was reading. "You've no time to sit down. We must start in fifteen minutes."

He shaded his eyes from the glaring overhead light.

"I'm afraid I can't go anywhere tonight. I'm all in."

Mrs. Bixby rattled her paper, and turned from the theatrical page to the fashions.

"You'll feel better after you dress. We won't stay late."

Her even persistence usually conquered her husband. She never forgot anything she had once decided to do. Her manner of following it up grew more chilly, but never weaker. Tonight there was no spring in Percy. He closed his eyes and replied without moving:

"I can't go. You had better telephone the Burks we aren't coming. I have to tell you something disagreeable."

Stella rose.

"I certainly am not going to disappoint the Burks and stay at home to talk about anything disagreeable."

"You're not very sympathetic, Stella."

She turned away.

"If I were, you'd soon settle down into a pretty dull proposition. We'd have no social life now if I didn't keep at you."

Percy roused himself a little.

"Social life? Well, we'll have to trim that pretty close for a while. I'm in debt to the company. We've been living beyond our means ever since we were married."

"We can't live on less than we do," Stella said quietly. "No use in taking that up again."

Percy sat up, clutching the arms of his chair.

"We'll have to take it up. I'm seven hundred dollars short, and the books are to be audited tomorrow. I told young Remsen and he's going to take my note and hold the money out of my pay-checks. He could send me to jail, of course."

Stella turned and looked down at him with a gleam of interest.

"Oh, you've been playing solitaire with the books, have you? And he's found you out! I hope I'll never see that man again. Sugar face!" She said this with intense acrimony. Her forehead flushed delicately, and her eyes were full of hate. Young Remsen was not her idea of a "business man."

Stella went into the other room. When she came back she wore her evening coat and carried long gloves and a black scarf. This she began to arrange over her hair before the mirror above the false fireplace. Percy lay inert in the Morris chair and watched her. Yes, he understood; it was very difficult for a woman with hair like that to be shabby and to go without things. Her hair made her conspicuous, and it had to be lived up to. It had been the deciding factor in his fate.

Stella caught the lace over one ear with a large gold hair-pin. She repeated this until she got a good effect. Then turning to Percy, she began to draw on her gloves.

"I'm not worrying any, because I'm going back into business," she said firmly. "I meant to, anyway, if you didn't get a raise the first of the year. I have the offer of a good position, and we can live in an apartment hotel."

Percy was on his feet in an instant.

"I won't have you grinding in any office. That's flat."

Stella's lower lip quivered in a commiserating smile. "Oh, I won't lose my health. Charley Greengay's a partner in his concern now, and he wants a private secretary."

Percy drew back.

"You can't work for Greengay. He's got too bad a reputation. You've more pride than that, Stella."

The thin sweep of color he knew so well went over Stella's face.

"His business reputation seems to be all right," she commented, working the kid on with her left hand.

"What if it is?" Percy broke out. "He's the cheapest kind of a skate. He gets into scrapes with the girls in his own office. The last one got into the newspapers, and he had to pay the girl a wad."

"He don't get into scrapes with his books, anyway, and he seems to be able to stand getting into the papers. I excuse Charley. His wife's a pill."

"I suppose you think he'd have been all right if he'd married you," said Percy, bitterly.

"Yes, I do." Stella buttoned her glove with an air of finishing something, and then looked at Percy without animosity. "Charley and I both have sporty tastes, and we like excitement. You might as well live in Newark if you're going to sit at home in the evening. You oughtn't to have married a business woman; you need somebody domestic. There's nothing in this sort of life for either of us."

"That means, I suppose, that you're going around with Greengay and his crowd?"

"Yes, that's my sort of crowd, and you never did fit into it. You're too intellectual. I've always been proud of you, Percy. You're better style than Charley, but that gets tiresome. You will never burn much red fire in New York, now, will you?"

Percy did not reply. He sat looking at the minute-hand of the eviscerated Mission clock. His wife almost never took the trouble to argue with him.

"You're old style, Percy," she went on. "Of course everybody marries and wishes they hadn't, but nowadays people get over it. Some women go ahead on the quiet, but I'm giving it to you straight. I'm going to work for Greengay. I like his line of business, and I meet people well. Now I'm going to the Burks'."

Percy dropped his hands limply between his knees.

"I suppose," he brought out, "the real trouble is that you've decided my earning power is not very great."

"That's part of it, and part of it is you're old-fashioned." Stella paused at the door and looked back. "What made you rush me, anyway, Percy?" she asked indulgently. "What did you go and pretend to be a spender and get tied up with me for?"

"I guess everybody wants to be a spender when he's in love," Percy replied.

Stella shook her head mournfully.

"No, you're a spender or you're not. Greengay has been broke three times, fired, down and out, black-listed. But he's always come back, and he always will. You will never be fired, but you'll always be poor." She turned and looked back again before she went out.

Six months later Bixby came to young Oliver Remsen one afternoon and said he would like to have twenty dollars a week held out of his pay until his debt was cleared off.

Oliver looked up at his sallow employee and asked him how he could spare as much as that.

"My expenses are lighter," Bixby replied. "My wife has gone into business with a ready-to-wear firm. She is not living with me any more."

Oliver looked annoyed, and asked him if nothing could be done to readjust his domestic affairs. Bixby said no; they would probably remain as they were.

"But where are you living, Bixby? How have you arranged things?" the young man asked impatiently.

"I'm very comfortable. I live in a boarding-house and have my own furniture. There are several fellows there who are fixed the same way. Their wives went back into business, and they drifted apart."

With a baffled expression Remsen stared at the uneven shoulders under the skin-fitting alpaca desk coat as his bookkeeper went out. He had meant to do something for Percy, but somehow, he reflected, one never did do anything for a fellow who had been stung as hard as that.

Century 92 (May 1916): 51–59

Ardessa

�֎ ✖ ✖

The grand-mannered old man who sat at a desk in the reception-room of "The Outcry" offices to receive visitors and incidentally to keep the time-book of the employees, looked up as Miss Devine entered at ten minutes past ten and condescendingly wished him good morning. He bowed profoundly as she minced past his desk, and with an indifferent air took her course down the corridor that led to the editorial offices. Mechanically he opened the flat, black book at his elbow and placed his finger on D, running his eye along the line of figures after the name Devine. "It's banker's hours she keeps, indeed," he muttered. What was the use of entering so capricious a record? Nevertheless, with his usual preliminary flourish he wrote 10:10 under this, the fourth day of May.

The employee who kept banker's hours rustled on down the corridor to her private room, hung up her lavender jacket and her trim spring hat, and readjusted her side combs by the mirror inside her closet door. Glancing at her desk, she rang for an office boy, and reproved him because he had not dusted more carefully and because there were lumps in her paste. When he disappeared with the paste-jar, she sat down to decide which of her employer's letters he should see and which he should not.

Ardessa was not young and she was certainly not handsome. The coquettish angle at which she carried her head was a mannerism surviving from a time when it was more becoming. She shuddered at the cold candor of the new business woman, and was insinuatingly feminine.

Ardessa's employer, like young Lochinvar, had come out of the West, and he had done a great many contradictory things before he became proprietor and editor of "The Outcry." Before he decided to go to New York and make the East take notice of him, O'Mally had acquired a punctual, reliable silver-mine in South Dakota. This silent friend in the background made his journalistic success comparatively easy. He had figured out, when he was a rich nobody in Nevada, that the quickest way to cut into the known world was through the printing-press. He arrived in New York, bought a highly respectable publication, and turned it into a red-hot magazine of protest, which he called "The Outcry." He knew what the West wanted, and it proved to be what everybody secretly wanted. In six years he had done the thing that had hitherto seemed impossible: built up a national weekly, out on the news-stands the same day in New York and San Francisco; a magazine the people howled for, a moving-picture film of their real tastes and interests.

O'Mally bought "The Outcry" to make a stir, not to make a career, but he had got built into the thing more than he ever intended. It had made him a public man and put him into politics. He found the publicity game diverting, and it held him longer than any other game had ever done. He had built up about him an organization of which he was somewhat afraid and with which he was vastly bored. On his staff there were five famous men, and he had made every one of them. At first it amused him to manufacture celebrities. He found he could take an average reporter from the daily press, give him a "line" to follow, a trust to fight, a vice to expose,—this was all in that good time when people were eager to read about their own wickedness,—and in two years the reporter would be recognized as an authority. Other people—Napoleon, Disraeli, Sarah Bernhardt—had discovered that advertising would go a long way; but Marcus O'Mally discovered that in America it would go all the way— as far as you wished to pay its passage. Any human countenance, plastered in three-sheet posters from sea to sea, would be revered by the American people. The strangest thing was that the owners of these grave countenances, staring at their own faces on news-stands and billboards, fell to venerating themselves; and even he, O'Mally, was more or less constrained by these reputations that he had created out of cheap paper and cheap ink.

Constraint was the last thing O'Mally liked. The most engaging and unusual thing about the man was that he couldn't be fooled by the success of his own methods, and no amount of "recognition" could make a stuffed shirt of him. No matter how much he was advertised as a great medicine-man in the councils of the nation, he knew that he was a born gambler and a soldier of fortune. He left his dignified office to take care of itself for a good many months of the year while he played about on the outskirts of social order. He liked being a great man from the East in rough-and-tumble Western cities where he had once been merely an unconsidered spender.

O'Mally's long absences constituted one of the supreme advantages of Ardessa Devine's position. When he was at his post her duties were not heavy, but when he was giving balls in Goldfield, Nevada, she lived an ideal life. She came to the office every day, indeed, to forward such of O'Mally's letters as she thought best, to attend to his club notices and tradesmen's bills, and to taste the sense of her high connections. The great men of the staff were all about her, as contemplative as Buddhas in their private offices, each meditating upon the particular trust or form of vice confided to his care. Thus surrounded, Ardessa had a pleasant sense of being at the heart of things. It was like a mental massage, exercise without exertion. She read and she embroidered. Her room was pleasant, and she liked to be seen at ladylike tasks and to feel herself a graceful contrast to the crude girls in the advertising and circulation departments across the hall. The younger stenographers, who had to get through with the enormous office correspondence, and who rushed about from one editor to another with wire baskets full of letters, made faces as they passed Ardessa's door and saw her cool and cloistered, daintily plying her needle. But no matter how hard the other stenographers were driven, no one, not even one of the five oracles of the staff, dared dictate so much as a letter to Ardessa. Like a sultan's bride, she was inviolate in her lord's absence; she had to be kept for him.

Naturally the other young women employed in "The Outcry" offices disliked Miss Devine. They were all competent girls, trained in the exacting methods of modern business, and they had to make good every day in the week, had to get through with a great deal of work or lose their position. O'Mally's private secretary was a mystery to them. Her exemptions and privileges, her patronizing remarks, formed an exhaustless subject of conversation at the lunch-hour. Ardessa had, indeed, as they knew she must have, a kind of "purchase" on her employer.

When O'Mally first came to New York to break into publicity, he engaged Miss Devine upon the recommendation of the editor whose ailing publication he bought and rechristened. That editor was a conservative, scholarly gentleman of the old school, who was retiring because he felt out of place in the world of brighter, breezier magazines that had been flowering since the new century came in. He believed that in this vehement world young O'Mally would make himself heard and that Miss Devine's training in an editorial office would be of use to him.

. When O'Mally first sat down at a desk to be an editor, all the cards that were brought in looked pretty much alike to him. Ardessa was at his elbow. She had long been steeped in literary distinctions and in the social distinctions which used to count for much more than they do now. She knew all the great men, all the nephews and clients of great men. She knew which must be seen, which must be made welcome, and which could safely be sent away. She could give O'Mally on the instant the former rating in magazine offices of nearly every name that was brought in to him. She could give him an idea of the man's connections, of the price his work commanded, and insinuate whether he ought to be met with the old punctiliousness or with the new joviality. She was useful in explaining to her employer the significance of various invitations, and the standing of clubs and associations. At first she was virtually the social mentor of the bullet-headed young Westerner who wanted to break into everything, the solitary person about the office of the humming new magazine who knew anything about the editorial traditions of the eighties and nineties which, antiquated as they now were, gave an editor, as O'Mally said, a background.

Despite her indolence, Ardessa was useful to O'Mally as a social reminder. She was the card catalogue of his ever-changing personal relations. O'Mally went in for everything and got tired of everything; that was why he made a good editor. After he was through with people, Ardessa was very skilful in covering his retreat. She read and answered the letters of admirers who had begun to bore him. When great authors, who had been dined and fêted the month before, were suddenly left to cool their heels in the reception-room, thrown upon the suave hospitality of the grand old man at the desk, it was Ardessa who went out and made soothing and plausible explanations as to why the editor could not see them. She was the brake that checked the too-eager neophyte, the emollient that eased the severing of relationships, the gentle extinguisher of the lights that failed. When there were no longer messages of hope and cheer to be sent to ardent young writers and reformers, Ardessa delivered, as sweetly as possible, whatever messages were left.

In handling these people with whom O'Mally was quite through, Ardessa had gradually developed an industry which was immensely gratifying to her own vanity. Not only did she not crush them; she even fostered them a little. She continued to advise them in the reception-room and "personally" received their manuscripts long after O'Mally had declared that he would never read another line they wrote. She let them outline their plans for stories and articles to her, promising to bring these suggestions to the editor's attention. She denied herself to nobody, was gracious even to the Shakespere-Bacon man, the perpetual-motion man, the travel-article man, the ghosts which haunt every magazine office. The writers who had had their happy hour of O'Mally's favor kept feeling that Ardessa might reinstate them. She answered their letters of inquiry in her most polished and elegant style, and even gave them hints as to the subjects in which the restless editor was or was not interested at the moment: she feared it would be useless to send him an article on "How to Trap Lions," because he had just bought an article on "Elephant-Shooting in Majuba Land," etc.

So when O'Mally plunged into his office at 11:30 on this, the fourth day of May, having just got back from three-days' fishing, he found

Ardessa in the reception-room, surrounded by a little court of discards. This was annoying, for he always wanted his stenographer at once. Telling the office boy to give her a hint that she was needed, he threw off his hat and top-coat and began to race through the pile of letters Ardessa had put on his desk. When she entered, he did not wait for her polite inquiries about his trip, but broke in at once.

"What is that fellow who writes about phossy jaw still hanging round here for? I don't want any articles on phossy jaw, and if I did, I wouldn't want his."

"He has just sold an article on the match industry to 'The New Age,' Mr. O'Mally," Ardessa replied as she took her seat at the editor's right.

"Why does he have to come and tell us about it? We've nothing to do with 'The New Age.' And that prison-reform guy, what's he loafing about for?"

Ardessa bridled.

"You remember, Mr. O'Mally, he brought letters of introduction from Governor Harper, the reform Governor of Mississippi."

O'Mally jumped up, kicking over his waste-basket in his impatience.

"That was months ago. I went through his letters and went through him, too. He hasn't got anything we want. I've been through with Governor Harper a long while. We're asleep at the switch in here. And let me tell you, if I catch sight of that causes-of-blindness-in-babies woman around here again, I'll do something violent. Clear them out, Miss Devine! Clear them out! We need a traffic policeman in this office. Have you got that article on 'Stealing Our National Water Power' ready for me?"

"Mr. Gerrard took it back to make modifications. He gave it to me at noon on Saturday, just before the office closed. I will have it ready for you tomorrow morning, Mr. O'Mally, if you have not too many letters for me this afternoon," Ardessa replied pointedly.

"Holy Mike!" muttered O'Mally, "we need a traffic policeman for the staff, too. Gerrard's modified that thing half a dozen times already. Why don't they get accurate information in the first place?"

He began to dictate his morning mail, walking briskly up and down the floor by way of giving his stenographer an energetic example. Her indolence and her ladylike deportment weighed on him. He wanted to take her by the elbows and run her around the block. He didn't mind that she loafed when he was away, but it was becoming harder and harder to speed her up when he was on the spot. He knew his correspondence was not enough to keep her busy, so when he was in town he made her type his own breezy editorials and various articles by members of his staff.

Transcribing editorial copy is always laborious, and the only way to make it easy is to farm it out. This Ardessa was usually clever enough to do. When she returned to her own room after O'Mally had gone out to lunch, Ardessa rang for an office boy and said languidly, "James, call Becky, please."

In a moment a thin, tense-faced Hebrew girl of eighteen or nineteen came rushing in, carrying a wire basket full of typewritten sheets. She was as gaunt as a plucked spring chicken, and her cheap, gaudy clothes might have been thrown on her. She looked as if she were running to catch a train and in mortal dread of missing it. While Miss Devine examined the pages in the basket, Becky stood with her shoulders drawn up and her elbows drawn in, apparently trying to hide herself in her insufficient open-work waist. Her wild, black eyes followed Miss Devine's hands desperately. Ardessa sighed.

"This seems to be very smeary copy again, Becky. You don't keep your mind on your work, and so you have to erase continually."

Becky spoke up in wailing self-vindication.

"It ain't that, Miss Devine. It's so many hard words he uses that I have to be at the dictionary all the time. Look! Look!" She produced a bunch of manuscript faintly scrawled in pencil, and thrust it under Ardessa's eyes. "He don't write out the words at all. He just begins a word, and then makes waves for you to guess."

"I see you haven't always guessed correctly, Becky," said Ardessa, with a weary smile. "There are a great many words here that would surprise Mr. Gerrard, I am afraid."

"And the inserts," Becky persisted. "How is anybody to tell where they go, Miss Devine? It's mostly inserts; see, all over the top and sides and back."

Ardessa turned her head away.

"Don't claw the pages like that, Becky. You make me nervous. Mr. Gerrard has not time to dot his i's and cross his t's. That is what we keep copyists for. I will correct these sheets for you,—it would be terrible if Mr. O'Mally saw them,—and then you can copy them over again. It must be done by tomorrow morning, so you may have to work late. See that your hands are clean and dry, and then you will not smear it."

"Yes, ma'am. Thank you, Miss Devine. Will you tell the janitor, please, it's all right if I have to stay? He was cross because I was here

Saturday afternoon doing this. He said it was a holiday, and when everybody else was gone I ought to—"

"That will do, Becky. Yes, I will speak to the janitor for you. You may go to lunch now."

Becky turned on one heel and then swung back.

"Miss Devine," she said anxiously, "will it be all right if I get white shoes for now?"

Ardessa gave her kind consideration.

"For office wear, you mean? No, Becky. With only one pair, you could not keep them properly clean; and black shoes are much less conspicuous. Tan, if you prefer."

Becky looked down at her feet. They were too large, and her skirt was as much too short as her legs were too long.

"Nearly all the girls I know wear white shoes to business," she pleaded.

"They are probably little girls who work in factories or department stores, and that is quite another matter. Since you raise the question, Becky, I ought to speak to you about your new waist. Don't wear it to the office again, please. Those cheap open-work waists are not appropriate in an office like this. They are all very well for little chorus girls."

"But Miss Kalski wears expensive waists to business more open than this, and jewelry—"

Ardessa interrupted. Her face grew hard.

"Miss Kalski," she said coldly, "works for the business department. You are employed in the editorial offices. There is a great difference. You see, Becky, I might have to call you in here at any time when a scientist or a great writer or the president of a university is here talking over editorial matters, and such clothes as you have on today would make a bad impression. Nearly all our connections are with important people of that kind, and we ought to be well, but quietly, dressed."

"Yes, Miss Devine. Thank you," Becky gasped and disappeared. Heaven knew she had no need to be further impressed with the greatness of "The Outcry" office. During the year and a half she had been there she had never ceased to tremble. She knew the prices all the authors got as well as Miss Devine did, and everything seemed to her to be done on a magnificent scale. She hadn't a good memory for long technical words, but she never forgot dates or prices or initials or telephone numbers.

Becky felt that her job depended on Miss Devine, and she was so glad to have it that she scarcely realized she was being bullied. Besides, she was grateful for all that she had learned from Ardessa; Ardessa had taught her to do most of the things that she was supposed to do herself. Becky wanted to learn, she had to learn; that was the train she was always running for. Her father, Isaac Tietelbaum, the tailor, who pressed Miss Devine's skirts and kept her ladylike suits in order, had come to his client two years ago and told her he had a bright girl just out of a commercial high school. He implored Ardessa to find some office position for his daughter. Ardessa told an appealing story to O'Mally, and brought Becky into the office, at a salary of six dollars a week, to help with the copying and to learn business routine. When Becky first came she was as ignorant as a young savage. She was rapid at her shorthand and typing, but a Kaffir girl would have known as much about the English language. Nobody ever wanted to learn more than Becky. She fairly wore the dictionary out. She dug up her old school grammar and worked over it at night. She faithfully mastered Miss Devine's fussy system of punctuation.

There were eight children at home, younger than Becky, and they were all eager to learn. They wanted to get their mother out of the three dark rooms behind the tailor shop and to move into a flat upstairs, where they could, as Becky said, "live private." The young Tietelbaums doubted their father's ability to bring this change about, for the more things he declared himself ready to do in his window placards, the fewer were brought to him to be done. "Dyeing, Cleaning, Ladies' Furs Remodeled"—it did no good.

Rebecca was out to "improve herself," as her father had told her she must. Ardessa had easy way with her. It was one of those rare relationships from which both persons profit. The more Becky could learn from Ardessa, the happier she was; and the more Ardessa could unload on Becky, the greater was her contentment. She easily broke Becky of the gum-chewing habit, taught her to walk quietly, to efface herself at the proper moment, and to hold her tongue. Becky had been raised to eight dollars a week; but she didn't care half so much about that as she did about her own increasing efficiency. The more work Miss Devine handed over to her the happier she was, and the faster she was able to eat it up. She tested and tried herself in every possible way. She now had full confidence that she would surely one day be a high-priced stenographer, a real "business woman."

Becky would have corrupted a really industrious person, but a bilious temperament like Ardessa's couldn't make even a feeble stand against such willingness. Ardessa had grown soft and had lost the knack of turning out work. Sometimes, in her importance and serenity, she shivered. What if O'Mally should die, and she were thrust out into the world to work in competition with the brazen, competent young women she saw about her everywhere? She believed herself indispensable, but she knew that in such a mischanceful world as this the very powers of darkness might rise to separate her from this pearl among jobs.

When Becky came in from lunch she went down the long hall to the wash-room, where all the little girls who worked in the advertising and circulation departments kept their hats and jackets. There were shelves and shelves of bright spring hats, piled on top of one another, all as stiff as sheet-iron and trimmed with gay flowers. At the marble wash-stand stood Rena Kalski, the right bower of the business manager, polishing her diamond rings with a nail-brush.

"Hullo, kid," she called over her shoulder to Becky. "I've got a ticket for you for Thursday afternoon."

Becky's black eyes glowed, but the strained look on her face drew tighter than ever.

"I'll never ask her, Miss Kalski," she said rapidly. "I don't dare. I have to stay late tonight again; and I know she'd be hard to please after, if I was to try to get off on a week-day. I thank you, Miss Kalski, but I'd better not."

Miss Kalski laughed. She was a slender young Hebrew, handsome in an impudent, Tenderloin sort of way, with a small head, reddish-brown almond eyes, a trifle tilted, a rapacious mouth, and a beautiful chin.

"Ain't you under that woman's thumb, though! Call her bluff. She isn't half the prima donna she thinks she is. On my side of the hall we know who's who about this place."

The business and editorial departments of "The Outcry" were separated by a long corridor and a great contempt. Miss Kalski dried her rings with tissue-paper and studied them with an appraising eye.

"Well, since you're such a 'fraidy-calf,'" she went on, "maybe I can get a rise out of her myself. Now I've got you a ticket out of that shirt-front, I want you to go. I'll drop in on Devine this afternoon."

When Miss Kalski went back to her desk in the business manager's private office, she turned to him familiarly, but not impertinently.

"Mr. Henderson, I want to send a kid over in the editorial stenographers' to the Palace Thursday afternoon. She's a nice kid, only she's scared out of her skin all the time. Miss Devine's her boss, and she'll be just mean enough not to let the young one off. Would you say a word to her?"

The business manager lit a cigar.

"I'm not saying words to any of the high-brows over there. Try it out with Devine yourself. You're not bashful."

Miss Kalski shrugged her shoulders and smiled.

"Oh, very well." She serpentined out of the room and crossed the Rubicon into the editorial offices. She found Ardessa typing O'Mally's letters and wearing a pained expression.

"Good afternoon, Miss Devine," she said carelessly. "Can we borrow Becky over there for Thursday afternoon? We're short."

Miss Devine looked piqued and tilted her head.

"I don't think it's customary, Miss Kalski, for the business department to use our people. We never have girls enough here to do the work. Of course if Mr. Henderson feels justified—"

"Thanks awfully, Miss Devine,"—Miss Kalski interrupted her with the perfectly smooth, good-natured tone which never betrayed a hint of the scorn every line of her sinuous figure expressed,—"I will tell Mr. Henderson. Perhaps we can do something for you some day." Whether this was a threat, a kind wish, or an insinuation, no mortal could have told. Miss Kalski's face was always suggesting insolence without being quite insolent. As she returned to her own domain she met the cashier's head clerk in the hall. "That Devine woman's a crime," she murmured. The head clerk laughed tolerantly.

That afternoon as Miss Kalski was leaving the office at 5:15, on her way down the corridor she heard a typewriter clicking away in the empty, echoing editorial offices. She looked in, and found Becky bending forward over the machine as if she were about to swallow it.

"Hello, kid. Do you sleep with that?" she called. She walked up to Becky and glanced at her copy. "What do you let 'em keep you up nights over that stuff for?" she asked contemptuously. "The world wouldn't suffer if that stuff never got printed."

Rebecca looked up wildly. Not even Miss Kalski's French pansy hat or her ear-rings and landscape veil could loosen Becky's tenacious mind from Mr. Gerrard's article on water power. She scarcely knew what Miss Kalski had said to her, certainly not what she meant.

"But I must make progress already, Miss Kalski," she panted.

Miss Kalski gave her low, siren laugh.

"I should say you must!" she ejaculated.

Ardessa decided to take her vacation in June, and she arranged that Miss Milligan should do O'Mally's work while she was away. Miss Milligan was blunt and noisy, rapid and inaccurate. It would be just as well for O'Mally to work with a coarse instrument for a time; he would be more appreciative, perhaps, of certain qualities to which he had seemed insensible of late. Ardessa was to leave for East Hampton on Sunday, and she spent Saturday morning instructing her substitute as to the state of the correspondence. At noon O'Mally burst into her room. All the morning he had been closeted with a new writer of mystery-stories just over from England.

"Can you stay and take my letters this afternoon, Miss Devine? You're not leaving until tomorrow."

Ardessa pouted, and tilted her head at the angle he was tired of.

"I'm sorry, Mr. O'Mally, but I've left all my shopping for this afternoon. I think Becky Tietelbaum could do them for you. I will tell her to be careful."

"Oh, all right." O'Mally bounced out with a reflection of Ardessa's disdainful expression on his face. Saturday afternoon was always a half-holiday, to be sure, but since she had weeks of freedom when he was away —However—

At two o'clock Becky Tietelbaum appeared at his door, clad in the sober office suit which Miss Devine insisted she should wear, her note-book in her hand, and so frightened that her fingers were cold and her lips were pale. She had never taken dictation from the editor before. It was a great and terrifying occasion.

"Sit down," he said encouragingly. He began dictating while he shook from his bag the manuscripts he had snatched away from the amazed English author that morning. Presently he looked up.

"Do I go too fast?"

"No, sir," Becky found strength to say.

At the end of an hour he told her to go and type as many of the letters as she could while he went over the bunch of stuff he had torn from the Englishman. He was with the Hindu detective in an opium den in Shanghai when Becky returned and placed a pile of papers on his desk.

"How many?" he asked, without looking up.

"All you gave me, sir."

"All, so soon? Wait a minute and let me see how many mistakes." He went over the letters rapidly, signing them as he read. "They seem to be all right. I thought you were the girl that made so many mistakes."

Rebecca was never too frightened to vindicate herself.

"Mr. O'Mally, sir, I don't make mistakes with letters. It's only copying the articles that have so many long words, and when the writing isn't plain, like Mr. Gerrard's. I never make many mistakes with Mr. Johnson's articles, or with yours I don't."

O'Mally wheeled round in his chair, looked with curiosity at her long, tense face, her black eyes, and straight brows.

"Oh, so you sometimes copy articles, do you? How does that happen?"

"Yes, sir. Always Miss Devine gives me the articles to do. It's good practice for me."

"I see." O'Mally shrugged his shoulders. He was thinking that he could get a rise out of the whole American public any day easier than he could get a rise out of Ardessa. "What editorials of mine have you copied lately, for instance?"

Rebecca blazed out at him, reciting rapidly:

"Oh, 'A Word about the Rosenbaums,' 'Useless Navy-Yards,' 'Who Killed Cock Robin'—"

"Wait a minute." O'Mally checked her flow. "What was that one about—Cock Robin?"

"It was all about why the secretary of the interior dismissed—"

"All right, all right. Copy those letters, and put them down the chute as you go out. Come in here for a minute on Monday morning."

Becky hurried home to tell her father that she had taken the editor's letters and had made no mistakes. On Monday she learned that she was to do O'Mally's work for a few days. He disliked Miss Milligan, and he was annoyed with Ardessa for trying to put her over on him when there was better material at hand. With Rebecca he got on very well; she was impersonal, unreproachful, and she fairly panted for work. Everything was done almost before he told her what he wanted. She raced ahead with him; it was like riding a good modern bicycle after pumping along on an old hard tire.

On the day before Miss Devine's return O'Mally strolled over for a chat with the business office.

"Henderson, your people are taking vacations now, I suppose? Could you use an extra girl?"

"If it's that thin black one, I can."

O'Mally gave him a wise smile.

"It isn't. To be honest, I want to put one over on you. I want you to take Miss Devine over here for a while and speed her up. I can't do anything. She's got the upper hand of me. I don't want to fire her, you understand, but she makes my life too difficult. It's my fault, of course. I've pampered her. Give her a chance over here; maybe she'll come back. You can be firm with 'em, can't you?"

Henderson glanced toward the desk where Miss Kalski's lightning eye was skimming over the printing-house bills that he was supposed to verify himself.

"Well, if I can't, I know who can," he replied, with a chuckle.

"Exactly," O'Mally agreed. "I'm counting on the force of Miss Kalski's example. Miss Devine's all right, Miss Kalski, but she needs regular exercise. She owes it to her complexion. I can't discipline people."

Miss Kalski's only reply was a low, indulgent laugh.

O'Mally braced himself on the morning of Ardessa's return. He told the waiter at his club to bring him a second pot of coffee and to bring it hot. He was really afraid of her. When she presented herself at his office at 10:30 he complimented her upon her tan and asked about her vacation. Then he broke the news to her.

"We want to make a few temporary changes about here, Miss Devine, for the summer months. The business department is short of help. Henderson is going to put Miss Kalski on the books for a while to figure out some economies for him, and he is going to take you over. Meantime I'll get Becky broken in so that she could take your work if you were sick or anything."

Ardessa drew herself up.

"I've not been accustomed to commercial work, Mr. O'Mally. I've no interest in it, and I don't care to brush up in it."

"Brushing up is just what we need, Miss Devine." O'Mally began tramping about his room expansively. "I'm going to brush everybody up. I'm going to brush a few people out; but I want you to stay with us, of course. You belong here. Don't be hasty now. Go to your room and think it over."

Ardessa was beginning to cry, and O'Mally was afraid he would lose his nerve. He looked out of the window at a new skyscraper that was building, while she retired without a word.

At her own desk Ardessa sat down breathless and trembling. The one thing she had never doubted was her unique value to O'Mally. She had, as she told herself, taught him everything. She would say a few things to Becky Tietelbaum, and to that pigeon-breasted tailor, her father, too! The worst of it was that Ardessa had herself brought it all about; she could see that clearly now. She had carefully trained and qualified her successor. Why had she ever civilized Becky? Why had she taught her manners and deportment, broken her of the gum-chewing habit, and made her presentable? In her original state O'Mally would never have put up with her, no matter what her ability.

Ardessa told herself that O'Mally was notoriously fickle; Becky amused him, but he would soon find out her limitations. The wise thing, she knew, was to humor him; but it seemed to her that she could not swallow her pride. Ardessa grew yellower within the hour. Over and over in her mind she bade O'Mally a cold adieu and minced out past the grand old man at the desk for the last time. But each exit she rehearsed made her feel sorrier for herself. She thought over all the offices she knew, but she realized that she could never meet their inexorable standards of efficiency.

While she was bitterly deliberating, O'Mally himself wandered in, rattling his keys nervously in his pocket. He shut the door behind him.

"Now, you're going to come through with this all right, aren't you, Miss Devine? I want Henderson to get over the notion that my people over here are stuck up and think the business department are old shoes. That's where we get our money from, as he often reminds me. You'll be the best-paid girl over there; no reduction, of course. You don't want to go wandering off to some new office where personality doesn't count for anything." He sat down confidentially on the edge of her desk. "Do you, now, Miss Devine?"

Ardessa simpered tearfully as she replied.

"Mr. O'Mally," she brought out, "you'll soon find that Becky is not the sort of girl to meet people for you when you are away. I don't see how you can think of letting her."

"That's one thing I want to change, Miss Devine. You're too soft-handed with the has-beens and the never-was-ers. You're too much of a lady for this rough game. Nearly everybody who comes in here wants to sell us a gold-brick, and you treat them as if they were bringing in wedding presents. Becky is as rough as sandpaper, and she'll clear out a lot of dead wood." O'Mally rose, and tapped Ardessa's shrinking shoulder. "Now, be a sport and go through with it, Miss Devine. I'll see that you don't lose. Henderson thinks you'll refuse to do his work, so I want you to get moved in there before he comes back from lunch. I've had a desk put in his office for you. Miss Kalski is in the bookkeeper's room half the time now."

ARDESSA

Rena Kalski was amazed that afternoon when a line of office boys
entered, carrying Miss Devine's effects, and when Ardessa herself coldly
followed them. After Ardessa had arranged her desk, Miss Kalski went
over to her and told her about some matters of routine very good-
naturedly. Ardessa looked pretty badly shaken up, and Rena bore no
grudges.

"When you want the dope on the correspondence with the paper
men, don't bother to look it up. I've got it all in my head, and I can save
time for you. If he wants you to go over the printing bills every week,
you'd better let me help you with that for a while. I can stay almost any
afternoon. It's quite a trick to figure out the plates and over-time charges
till you get used to it. I've worked out a quick method that saves trouble."

When Henderson came in at three he found Ardessa, chilly, but civil,
awaiting his instructions. He knew she disapproved of his tastes and his
manners, but he didn't mind. What interested and amused him was that
Rena Kalski, whom he had always thought as cold-blooded as an adding-
machine, seemed to be making a hair-mattress of herself to break Ardessa's
fall.

At five o'clock, when Ardessa rose to go, the business manager said
breezily:

"See you at nine in the morning, Miss Devine. We begin on the
stroke."

Ardessa faded out of the door, and Miss Kalski's slender back squirmed
with amusement.

"I never thought to hear such words spoken," she admitted; "but I
guess she'll limber up all right. The atmosphere is bad over there. They
get moldy."

After the next monthly luncheon of the heads of departments,
O'Mally said to Henderson, as he feed the coat-boy:

"By the way, how are you making it with the bartered bride?"

Henderson smashed on his Panama as he said:

"Any time you want her back, don't be delicate."

But O'Mally shook his red head and laughed.

"Oh, I'm no Indian giver!"

Century 96 (May 1918): 105–16

Her Boss

✳ ✳ ✳

Paul Wanning opened the front door of his house in Orange, closed it softly behind him, and stood looking about the hall as he drew off his gloves.

Nothing was changed there since last night, and yet he stood gazing about him with an interest which a long-married man does not often feel in his own reception hall. The rugs, the two pillars, the Spanish tapestry chairs, were all the same. The Venus di Medici stood on her column as usual and there, at the end of the hall (opposite the front door), was the full-length portrait of Mrs. Wanning, maturely blooming forth in an evening gown, signed with the name of a French painter who seemed purposely to have made his signature indistinct. Though the signature was largely what one paid for, one couldn't ask him to do it over.

In the dining-room the colored man was moving about the table set for dinner, under the electric cluster. The candles had not yet been lighted. Wanning watched him with a homesick feeling in his heart. They had had Sam a long while, twelve years, now. His warm hall, the lighted dining-room, the drawing room where only the flicker of the wood fire played upon the shining surfaces of many objects—they seemed to Wanning like a haven of refuge. It had never occurred to him that his house was too full of things. He often said, and he believed, that the women of his household had "perfect taste." He had paid for these objects, sometimes with difficulty, but always with pride. He carried a heavy life-insurance and permitted himself to spend most of the income from a good law practise. He wished, during his life-time, to enjoy the benefits of his wife's discriminating extravagance.

Yesterday Wanning's doctor had sent him to a specialist. Today the specialist, after various laboratory tests, had told him most disconcerting things about the state of very necessary, but hitherto wholly uninteresting, organs of his body.

The information pointed to something incredible; insinuated that his residence in this house was only temporary; that he, whose time was so full, might have to leave not only his house and his office and his club, but a world with which he was extremely well satisfied—the only world he knew anything about.

Wanning unbuttoned his overcoat, but did not take it off. He stood folding his muffler slowly and carefully. What he did not understand was, how he could go while other people stayed. Sam would be moving about the table like this, Mrs. Wanning and her daughters would be dressing upstairs, when he would not be coming home to dinner any more; when he would not, indeed, be dining anywhere.

Sam, coming to turn on the parlor lights, saw Wanning and stepped behind him to take his coat.

"Good evening, Mr. Wanning, sah, excuse me. You entahed so quietly, sah, I didn't heah you."

The master of the house slipped out of his coat and went languidly upstairs.

He tapped at the door of his wife's room, which stood ajar.

"Come in, Paul," she called from her dressing table.

She was seated, in a violet dressing gown, giving the last touches to her coiffure, both arms lifted. They were firm and white, like her neck and shoulders. She was a handsome woman of fifty-five,—still a woman, not an old person, Wanning told himself, as he kissed her cheek. She was heavy in figure, to be sure, but she had kept, on the whole, presentable outlines. Her complexion was good, and she wore less false hair than either of her daughters.

Wanning himself was five years older, but his sandy hair did not show the gray in it, and since his mustache had begun to grow white he kept it clipped so short that it was unobtrusive. His fresh skin made him look younger than he was. Not long ago he had overheard the stenographers in his law office discussing the ages of their employers. They had put him down at fifty, agreeing that his two partners must be considerably older than he—which was not the case. Wanning had an especially kindly feeling for the little new girl, a copyist, who had exclaimed that "Mr. Wanning couldn't be fifty; he seemed so boyish!"

Wanning lingered behind his wife, looking at her in the mirror.

"Well, did you tell the girls, Julia?" he asked, trying to speak casually.

Mrs. Wanning looked up and met his eyes in the glass. "The girls?"

She noticed a strange expression come over his face.

"About your health, you mean? Yes, dear, but I tried not to alarm them. They feel dreadfully. I'm going to have a talk with Dr. Seares myself. These specialists are all alarmists, and I've often heard of his frightening people."

She rose and took her husband's arm, drawing him toward the fireplace.

"You are not going to let this upset you, Paul? If you take care of yourself, everything will come out all right. You have always been so strong. One has only to look at you."

"Did you," Wanning asked, "say anything to Harold?"

"Yes, of course. I saw him in town today, and he agrees with me that Seares draws the worst conclusions possible. He says even the young men are always being told the most terrifying things. Usually they laugh at the doctors and do as they please. You certainly don't look like a sick man, and you don't feel like one, do you?"

She patted his shoulder, smiled at him encouragingly, and rang for the maid to come and hook her dress.

When the maid appeared at the door, Wanning went out through the bath-room to his own sleeping chamber. He was too much dispirited to put on a dinner coat, though such remissness was always noticed. He sat down and waited for the sound of the gong, leaving his door open, on the chance that perhaps one of his daughters would come in.

When Wanning went down to dinner he found his wife already at her chair, and the table laid for four.

"Harold," she explained, "is not coming home. He has to attend a first night in town."

A moment later their two daughters entered, obviously "dressed." They both wore earrings and masses of hair. The daughters' names were Roma and Florence,—Roma, Firenze, one of the young men who came to the house often, but not often enough, had called them. Tonight they were going to a rehearsal of "The Dances of the Nations,"—a benefit performance in which Miss Roma was to lead the Spanish dances, her sister the Grecian.

The elder daughter had often been told that her name suited her admirably. She looked, indeed, as we are apt to think the unrestrained beauties of later Rome must have looked,—but as their portrait busts emphatically declare they did not. Her head was massive, her lips full and crimson, her eyes large and heavy-lidded, her forehead low. At costume balls and in living pictures she was always Semiramis, or Poppea, or Theodora. Barbaric accessories brought out something cruel and even rather brutal in her handsome face. The men who were attracted to her were somehow afraid of her.

Florence was slender, with a long, graceful neck, a restless head, and a flexible mouth—discontent lurked about the corners of it. Her shoulders were pretty, but her neck and arms were too thin. Roma was always struggling to keep within a certain weight—her chin and upper arms grew persistently more solid—and Florence was always striving to attain a certain weight. Wanning used sometimes to wonder why these disconcerting fluctuations could not go the other way; why Roma could not melt away as easily as did her sister, who had to be sent to Palm Beach to save the precious pounds.

"I don't see why you ever put Rickie Allen in charge of the English country dances," Florence said to her sister, as they sat down. "He knows the figures, of course, but he has no real style."

Roma looked annoyed. Rickie Allen was one of the men who came to the house almost often enough.

"He is absolutely to be depended upon, that's why," she said firmly.

"I think he is just right for it, Florence," put in Mrs. Wanning. "It's remarkable he should feel that he can give up the time; such a busy man. He must be very much interested in the movement."

Florence's lip curled drolly under her soup spoon. She shot an amused glance at her mother's dignity.

"Nothing doing," her keen eyes seemed to say.

Though Florence was nearly thirty and her sister a little beyond, there was, seriously, nothing doing. With so many charms and so much preparation, they never, as Florence vulgarly said, quite pulled it off. They had been rushed, time and again, and Mrs. Wanning had repeatedly steeled herself to bear the blow. But the young men went to follow a career in Mexico or the Philippines, or moved to Yonkers, and escaped without a mortal wound.

Roma turned graciously to her father.

"I met Mr. Lane at the Holland House today, where I was lunching with the Burtons, father. He asked about you, and when I told him you were not so well as usual, he said he would call you up. He wants to tell you about some doctor he discovered in Iowa, who cures everything with massage and hot water. It sounds freakish, but Mr. Lane is a very clever man, isn't he?"

"Very," assented Wanning.

"I should think he must be!" sighed Mrs. Wanning. "How in the world did he make all that money, Paul? He didn't seem especially promising years ago, when we used to see so much of them."

"Corporation business. He's attorney for the P. L. and G.," murmured her husband.

"What a pile he must have!" Florence watched the old negro's slow movements with restless eyes. "Here is Jenny, a Contessa, with a glorious palace in Genoa that her father must have bought her. Surely Aldrini had nothing. Have you seen the baby count's pictures, Roma? They're very cunning. I should think you'd go to Genoa and visit Jenny."

"We must arrange that, Roma. It's such an opportunity." Though Mrs. Wanning addressed her daughter, she looked at her husband. "You would get on so well among their friends. When Count Aldrini was here you spoke Italian much better than poor Jenny. I remember when we entertained him, he could scarcely say anything to her at all."

Florence tried to call up an answering flicker of amusement upon her sister's calm, well-bred face. She thought her mother was rather outdoing herself tonight,—since Aldrini had at least managed to say the one important thing to Jenny, somehow, somewhere. Jenny Lane had been Roma's friend and schoolmate, and the Count was an ephemeral hope in Orange. Mrs. Wanning was one of the first matrons to declare that she had no prejudices against foreigners, and at the dinners that were given for the Count, Roma was always put next him to act as interpreter.

Roma again turned to her father.

"If I were you, dear, I would let Mr. Lane tell me about his doctor. New discoveries are often made by queer people."

Roma's voice was low and sympathetic; she never lost her dignity.

Florence asked if she might have her coffee in her room, while she dashed off a note, and she ran upstairs humming "Bright Lights" and wondering how she was going to stand her family until the summer scattering. Why could Roma never throw off her elegant reserve and call things by their names? She sometimes thought she might like her sister, if she would only come out in the open and howl about her disappointments.

Roma, drinking her coffee deliberately, asked her father if they might have the car early, as they wanted to pick up Mr. Allen and Mr. Rydberg on their way to rehearsal.

Wanning said certainly. Heaven knew he was not stingy about his car, though he could never quite forget that in his day it was the young men who used to call for the girls when they went to rehearsals.

"You are going with us, Mother?" Roma asked as they rose.

"I think so, dear. Your father will want to go to bed early, and I shall sleep better if I go out. I am going to town tomorrow to pour tea for Harold. We must get him some new silver, Paul. I am quite ashamed of his spoons."

Harold, the only son, was a playwright—as yet "unproduced"—and he had a studio in Washington Square.

A half-hour later, Wanning was alone in his library. He would not permit himself to feel aggrieved. What was more commendable than a mother's interest in her children's pleasures? Moreover, it was his wife's way of following things up, of never letting the grass grow under her feet, that had helped to push him along in the world. She was more ambitious than he,—that had been good for him. He was naturally indolent, and Julia's childlike desire to possess material objects, to buy what other people were buying, had been the spur that made him go after business. It had, moreover, made his house the attractive place he believed it to be.

"Suppose," his wife sometimes said to him when the bills came in from Céleste or Mme. Blanche, "suppose you had plain daughters; how would you like that?"

He wouldn't have liked it. When he went anywhere with his three ladies, Wanning always felt very well done by. He had no complaint to make about them, or about anything. That was why it seemed so unreasonable—He felt along his back incredulously with his hand. Harold, of course, was a trial; but among all his business friends, he knew scarcely one who had a promising boy.

The house was so still that Wanning could hear a faint, metallic tinkle from the butler's pantry. Old Sam was washing up the silver, which he put away himself every night.

Wanning rose and walked aimlessly down the hall and out through the dining-room.

"Any Apollinaris on ice, Sam? I'm not feeling very well tonight."

The old colored man dried his hands.

"Yessah, Mistah Wanning. Have a little rye with it, sah?"

"No, thank you, Sam. That's one of the things I can't do any more. I've been to see a big doctor in the city, and he tells me there's something seriously wrong with me. My kidneys have sort of gone back on me."

It was a satisfaction to Wanning to name the organ that had betrayed him, while all the rest of him was so sound.

Sam was immediately interested. He shook his grizzled head and looked full of wisdom.

"Don't seem like a gen'leman of such a temperate life ought to have anything wrong thar, sah."

"No, it doesn't, does it?"

Wanning leaned against the china closet and talked to Sam for nearly half an hour. The specialist who condemned him hadn't seemed half so much interested. There was not a detail about the examination and the laboratory tests in which Sam did not show the deepest concern. He kept asking Wanning if he could remember "straining himself" when he was a young man.

"I've knowed a strain like that to sleep in a man for yeahs and yeahs, and then come back on him, 'deed I have," he said, mysteriously. "An' again, it might be you got a floatin' kidney, sah. Aftah dey once teah loose, dey sometimes don't make no trouble for quite a while."

When Wanning went to his room he did not go to bed. He sat up until he heard the voices of his wife and daughters in the hall below. His own bed somehow frightened him. In all the years he had lived in this house he had never before looked about his room, at that bed, with the thought that he might one day be trapped there, and might not get out again. He had been ill, of course, but his room had seemed a particularly pleasant place for a sick man; sunlight, flowers,—agreeable, well-dressed women coming in and out.

Now there was something sinister about the bed itself, about its position, and its relation to the rest of the furniture.

II

The next morning, on his way downtown, Wanning got off the subway train at Astor Place and walked over to Washington Square. He climbed three flights of stairs and knocked at his son's studio. Harold, dressed, with his stick and gloves in his hand, opened the door. He was just going over to the Brevoort for breakfast. He greeted his father with the cordial familiarity practised by all the "boys" of his set, clapped him on the shoulder and said in his light, tonsillitis voice:

"Come in, Governor, how delightful! I haven't had a call from you in a long time."

He threw his hat and gloves on the writing table. He was a perfect gentleman, even with his father.

Florence said the matter with Harold was that he had heard people say he looked like Byron, and stood for it.

What Harold would stand for in such matters was, indeed, the best definition of him. When he read his play "The Street Walker" in drawing rooms and one lady told him it had the poetic symbolism of Tchekhov, and another said that it suggested the biting realism of Brieux, he never, in his most secret thoughts, questioned the acumen of either lady. Harold's speech, even if you heard it in the next room and could not see him, told you that he had no sense of the absurd,—a throaty staccato, with never a downward inflection, trustfully striving to please.

"Just going out?" his father asked. "I won't keep you. Your mother told you I had a discouraging session with Seares?"

"So awfully sorry you've had this bother, Governor; just as sorry as I can be. No question about its coming out all right, but it's a downright nuisance, your having to diet and that sort of thing. And I suppose you ought to follow directions, just to make us all feel comfortable, oughtn't you?" Harold spoke with fluent sympathy.

Wanning sat down on the arm of a chair and shook his head. "Yes, they do recommend a diet, but they don't promise much from it."

Harold laughed precipitately. "Delicious! All doctors are, aren't they? So profound and oracular! The medicine-man; it's quite the same idea, you see; with tom-toms."

Wanning knew that Harold meant something subtle,—one of the subtleties which he said were only spoiled by being explained—so he came bluntly to one of the issues he had in mind.

"I would like to see you settled before I quit the harness, Harold."

Harold was absolutely tolerant.

He took out his cigarette case and burnished it with his handkerchief.

"I perfectly understand your point of view, dear Governor, but perhaps you don't altogether get mine. Isn't it so? I am settled. What you mean by being settled, would unsettle me, completely. I'm cut out for just such an existence as this; to live four floors up in an attic, get my own breakfast, and have a charwoman to do for me. I should be awfully bored with an establishment. I'm quite content with a little diggings like this."

Wanning's eyes fell. Somebody had to pay the rent of even such modest quarters as contented Harold, but to say so would be rude, and Harold himself was never rude. Wanning did not, this morning, feel equal to hearing a statement of his son's uncommercial ideals.

"I know," he said hastily. "But now we're up against hard facts, my boy. I did not want to alarm your mother, but I've had a time limit put on me, and it's not a very long one."

Harold threw away the cigarette he had just lighted in a burst of indignation.

"That's the sort of thing I consider criminal, Father, absolutely criminal! What doctor has a right to suggest such a thing? Seares himself may be knocked out tomorrow. What have laboratory tests got to do with a man's will to live? The force of that depends upon his entire personality, not on any organ or pair of organs."

Harold thrust his hands in his pockets and walked up and down, very much stirred. "Really, I have a very poor opinion of scientists. They ought to be made serve an apprenticeship in art, to get some conception of the power of human motives. Such brutality!"

Harold's plays dealt with the grimmest and most depressing matters, but he himself was always agreeable, and he insisted upon high cheerfulness as the correct tone of human intercourse.

Wanning rose and turned to go. There was, in Harold, simply no reality, to which one could break through. The young man took up his hat and gloves.

"Must you go? Let me step along with you to the sub. The walk will do me good."

Harold talked agreeably all the way to Astor Place. His father heard little of what he said, but he rather liked his company and his wish to be pleasant.

Wanning went to his club for luncheon, meaning to spend the afternoon with some of his friends who had retired from business and who read the papers there in the empty hours between two and seven. He got no satisfaction, however. When he tried to tell these men of his present predicament, they began to describe ills of their own in which he could not feel interested. Each one of them had a treacherous organ of which he spoke with animation, almost with pride, as if it were a crafty business competitor whom he was constantly outwitting. Each had a doctor, too, for whom he was ardently soliciting business. They wanted either to telephone their doctor and make an appointment for Wanning, or to take him then and there to the consulting room. When he did not accept these invitations, they lost interest in him and remembered engagements. He called a taxi and returned to the offices of McQuiston, Wade, and Wanning.

Settled at his desk, Wanning decided that he would not go home to dinner, but would stay at the office and dictate a long letter to an old college friend who lived in Wyoming. He could tell Douglas Brown things that he had not succeeded in getting to any one else. Brown, out in the Wind River Mountains, couldn't defend himself, couldn't slap Wanning on the back and tell him to gather up the sunbeams.

He called up his house in Orange to say that he would not be home until late. Roma answered the telephone. He spoke mournfully, but she was not disturbed by it.

"Very well, Father. Don't get too tired," she said in her well modulated voice.

When Wanning was ready to dictate his letter, he looked out from his private office into the reception room and saw that his stenographer in her hat and gloves, and furs of the newest cut, was just leaving.

"Good-night, Mr. Wanning," she said, drawing down her dotted veil.

Had there been important business letters to be got off on the night mail, he would have felt that he could detain her, but not for anything personal. Miss Doane was an expert legal stenographer, and she knew her value. The slightest delay in dispatching office business annoyed her. Letters that were not signed until the next morning awoke her deepest contempt. She was scrupulous in professional etiquette, and Wanning felt that their relations, though pleasant, were scarcely cordial.

As Miss Doane's trim figure disappeared through the outer door, little Annie Wooley, the copyist, came in from the stenographers' room. Her hat was pinned over one ear, and she was scrambling into her coat as she came, holding her gloves in her teeth and her battered handbag in the fist that was already through a sleeve.

"Annie, I wanted to dictate a letter. You were just leaving, weren't you?"

"Oh, I don't mind!" she answered cheerfully, and pulling off her old coat, threw it on a chair. "I'll get my book."

She followed him into his room and sat down by a table,—though she wrote with her book on her knee.

Wanning had several times kept her after office hours to take his private letters for him, and she had always been good-natured about it. On each occasion, when he gave her a dollar to get her dinner, she protested, laughing, and saying that she could never eat so much as that.

She seemed a happy sort of little creature, didn't pout when she was scolded, and giggled about her own mistakes in spelling. She was plump and undersized, always dodging under the elbows of taller people and clattering about on high heels, much run over. She had bright black eyes and fuzzy black hair in which, despite Miss Doane's reprimands, she often stuck her pencil. She was the girl who couldn't believe that Wanning was fifty, and he had liked her ever since he overheard that conversation.

Tilting back his chair—he never assumed this position when he dictated to Miss Doane—Wanning began: "To Mr. D. E. Brown, South Forks, Wyoming."

He shaded his eyes with his hand and talked off a long letter to this man who would be sorry that his mortal frame was breaking up. He recalled to him certain fine months they had spent together on the Wind River when they were young men, and said he sometimes wished that like D. E. Brown, he had claimed his freedom in a big country where the wheels did not grind a man as hard as they did in New York. He had spent all these years hustling about and getting ready to live the way he wanted to live, and now he had a puncture the doctors couldn't mend. What was the use of it?

Wanning's thoughts were fixed on the trout streams and the great silver-firs in the canyons of the Wind River Mountains, when he was disturbed by a soft, repeated sniffling. He looked out between his fingers. Little Annie, carried away by his eloquence, was fairly panting to make dots and dashes fast enough, and she was sopping her eyes with an unpresentable, end-of-the-day handkerchief.

Wanning rambled on in his dictation. .Why was she crying? What did it matter to her? He was a man who said good-morning to her, who sometimes took an hour of the precious few she had left at the end of the day and then complained about her bad spelling. When the letter was finished, he handed her a new two dollar bill.

"I haven't got any change tonight; and anyhow, I'd like you to eat a whole lot. I'm on a diet, and I want to see everybody else eat."

Annie tucked her notebook under her arm and stood looking at the bill which she had not taken up from the table.

"I don't like to be paid for taking letters to your friends, Mr. Wanning," she said impulsively. "I can run personal letters off between times. It ain't as if I needed the money," she added carelessly.

"Get along with you! Anybody who is eighteen years old and has a sweet tooth needs money, all they can get."

Annie giggled and darted out with the bill in her hand.

Wanning strolled aimlessly after her into the reception room.

"Let me have that letter before lunch tomorrow, please, and be sure that nobody sees it." He stopped and frowned. "I don't look very sick, do I?"

"I should say you don't!" Annie got her coat on after considerable tugging. "Why don't you call in a specialist? My mother called a specialist for my father before he died."

"Oh, is your father dead?"

"I should say he is! He was a painter by trade, and he fell off a seventy-foot stack into the East River. Mother couldn't get anything out of the company, because he wasn't buckled. He lingered for four months, so I know all about taking care of sick people. I was attending business college then, and sick as he was, he used to give me dictation for practise. He made us all go into professions; the girls, too. He didn't like us to just run."

Wanning would have liked to keep Annie and hear more about her family, but it was nearly seven o'clock, and he knew he ought, in mercy, to let her go. She was the only person to whom he had talked about his illness who had been frank and honest with him, who had looked at him with eyes that concealed nothing. When he broke the news of his condition to his partners that morning, they shut him off as if he were uttering indecent ravings. All day they had met him with a hurried, abstracted manner. McQuiston and Wade went out to lunch together, and he knew what they were thinking, perhaps talking, about. Wanning had brought into the firm valuable business, but he was less enterprising than either of of his partners.

III

In the early summer Wanning's family scattered. Roma swallowed her pride and sailed for Genoa to visit the Contessa Jenny. Harold went to Cornish to be in an artistic atmosphere. Mrs. Wanning and Florence took a cottage at York Harbor where Wanning was supposed to join them whenever he could get away from town. He did not often get away. He felt most at ease among his accustomed surroundings. He kept his car in the city and went back and forth from his office to the club where he was living. Old Sam, his butler, came in from Orange every night to put his clothes in order and make him comfortable.

Wanning began to feel that he would not tire of his office in a hundred years. Although he did very little work, it was pleasant to go downtown every morning when the streets were crowded, the sky clear, and the sunshine bright. From the windows of his private office he could see the harbor and watch the ocean liners come down the North River and go out to sea.

While he read his mail, he often looked out and wondered why he had been so long indifferent to that extraordinary scene of human activity and hopefulness. How had a short-lived race of beings the energy and courage valiantly to begin enterprises which they could follow for only a few years; to throw up towers and build sea-monsters and found great businesses, when the frailest of the materials with which they worked, the paper upon which they wrote, the ink upon their pens, had more permanence in this world than they? All this material rubbish lasted. The linen clothing and cosmetics of the Egyptians had lasted. It was only the human flame that certainly, certainly went out. Other things had a fighting chance; they might meet with mishap and be destroyed, they might not. But the human creature who gathered and shaped and hoarded and foolishly loved these things, he had no chance—absolutely none. Wanning's cane, his hat, his top-coat, might go from beggar to beggar and knock about in this world for another fifty years or so; but not he.

In the late afternoon he never hurried to leave his office now. Wonderful sunsets burned over the North River, wonderful stars trembled up among the towers; more wonderful than anything he could hurry away to. One of his windows looked directly down upon the spire of Old Trinity, with the green churchyard and the pale sycamores far below. Wanning often dropped into the church when he was going out to lunch; not because he was trying to make his peace with Heaven, but because the church was old and restful and familiar, because it and its gravestones had sat in the same place for a long while. He bought flowers from the street boys and kept them on his desk, which his partners thought strange behavior, and which Miss Doane considered a sign that he was failing.

But there were graver things than bouquets for Miss Doane and the senior partner to ponder over.

The senior partner, McQuiston, in spite of his silvery hair and mustache and his important church connections, had rich natural taste for scandal.—After Mr. Wade went away for his vacation, in May, Wanning took Annie Wooley out of the copying room, put her at a desk in his private office, and raised her pay to eighteen dollars a week, explaining to McQuiston that for the summer months he would need a secretary. This explanation satisfied neither McQuiston nor Miss Doane.

Annie was also paid for overtime, and although Wanning attended to very little of the office business now, there was a great deal of overtime. Miss Doane was, of course, "above" questioning a chit like Annie; but what was he doing with his time and his new secretary, she wanted to know?

If anyone had told her that Wanning was writing a book, she would have said bitterly that it was just like him. In his youth Wanning had hankered for the pen. When he studied law, he had intended to combine that profession with some tempting form of authorship. Had he remained a bachelor, he would have been an unenterprising literary lawyer to the end of his days. It was his wife's restlessness and her practical turn of mind that had made him a money-getter. His illness seemed to bring back to him the illusions with which he left college.

As soon as his family were out of the way and he shut up the Orange house, he began to dictate his autobiography to Annie Wooley. It was not only the story of his life, but an expression of all his theories and opinions, and a commentary on the fifty years of events which he could remember.

Fortunately, he was able to take great interest in this undertaking. He had the happiest convictions about the clear-cut style he was developing and his increasing felicity in phrasing. He meant to publish the work handsomely, at his own expense and under his own name. He rather enjoyed the thought of how greatly disturbed Harold would be. He and Harold differed in their estimates of books. All the solid works which made up Wanning's library, Harold considered beneath contempt. Anybody, he said, could do that sort of thing.

When Wanning could not sleep at night, he turned on the light beside his bed and made notes on the chapter he meant to dictate the next day.

When he returned to the office after lunch, he gave instructions that he was not to be interrupted by telephone calls, and shut himself up with his secretary.

After he had opened all the windows and taken off his coat, he fell to dictating. He found it a delightful occupation, the solace of each day. Often he had sudden fits of tiredness; then he would lie down on the leather sofa and drop asleep, while Annie read "The Leopard's Spots" until he awoke.

Like many another business man Wanning had relied so long on stenographers that the operation of writing with a pen had become laborious to him. When he undertook it, he wanted to cut everything short. But walking up and down his private office, with the strong after-noon sun pouring in at his windows, a fresh air stirring, all the people and boats moving restlessly down there, he could say things he wanted to say. It was like living his life over again.

He did not miss his wife or his daughters. He had become again the mild, contemplative youth he was in college, before he had a profession and a family to grind for, before the two needs which shape our destiny had made of him pretty much what they make of every man.

At five o'clock Wanning sometimes went out for a cup of tea and took Annie along. He felt dull and discouraged as soon as he was alone. So long as Annie was with him, he could keep a grip on his own thoughts. They talked about what he had just been dictating to her. She found that he liked to be questioned, and she tried to be greatly interested in it all.

After tea, they went back to the office. Occasionally Wanning lost track of time and kept Annie until it grew dark. He knew he had old McQuiston guessing, but he didn't care. One day the senior partner came to him with a reproving air.

"I am afraid Miss Doane is leaving us, Paul. She feels that Miss Wooley's promotion is irregular."

"How is that any business of hers, I'd like to know? She has all my legal work. She is always disagreeable enough about doing anything else."

McQuiston's puffy red face went a shade darker.

"Miss Doane has a certain professional pride; a strong feeling for office organization. She doesn't care to fill an equivocal position. I don't know that I blame her. She feels that there is something not quite regular about the confidence you seem to place in this inexperienced young woman."

Wanning pushed back his chair.

"I don't care a hang about Miss Doane's sense of propriety. I need a stenographer who will carry out my instructions. I've carried out Miss Doane's long enough. I've let that schoolma'am hector me for years. She can go when she pleases."

That night McQuiston wrote to his partner that things were in a bad way, and they would have to keep an eye on Wanning. He had been seen at the theater with his new stenographer.

That was true. Wanning had several times taken Annie to the Palace on Saturday afternoon. When all his acquaintances were off motoring or playing golf, when the downtown offices and even the streets were deserted, it amused him to watch a foolish show with a delighted, cheerful little person beside him.

Beyond her generosity, Annie had no shining merits of character, but she had the gift of thinking well of everything, and wishing well. When she was there Wanning felt as if there were someone who cared whether this was a good or a bad day with him. Old Sam, too, was like that. While the old black man put him to bed and made him comfortable, Wanning could talk to him as he talked to little Annie. Even if he dwelt upon his illness, in plain terms, in detail, he did not feel as if he were imposing on them.

People like Sam and Annie admitted misfortune,—admitted it almost cheerfully. Annie and her family did not consider illness or any of its hard facts vulgar or indecent. It had its place in their scheme of life, as it had not in that of Wanning's friends.

Annie came out of a typical poor family of New York. Of eight children, only four lived to grow up. In such families the stream of life is broad enough, but runs shallow. In the children, vitality is exhausted early. The roots do not go down into anything very strong. Illness and deaths and funerals, in her own family and in those of her friends, had come at frequent intervals in Annie's life. Since they had to be, she and her sisters made the best of them. There was something to be got out of funerals, even, if they were managed right. They kept people in touch with old friends who had moved uptown, and revived kindly feelings.

Annie had often given up things she wanted because there was sickness at home, and now she was patient with her boss. What he paid her for overtime work by no means made up to her what she lost.

Annie was not in the least thrifty, nor were any of her sisters. She had to make a living, but she was not interested in getting all she could for her time, or in laying up for the future. Girls like Annie know that the future is a very uncertain thing, and they feel no responsibility about it. The present is what they have—and it is all they have. If Annie missed a chance to go sailing with the plumber's son on Saturday afternoon, why, she missed it. As for the two dollars her boss gave her, she handed them over to her mother. Now that Annie was getting more money, one of her sisters quit a job she didn't like and was staying at home for a rest. That was all promotion meant to Annie.

The first time Annie's boss asked her to work on Saturday afternoon, she could not hide her disappointment. He suggested that they might knock off early and go to a show, or take a run in his car, but she grew tearful and said it would be hard to make her family understand. Wanning thought perhaps he could explain to her mother. He called his motor and took Annie home.

When his car stopped in front of the tenement house on Eighth Avenue, heads came popping out of the windows for six storys up, and all the neighbor women, in dressing sacks and wrappers, gazed down at the machine and at the couple alighting from it. A motor meant a wedding or the hospital.

The plumber's son, Willy Steen, came over from the corner saloon to see what was going on, and Annie introduced him at the doorstep.

Mrs. Wooley asked Wanning to come into the parlor and invited him to have a chair of ceremony between the folding bed and the piano.

Annie, nervous and tearful, escaped to the dining-room—the cheerful spot where the daughters visited with each other and with their friends. The parlor was a masked sleeping chamber and store room.

The plumber's son sat down on the sofa beside Mrs. Wooley, as if he were accustomed to share in the family councils. Mrs. Wooley waited expectant and kindly. She looked the sensible, hard-working woman that she was, and one could see she hadn't lived all her life on Eighth Avenue without learning a great deal.

Wanning explained to her that he was writing a book which he wanted to finish during the summer months when business was not so heavy. He was ill and could not work regularly. His secretary would have to take his dictation when he felt able to give it; must, in short, be a sort of companion to him. He would like to feel that she could go out in his car with him, or even to the theater, when he felt like it. It might have been better if he had engaged a young man for this work, but since he had begun it with Annie, he would like to keep her if her mother was willing.

Mrs. Wooley watched him with friendly, searching eyes. She glanced at Willy Steen, who, wise in such distinctions, had decided that there was nothing shady about Annie's boss. He nodded his sanction.

"I don't want my girl to conduct herself in any such way as will prejudice her, Mr. Wanning," she said thoughtfully. "If you've got daughters, you know how that is. You've been liberal with Annie, and it's a good position for her. It's right she should go to business every day, and I want her to do her work right, but I like to have her home after working hours. I always think a young girl's time is her own after business hours, and I try not to burden them when they come home. I'm willing she should do your work as suits you, if it's her wish; but I don't like to press her. The good times she misses now, it's not you nor me, sir, that can make them up to her. These young things has their feelings."

"Oh, I don't want to press her, either," Wanning said hastily. "I simply want to know that you understand the situation. I've made her a little present in my will as a recognition that she is doing more for me than she is paid for."

"That's something above me, sir. We'll hope there won't be no question of wills for many years yet," Mrs. Wooley spoke heartily. "I'm glad if my girl can be of any use to you, just so she don't prejudice herself."

The plumber's son rose as if the interview were over.

"It's all right, Mama Wooley, don't you worry," he said.

He picked up his canvas cap and turned to Wanning. "You see, Annie ain't the sort of girl that would want to be spotted circulating around with a monied party her folks didn't know all about. She'd lose friends by it."

After this conversation Annie felt a great deal happier. She was still shy and a trifle awkward with poor Wanning when they were outside the office building, and she missed the old freedom of her Saturday afternoons. But she did the best she could, and Willy Steen tried to make it up to her.

In Annie's absence he often came in of an afternoon to have a cup of tea and a sugar-bun with Mrs. Wooley and the daughter who was "resting." As they sat at the dining-room table, they discussed Annie's employer, his peculiarities, his health, and what he had told Mrs. Wooley about his will.

Mrs. Wooley said she sometimes felt afraid he might disinherit his children, as rich people often did, and make talk; but she hoped for the best. Whatever came to Annie, she prayed it might not be in the form of taxable property.

IV

Late in September Wanning grew suddenly worse. His family hurried home, and he was put to bed in his house in Orange. He kept asking the doctors when he could get back to the office, but he lived only eight days.

The morning after his father's funeral, Harold went to the office to consult Wanning's partners and to read the will. Everything in the will was as it should be. There were no surprises except a codicil in the form of a letter to Mrs. Wanning, dated July 8th, requesting that out of the estate she should pay the sum of one thousand dollars to his stenographer, Annie Wooley, "in recognition of her faithful services."

"I thought Miss Doane was my father's stenographer," Harold exclaimed.

Alec McQuiston looked embarrassed and spoke in a low, guarded tone.

"She was, for years. But this spring,—" he hesitated.

McQuiston loved a scandal. He leaned across his desk toward Harold.

"This spring your father put this little girl, Miss Wooley, a copyist, utterly inexperienced, in Miss Doane's place. Miss Doane was indignant and left us. The change made comment here in the office. It was slightly— No, I will be frank with you, Harold, it was very irregular."

Harold also looked grave. "What could my father have meant by such a request as this to my mother?"

The silver haired senior partner flushed and spoke as if he were trying to break something gently.

"I don't understand it, my boy. But I think, indeed I prefer to think, that your father was not quite himself all this summer. A man like your father does not, in his right senses, find pleasure in the society of an ignorant, common little girl. He does not make a practise of keeping her at the office after hours, often until eight o'clock, or take her to restaurants and to the theater with him; not, at least, in a slanderous city like New York."

Harold flinched before McQuiston's meaning gaze and turned aside in pained silence. He knew, as a dramatist, that there are dark chapters in all men's lives, and this but too clearly explained why his father had stayed in town all summer instead of joining his family.

McQuiston asked if he should ring for Annie Wooley.

Harold drew himself up. "No. Why should I see her? I prefer not to. But with your permission, Mr. McQuiston, I will take charge of this request to my mother. It could only give her pain, and might awaken doubts in her mind."

"We hardly know," murmured the senior partner, "where an investigation would lead us. Technically, of course, I cannot agree with you. But if, as one of the executors of the will, you wish to assume personal responsibility for this bequest, under the circumstances— irregularities beget irregularities."

"My first duty to my father," said Harold, "is to protect my mother."

That afternoon McQuiston called Annie Wooley into his private office and told her that her services would not be needed any longer, and that in lieu of notice the clerk would give her two weeks' salary.

"Can I call up here for references?" Annie asked.

"Certainly. But you had better ask for me, personally. You must know there has been some criticism of you here in the office, Miss Wooley."

"What about?" Annie asked boldly.

"Well, a young girl like you cannot render so much personal service to her employer as you did to Mr. Wanning without causing unfavorable comment. To be blunt with you, for your own good, my dear young lady, your services to your employer should terminate in the office, and at the close of office hours. Mr. Wanning was a very sick man and his judgment was at fault, but you should have known what a girl in your station can do and what she cannot do."

The vague discomfort of months flashed up in little Annie. She had no mind to stand by and be lectured without having a word to say for herself.

"Of course he was sick, poor man!" she burst out. "Not as anybody seemed much upset about it. I wouldn't have given up my half-holidays for anybody if they hadn't been sick, no matter what they paid me. There wasn't anything in it for me."

McQuiston raised his hand warningly.

"That will do, young lady. But when you get another place, remember this: it is never your duty to entertain or to provide amusement for your employer."

He gave Annie a look which she did not clearly understand, although she pronounced him a nasty old man as she hustled on her hat and jacket.

When Annie reached home she found Willy Steen sitting with her mother and sister at the dining-room table. This was the first day that Annie had gone to the office since Wanning's death, and her family awaited her return with suspense.

"Hello yourself," Annie called as she came in and threw her handbag into an empty armchair.

"You're off early, Annie," said her mother gravely. "Has the will been read?"

"I guess so. Yes, I know it has. Miss Wilson got it out of the safe for them. The son came in. He's a pill."

"Was nothing said to you, daughter?"

"Yes, a lot. Please give me some tea, mother." Annie felt that her swagger was failing.

"Don't tantalize us, Ann," her sister broke in. "Didn't you get anything?"

"I got the mit, all right. And some back talk from the old man that I'm awful sore about."

Annie dashed away the tears and gulped her tea.

Gradually her mother and Willy drew the story from her. Willy offered at once to go to the office building and take his stand outside the door and never leave it until he had punched old Mr. McQuiston's face. He rose as if to attend to it at once, but Mrs. Wooley drew him to his chair again and patted his arm.

"It would only start talk and get the girl in trouble, Willy. When it's lawyers, folks in our station is helpless. I certainly believed that man when he sat here; you heard him yourself. Such a gentleman as he looked."

Willy thumped his great fist, still in punching position, down on his knee.

"Never you be fooled again, Mama Wooley. You'll never get anything out of a rich guy that he ain't signed up in the courts for. Rich is tight. There's no exceptions."

Annie shook her head.

"I didn't want anything out of him. He was a nice, kind man, and he had his troubles, I guess. He wasn't tight."

"Still," said Mrs. Wooley sadly, "Mr. Wanning had no call to hold out promises. I hate to be disappointed in a gentleman. You've had confining work for some time, daughter; a rest will do you good."

Smart Set 90 (October 1919): 95–108

Coming, Eden Bower!

❖ ❖ ❖

CHAPTER I

Don Hedger had lived for four years on the top floor of an old house on the south side of Washington Square, and nobody had ever disturbed him. He occupied one big room with no outside exposure except on the north, where he had built in a many-paned studio window that looked upon a court and upon the roofs and walls of other buildings.

His room was very cheerless, since he never got a ray of direct sunlight; the south corners were always in shadow. In one of these corners was a clothes closet, built against the partition; in another a wide divan, serving as a seat by day and a bed by night. In the front corner, the one farther from the window, was a sink, and a table with two gas burners, where he sometimes cooked his food. There, too, in the perpetual dusk, was the dog's bed, and often a bone or two for his comfort.

The dog was a Boston bull terrier, and Hedger explained his surly disposition by the fact that he had been bred to the point where it told on his nerves. His name was Cæsar III, and he had taken prizes at very exclusive dog shows. When he and his master went out to prowl about University Place or to promenade along West Street, Cæsar III was invariably fresh and shining. His pink skin showed through his mottled coat, which glistened as if it had just been rubbed with olive oil, and he wore a brass-studded collar, bought at the smartest saddler's. Hedger, as often as not, was hunched up in an old striped blanket coat, with a shapeless felt hat pulled over his bushy hair, wearing black shoes that had become gray, or brown ones that had become black, and he never put on gloves unless the day was biting cold.

Early in May, Hedger learned that he was to have a new neighbour in the rear apartment—two rooms, one large and one small, that faced the west. His studio was shut off from the larger of these rooms by double doors which, though they were fairly tight, left him a good deal at the mercy of the occupant.

The rooms had been leased, long before he came there, by a trained nurse who considered herself knowing in old furniture. She went to auction sales and bought up mahogany and dirty brass and stored it away here, where she meant to live when she retired from nursing. Meanwhile, she sub-let her rooms, with their precious furniture, to young people who came to New York to write or to paint—who proposed to live by the sweat of the brow rather than of the hand, and who desired artistic surroundings. When Hedger first moved in, these rooms were occupied by a young man who tried to write plays, and who had kept on trying until a week ago, when the nurse had put him out for unpaid rent.

A few days after the playwright left, Hedger heard an ominous murmur of voices through the bolted double doors; the lady-like intonation of the nurse—doubtless exhibiting her treasures—and another voice, also a woman's, but very different, young, fresh, unguarded, confident. All the same, it would be very annoying to have a woman in there. The only bathroom on the floor was at the top of the stairs in the front hall, and he would always be running into her as he came or went from his bath. He would have to be more careful to see that Cæsar didn't leave bones around the hall, too; and she might object when he cooked steak and onions on his gas burner.

As soon as the talking ceased and the women left, he forgot them. He was absorbed in a picture of paradise fish at the Aquarium, staring out at people through the glass and green water of their tank. It was a highly gratifying idea; the incommunicability of one stratum of animal life with another—though Hedger pretended it was only an experiment in unusual lighting. When he heard trunks knocking against the sides of the narrow hall, then he realized that she was moving in at once.

Toward noon, groans and deep gasps and the creaking of ropes made him aware that a piano was arriving. After the tramp of the movers died away down the stairs, somebody touched off a few scales and chords on the instrument, and then there was peace. Presently he heard her lock her door and go down the hall humming something; going out to lunch, probably. He stuck his brushes in a can of turpentine and put on his hat, not stopping to wash his hands. Cæsar was smelling along the crack under the bolted doors; his bony tail stuck out hard as a hickory withe and the hair was standing up about his elegant collar.

Hedger encouraged him. "Come along, Cæsar. You'll soon get used to a new aroma."

In the hall stood an enormous trunk, behind the ladder that led to the roof, just opposite Hedger's door. The dog flew at it with a growl of hurt amazement. They went down three flights of stairs and out into the brilliant May afternoon.

Behind the Square, Hedger and his dog descended into a basement oyster house where there were no tablecloths on the tables and no handles on the coffee cups, and the floor was covered with sawdust, and Cæsar was always welcome—not that he needed any such precautionary flooring. All the carpets of Persia would have been safe for him. Hedger ordered

steak and onions absent-mindedly, not realizing why he had an appre-
hension that this dish might be less readily at hand hereafter. While he ate,
Cæsar sat beside his chair, gravely disturbing the sawdust with his tail.

After lunch, Hedger strolled about the Square for the dog's health and
watched the stages pull out; that was almost the very last summer of the
old horse stages on Fifth Avenue. The fountain had but lately begun
operations for the season and was throwing up a mist of rainbow water
which now and then blew south and sprayed a bunch of Italian babies who
were being held up on the outer rim by older, very little older, brothers
and sisters. Plump robins were hopping about on the soil; the grass was
newly cut and blindingly green. Looking up the Avenue, through the
Arch, one could see the young poplars with their fresh, bright, un-
smoked leaves, and the Brevoort glistening in its spring coat of paint, and
shining horses and carriages—occasionally an automobile, misshapen and
sullen, like an ugly threat in a stream of things that were bright and
beautiful and alive.

While Cæsar and his master were standing by the fountain, a girl
approached them, crossing the Square. Hedger noticed her because she
wore a lavender cloth suit and carried in her arms a big bunch of fresh
lilacs. He saw that she was young and handsome—beautiful, in fact, with
a splendid figure and good action. She, too, paused by the fountain and
looked back through the Arch up the Avenue. She smiled rather patron-
izingly as she looked, and at the same time seemed delighted. Her slowly
curving upper lip and half-closed eyes seemed to say:

"You're gay, you're exciting, you are quite the right sort of thing;
but you're none too fine for me!"

In the moment she tarried, Cæsar stealthily approached her and
sniffed at the hem of her lavender skirt, then, when she went south like an
arrow, he ran back to his master and lifted a face full of emotion and
alarm, his lower lip twitching under his sharp white teeth and his hazel
eyes pointed with a very definite discovery. He stood thus, motionless,
while Hedger watched the lavender girl go up the steps and through the
door of the house in which he lived.

"You're right, my boy, it's she! She might be worse looking, you
know."

When they mounted to the studio, the new lodger's door at the back
of the hall was a little ajar, and Hedger caught the warm perfume of lilacs
just brought in out of the sun. He was used to the musty smell of the old
hall carpet. (The nurse-lessee had once knocked at his studio door and

complained that Cæsar must be somewhat responsible for the particular flavour of that mustiness, and Hedger had never spoken to her since.) He was used to the old smell, and he preferred it to that of lilacs, and so did his companion, whose nose was so much more discriminating. Hedger shut his door vehemently, and fell to work.

Most young men who dwell in obscure studios in New York have had a beginning, come out of something, have somewhere a home town, a family, a paternal roof. But Don Hedger had no such background. He was a foundling, and had grown up in a school for homeless boys, where book-learning was a negligible part of the curriculum. When he was sixteen, a Catholic priest took him to Greensburg, Pennsylvania, to keep house for him. The priest did something to fill in the large gaps in the boy's education—taught him to like Don Quixote and The Golden Legend, and encouraged him to mess with paints and crayons in his room up under the slope of the mansard.

When Don wanted to go to New York to study at the Art League, the priest got him a night job as a packer in one of the big department stores. Since then, Hedger had taken care of himself; that was his only responsibility. He was singularly unencumbered; had no family duties, no social ties, no obligations toward anyone but his landlord. Since he travelled light, he had travelled rather far. He had got over a good deal of the earth's surface, in spite of the fact that he never in his life had more than three hundred dollars ahead at any one time, and he had already outlived a succession of convictions and revelations about his art.

Though he was now but twenty-six years old, he had twice been on the verge of becoming a marketable product; once through some studies of New York streets he did for a magazine, and once through a collection of pastels he brought home from New Mexico, which Remington, then a great man in American art, happened to see and generously tried to push. But on both occasions Hedger decided that this was something he didn't wish to carry further—simply the old thing over again and got nowhere—so he took enquiring dealers something in a "later manner," and they put him out of the shop. When he ran short of money he could always get any amount of commercial work because he was an expert draughtsman and worked with lightning speed. The rest of his time he spent in groping his way from one kind of painting into another, or travelling about without luggage, like a tramp, and he was chiefly occupied with getting rid of ideas he had once thought very fine.

Hedger's circumstances, since he had moved to Washington Square, were affluent compared to anything he had ever known before. He was now able to pay advance rent and turn the key on his studio when he went away for four months at a stretch. It didn't occur to him to wish to be richer than this. To be sure, he did without a great many things that other people think necessary, but he didn't miss them because he had never had them. He belonged to no clubs, visited no houses, had no studio friends, and he ate his dinner alone in some decent little restaurant, even on Christmas and New Year's. For days together he talked to nobody but his dog and the janitress and the lame oysterman.

After he shut the door and settled down to his paradise fish on that first Tuesday in May, Hedger forgot all about his new neighbour. When the light failed, he took Cæsar out for a walk. On the way home he did his marketing on West Houston Street, with a one-eyed Italian woman he knew. After he had cooked his beans and scallopini, and drunk half a bottle of Chianti, he put his dishes in the sink and went up on the roof to smoke. He was the only person in the house who ever went to the roof, and he had a secret understanding with the janitress about it. He was to have "the privilege of the roof" as she said, if he opened the heavy trap-door on sunny days to air out the upper hall, and was watchful to close it when rain threatened. Mrs. Foley was fat and dirty and hated to climb stairs—besides, the roof was reached by a perpendicular iron ladder, definitely inaccessible to a woman of her bulk, and the iron door at the top of it was too heavy for any but Hedger's strong arm to lift. Hedger was not above medium height, but he practised with weights and dumb-bells and in the shoulders he was as strong as a gorilla.

So Hedger had the roof to himself. He and Cæsar often slept up there on hot nights, rolled in blankets he had brought home from Arizona. He mounted with Cæsar under his left arm. The dog had never learned to climb a perpendicular ladder, and never did he feel so much his master's greatness and his own dependence upon him as when he crept under his arm for this perilous ascent. Up there was even gravel to scratch in, and a dog could do whatever he liked so long as he did not bark. It was a kind of Heaven, which no one was strong enough to reach but his great, paint-smelling master.

On this blue May night there was a slender, girlish-looking young moon in the west, playing with a whole company of silver stars. Now and then one of them darted away from the group and shot off into the gauzy blue with a soft trail of light, like laughter. Hedger and his dog were delighted when a star did this. They were quite lost in watching the glittering game, when they were suddenly diverted by a sound—not from the stars, though it was music. It was not the prologue to "Pagliacci," which rose ever and anon on hot evenings from an Italian tenement on Thompson Street, with the gasps of the corpulent baritone who got behind it; nor was it the hurdy-gurdy man, who often played at the corner in the balmy twilight. No, this was a woman's voice, singing the tempestuous, overlapping phrases of Signor Puccini, then comparatively new in the world, but already so popular that even Hedger recognized his unmistakable gusts of breath.

He looked about over the roofs; all was blue and still, with the well-built chimneys that were never used now standing up dark and mournful. He moved softly toward the yellow quadrangle where the gas from the hall shone up through the half-lifted trapdoor. Oh, yes! It came up through the hole like a strong draught, a big, beautiful voice, and it sounded rather like a professional's. A piano had come in the morning, Hedger remembered. This might be a very great nuisance. It would be pleasant enough to listen to if you could turn it on and off as you wished; but you couldn't. Cæsar, with the gas light shining up on his collar and his ugly but sensitive face, panted and looked up for information. Hedger put down a reassuring hand.

"I don't know. We can't tell yet. It may not be so bad."

He stayed on the roof until all was still below, and finally descended with quite a new feeling about his neighbour. Her voice, like her figure, inspired respect—if one did not choose to call it admiration. Her door was shut, the transom was dark; nothing remained of her but the obtrusive trunk, unrightfully taking up room in the narrow hall.

CHAPTER II

For two days Hedger didn't see her. He was painting eight hours a day just then, and only went out to hunt for food. He noticed that she practised scales and exercises for about an hour in the morning. Then she locked her door, went humming down the hall, and left him in peace. He heard her getting her coffee ready at about the same time he got his. Earlier still, she passed his room on her way to her bath. In the evening she sometimes sang, but on the whole she didn't bother him.

When he was working well he did not notice anything much. The morning paper lay before his door until he reached out for his milk bottle, then he kicked the sheet inside and it lay on the floor until evening.

Sometimes he read it and sometimes he did not. He forgot there was anything of importance going on in the world outside of his third floor studio. Nobody had ever taught him that he ought to be interested in other people; in the Pittsburgh steel strike, in the Fresh Air Fund, in the scandal about the Babies' Hospital. A gray wolf, living in a Wyoming canyon, would hardly have been less concerned about these things than was Don Hedger.

One morning he was coming out of the bathroom at the front end of the hall, having just given Cæsar his bath and rubbed him into a glow with a heavy towel. Before the door, lying in wait for him as it were, stood a tall figure in a flowing blue silk dressing gown that fell away from her marble arms. In her hands she carried various accessories of the bath.

"I wish," she said distinctly, standing in his way, "I wish you wouldn't wash your dog in the tub. I never heard of such a thing! I've found his hair in the tub, and I've smelled a doggy smell, and now I've caught you at it. It's an outrage!"

Hedger was badly frightened. She was so tall and positive, and was fairly blazing with beauty and anger. He stood blinking, holding onto his sponge and dog-soap, feeling that he ought to bow very low to her. But what he actually said was:

"Nobody has ever objected before. I always wash the tub—and, anyhow, he's cleaner than most people."

"Cleaner than me?" her eyebrows went up, her white arms and neck and her fragrant person seemed to scream at him like a band of outraged nymphs. Something flashed through his mind about a man who was turned into a dog, or was pursued by dogs, because he unwittingly intruded upon the bath of beauty.

"No, I didn't mean that," he muttered, turning scarlet under the bluish stubble of his muscular jaws. "But I know he's cleaner than I am."

"That I don't doubt!" Her voice sounded like a soft shivering of crystal, and with a smile of pity she drew the folds of her voluminous blue robe against the wall and allowed the wretched man to pass. Even Cæsar was frightened; he darted like a streak down the hall, through the door and to his own bed in the corner among the bones.

Hedger stood still in the doorway, listening to indignant sniffs and coughs and a great swishing of water about the sides of the tub. He had washed it; but as he had washed it with Cæsar's sponge, it was quite possible that a few bristles remained; the dog was shedding now. The playwright had never objected, nor had the jovial illustrator who occupied the front apartment—but he, as he admitted, "was usually pie-eyed, when he wasn't in Buffalo." He went home to Buffalo sometimes to rest his nerves.

It had never occurred to Hedger that anyone would mind using the tub after Cæsar—but then, he had never seen a beautiful girl caparisoned for the bath before. As soon as he beheld her standing there, he realized the unfitness of it. For that matter, she ought not to step into a tub that any other mortal had bathed in; the illustrator was sloppy and left cigarette ends on the moulding.

All morning as he worked he was gnawed by a spiteful desire to get back at her. It rankled that he had been so vanquished by her disdain. When he heard her locking her door to go out for lunch, he stepped quickly into the hall in his messy painting coat, and addressed her.

"I don't wish to be exigent, Miss"—he had certain grand words that he used upon occasion—"but if this is your trunk, it's rather in the way here."

"Oh, very well!" she exclaimed carelessly, dropping her keys into her handbag. "I'll have it moved when I can get a man to do it," and she went down the hall with her free, roving stride.

Her name, Hedger discovered from her letters, which the postman left on the table in the lower hall, was Eden Bower.

CHAPTER III

In the closet that was built against the partition separating his room from Miss Bower's, Hedger kept all his wearing apparel, some of it on hooks and hangers, some of it on the floor. When he opened his closet door nowadays, little dust-coloured insects flew out on downy wing, and he suspected that a brood of moths were hatching in his winter overcoat. Mrs. Foley, the janitress, told him to bring down all his heavy clothes and she would give them a beating and hang them in the court. The closet was in such disorder that he shunned the encounter, but one hot afternoon he set himself to the task.

First he threw out a pile of forgotten laundry and tied it up in a sheet. The bundle stood as high as his middle when he had knotted the corners. Then he got his shoes and overshoes together. When he took his overcoat from its place against the partition, a long ray of yellow light shot across the dark enclosure, a knothole, evidently, in the high wainscoting of the west room. He had never noticed it before and without realizing what he was doing, he stooped and squinted through it.

Yonder, in a pool of sunlight, stood his new neighbour, clad in a pink chiffon cloud of some sort, doing gymnastic exercises before a long gilt mirror. Hedger did not think how unpardonable it was of him to watch her. A woman in negligée was not an improper object to a man who had worked so much from unclad models, and he continued to look simply because, except in old sculpture, he had never seen a human body so beautiful as this one—positively glorious in action. As she swung her arms and changed from one pivot of motion to another, muscular energy seemed to flow through her from her toes to her finger-tips. The soft flush of exercise and the gold of the afternoon sun played over her together, enveloped her in a luminous mist which, as she turned and twisted, made now an arm, now a shoulder, dissolve in pure light and instantly recover its outline with the next gesture.

Hedger's fingers curved as if he were holding a crayon; mentally he was doing the whole figure in a single running line, and the charcoal seemed to explode in his hand at the point where the energy of each gesture was discharged into the whirling disc of light.

He could not have told whether he watched her for six minutes or sixteen. When her gymnastics were over, she paused to catch up a lock of hair that had come down; then, with her hand on her hip, she walked unconcernedly across the room and disappeared through the door into her bedchamber.

Disappeared—Don Hedger was staring at the golden shower which poured in through the west windows, at the lake of gold on the faded Turkish carpet. The spot seemed enchanted; as if a vision out of Alexandria, out of the remote pagan past, had bathed itself there in Helianthine fire.

When he crawled out of his closet he stood blinking at the gray sheet stuffed with laundry. He felt a little sick as he contemplated the bundle. Everything here was different; he hated the disorder of the place, the gray prison light, his old shoes and himself and all his slovenly habits. The black calico curtains that ran on wires over his big window were white with dust. There were three frying pans in the sink, and the sink itself—. He felt desperate. He couldn't stand this another minute. He took up an armful of winter clothes and ran down four flights into the basement.

"Mrs. Foley," he began, "I want my room cleaned this afternoon, thoroughly cleaned. Can you get a woman for me right away?"

"Is it company you're having?" the fat, dirty janitress inquired.

Mrs. Foley was the widow of a useful Tammany man, and she owned real estate in Flatbush. She was huge and soft as a feather bed. Her face and arms were permanently coated with dust, grained like wood where the perspiration had trickled.

"Yes, company. That's it."

"Well, this is a queer time of the day to be asking for a cleaning woman. It's likely I can get you old Lizzie, if she's not drunk. I'll send Willy round to see."

Willy, the son of fourteen, roused from the stupor and stain of his third box of cigarettes by the gleam of a quarter, went out. In five minutes he returned with old Lizzie—she smelling strong of spirits and wearing several jackets which she had put on one over the other, and a number of skirts, long and short, which made her resemble an animated dish-clout.

She had, of course, to borrow her equipment from Mrs. Foley, and toiled up the long flights, dragging mop and pail and broom. She told Hedger to be of good cheer, for he had got the right woman for the job, and showed him a great leather strap she wore about her wrist to prevent dislocation of tendons. She swished about the place, scattering dust and splashing soapsuds, while he watched her in nervous despair. He stood over Lizzie and made her scour the sink, directing her roughly, then paid her and got rid of her. Shutting the door on his failure, he hurried off with his dog to lose himself among the stevedores and dock labourers on West Street.

A strange chapter began for Don Hedger. Day after day, at that hour in the afternoon, the hour before his neighbour dressed for dinner, he crouched in his closet to watch her go through with her mysterious exercises. It did not occur to him that his conduct was detestable; there was nothing shy or retreating about this girl—and these gymnastics had clearly a public purpose, were a part of her preparation for the stage.

Hedger scarcely regarded his action as conduct at all; it was something that had happened to him. More than once he went out and tried to stay away for the whole afternoon, but at about five o'clock he was sure to find himself among his old shoes in the dark. The pull of that aperture was stronger than his will—and he had always considered his will the strongest thing about him. When she threw herself upon the divan and lay resting, he still stared, holding his breath. His nerves were so on edge that a sudden noise made him start. The dog would come and tug at his sleeve, knowing that something was wrong with his master. If he attempted a mournful whine, those strong hands closed about his throat.

When Hedger came out of his closet, he sat down on the edge of the couch, sat for hours without moving. He was not painting at all now. This thing, whatever it was, drank him up as ideas had sometimes done, and he sank into a stupor of idleness as deep and dark as the stupor of work. He could not understand it; he was no boy, he had worked from models for years, and the beauty of women had disturbed him little more than any other form of beauty. Yet now his brain held but one image—vibrated, burned with it.

Women had come and gone in Hedger's life. Not having had a mother to begin with, his relations with them, whether amorous or friendly, had been casual. He got on well with janitresses and wash-women, with Indians and with the peasant women of foreign countries. He had friends among the shirtwaist factory girls who came to eat their lunch in Washington Square, and he sometimes took a model for a day into the country. He felt an unreasoning antipathy toward the well-dressed women he saw coming out of big shops, or driving in the Park. If, on his way to the Art Museum, he noticed a pretty girl standing on the steps of one of the houses in upper Fifth Avenue, he frowned at her and went by with his shoulders hunched up as if he were cold. He had never known such girls, or heard them talk, or seen the inside of the houses in which they lived; but he believed them all to be artificial and, in an æsthetic sense, perverted. He saw them enslaved by desire of merchandise and manufactured articles, effective only in making life complicated and insincere and in embroidering it with ugly and meaningless trivialities. They were enough, he thought, to make one almost forget woman as she existed in art, in thought and in the universe.

He had no desire to know the woman who had, for the time at least, so broken up his life, no curiosity about her every-day personality. He shunned any revelation of it, and he listened for Miss Bower's coming and going not to encounter but to avoid her. He wished that the girl who wore shirtwaists and got letters from Chicago would keep out of his way, that she did not exist. With her he had nought to make. But in a room full of sun, before an old mirror, on a little enchanted rug of sleeping colours, he had seen a woman emerge and give herself up to the primitive poetry of motion. And for him she had no geographical associations; unless with Crete, or Alexandria, or Veronese's Venice. She was the immortal conception, the perennial theme.

The first break in Hedger's lethargy occurred one afternoon when two young men came to take Eden Bower out to dine. They went into her music room, laughed and talked for a few minutes, and then took her away with them. They were gone a long while, but he did not go out for food himself; he waited for them to come back. At last he heard them coming down the hall, gayer and more talkative than when they left. One of them sat down at the piano, and they all began to sing. This Hedger found absolutely unendurable. He snatched up his hat and went running down the stairs. Cæsar leaped beside him, hoping that old times were coming back.

They had supper in the oysterman's basement and then sat down in front of their own doorway. The moon stood full over the Square, a thing of regal glory; but Hedger did not see the moon; he was looking, murderously, for men. Presently two, wearing straw hats and white trousers and carrying canes, came down the steps from his house. He rose and dogged them across the Square. They were laughing and seemed very much elated about something. As one stopped to light a cigarette, Hedger caught from the other:

"Don't you think she has a beautiful talent?"

His companion threw away his match. "She has a beautiful figure." They both ran to catch the stage.

Hedger went back to his studio. The light was shining from her transom. For the first time he violated her privacy at night and looked through that fatal aperture. She was sitting, fully dressed, in the window, smoking a cigarette and looking out over the housetops. He watched her until she rose, looked about her with a disdainful, crafty smile, and turned out the light.

The next morning, when Miss Bower went out, Hedger followed her. Her white skirt gleamed ahead of him as she sauntered about the Square. She sat down behind the Garibaldi statue and opened a music book she carried. She turned the leaves carelessly, and several times glanced in his direction. He was on the point of going over to her when she rose quickly and looked up at the sky. A flock of pigeons had risen from somewhere in the crowded Italian quarter to the south, and were wheeling rapidly up through the morning air, soaring and dropping, scattering and coming together, now gray, now white as silver, as they caught or intercepted the sunlight. She put up her hand to shade her eyes and followed them with a kind of defiant delight in her face.

Hedger came and stood beside her. "You've surely seen them before?"

"Oh, yes," she replied, still looking up. "I see them every day from my windows. They always come home about five o'clock. Where do they live?"

"I don't know. Probably some Italian raises them for the market. They were here long before I came, and I've been here four years."

"In that same gloomy room? Why didn't you take mine when it was vacant?"

"It isn't gloomy. That's the best light for painting."

"Oh, is it? I don't know anything about painting. I'd like to see your pictures some time. You have such a lot in there. Don't they get dusty, piled up against the wall like that?"

"Not very. I'd be glad to show them to you. Is your name really Eden Bower? I've seen your letters on the table."

"Well, it's the name I'm going to sing under. My father's name is Bowers, but my friend, Mr. Jones, a Chicago newspaper man who writes about music, told me to drop the 's.' He's crazy about my voice."

Miss Bower didn't usually tell the whole story—about anything. Her first name, when she lived in Huntington, Ill., was Edna, but Mr. Jones had persuaded her to change it to one which he felt would be worthy of her future. She was quick to take suggestions, though she told him she "didn't see what was the matter with Edna."

She explained to Hedger that she was going to Paris to study. She was waiting in New York for Chicago friends who were to take her over, but who had been detained.

"Did you study in Paris?" she asked.

"No, I've never been in Paris. But I was in the south of France all last summer, studying with C—. He's the biggest man among the moderns—at least I think so."

Miss Bower sat down and made room for him on the bench. "Do tell me about it. I expected to be there by this time, and I can't wait to find out what it's like."

Hedger began to relate how he had seen some of this Frenchman's work in an exhibition, and deciding at once that this was the man with whom he wanted to study, he had taken a boat for Marseilles the next week, going over steerage. He proceeded at once to the little town on the coast where his painter lived, and presented himself. The man never took pupils, but because Hedger had come so far he let him stay. Hedger lived at the master's house and every day they went out together to paint, sometimes on the blazing rocks down by the sea. They wrapped themselves in light woolen blankets and didn't feel the heat. Being there and working with C— was being in paradise, Hedger concluded; he learned more in three months than in all his life before.

Eden Bower laughed.

"You're a funny fellow. Didn't you do anything but work? Are the women very beautiful? Did you have awfully good things to eat and drink?"

Hedger said some of the women were fine looking, especially one girl who went about selling fish and lobsters. About the food there was nothing remarkable—except the ripe figs, he liked those. They drank sour wine, and used goat-butter, which was very strong.

"But don't they have parties or banquets? Aren't there any fine hotels down there?"

"Yes, but they are all closed in summer and the country people are poor. It's a beautiful country, though."

"How beautiful?" she persisted.

"If you want to go in, I'll show you some sketches and you'll see."

Miss Bower rose. "All right. I won't go to my fencing lesson this morning. Do you fence? Here comes your dog. You can't move but he's after you. He always makes a face at me when I meet him in the hall, and shows his nasty little teeth as if he wanted to bite me."

In the studio Hedger got out his sketches, but to Miss Bower, whose favourite pictures were "Christ Before Pilate" and a red-haired Magdalen of Henner, these landscapes were not at all beautiful, and they gave her no idea of any country whatsoever. She was careful not to commit herself, however. Her vocal teacher had already convinced her that she had a great deal to learn about many things.

"Why don't we go out to lunch somewhere?" Hedger asked, and began to dust his fingers with a handkerchief which he got out of sight as swiftly as possible.

"All right, the Brevoort," she said carelessly. "I think that's a good place and they have good wine. I don't care for cocktails."

Hedger felt his chin uneasily. "I'm afraid I haven't shaved this morning. If you could wait for me in the Square? It won't take me ten minutes."

Left alone, he found a clean collar and handkerchief, brushed his coat and blacked his shoes, and last of all dug up ten dollars from the bottom of an old copper kettle he had brought from Spain. His winter hat was of such a complexion that the Brevoort hall boy winked at the porter as he took it and placed it on the rack in a row of fresh straw ones.

CHAPTER IV

That afternoon Eden Bower was lying on the couch in her music room, her face turned to the window, watching the pigeons. Reclining thus, she could see none of the neighbouring roofs, only the sky itself and the birds that crossed and re-crossed her field of vision, white as scraps of paper blowing in the wind. She was thinking that she was young and handsome and had had a good luncheon, that a very easy-going, light-hearted city lay in the streets below her; and she was wondering why she found this queer painter chap, with his lean, bluish cheeks and heavy black eyebrows, more interesting than the smart young men she met at her teacher's studio.

Eden Bower was at twenty very much the same person that we all know her to be at forty, except that she knew a great deal less. But one thing she knew; that she was to be Eden Bower. She was like someone standing before a great show window full of beautiful and costly things, deciding which she will order. She understands that they will not all be delivered immediately, but one by one they will arrive at her door. She already knew some of the many things that were to happen to her; for instance, that the Chicago millionaire who was going to take her abroad with his sister as chaperon, would eventually press his claim in quite another manner. He was the most circumspect of bachelors, afraid of everything obvious, even of women who were too flagrantly handsome. He was a nervous collector of pictures and furniture, a nervous patron of music, and a nervous host; very cautious about his health and about any course of conduct that might make him ridiculous. But she knew that he would at last throw all his precautions to the winds.

People like Eden Bower are inexplicable. Her father sold farming machinery in Huntington, Ill., and she had grown up in that prairie town with no acquaintances or experiences outside of it. Yet from her earliest childhood she had not one conviction or opinion in common with the people about her—the only people she knew.

Before she was out of short dresses she had made up her mind that she was going to be an actress, that she would live far away in great cities, that she would be much admired by men and would have everything she wanted. When she was thirteen, and was already singing and reciting for church entertainments, she read in some illustrated magazine a long article about the late Czar of Russia, then just come to the throne or about to come to it. After that, lying in the hammock on the front porch on summer evenings, or sitting through a long sermon in the family pew, she amused herself by trying to make up her mind whether she would or would not be the Czar's mistress when she played in his capital.

Now, Edna had met this fascinating word only in the novels of Ouida—her hard-worked little mother kept a long row of them in the upstairs storeroom, behind the linen chest. In Huntington, women who bore that relation to men were called by a very different name, and their lot was not an enviable one; of all the shabby and poor, they were the shabbiest. But then, Edna had never lived in Huntington; not even before she began to find books like "Sapho" and "Mademoiselle de Maupin," secretly sold in paper covers throughout Illinois. It was as if she had come into Huntington, into the Bowers family, on one of the trains that puffed over the marshes behind their back fence all day long, and was waiting for another train to take her out.

As she grew older and handsomer, she had many beaux, but these small-town boys didn't interest her. If a lad kissed her when he brought her home from a dance, she was indulgent and she rather liked it. But if he pressed her further, she slipped away from him, laughing. After she began to sing in Chicago, she was consistently discreet. She stayed as a guest in rich people's houses, and she knew that she was being watched like a rabbit in a laboratory. Covered up in bed, with the lights out, she thought her own thoughts, and laughed.

This summer in New York was her first taste of freedom. The Chicago capitalist, after all his arrangements were made for sailing, had been compelled to go to Mexico to look after oil interests. His sister knew an excellent singing master in New York. Why should not a discreet, well-balanced girl like Miss Bower spend the summer there, studying quietly? The capitalist suggested that his sister might enjoy a summer on Long Island; he would rent the Griffiths place for her, with all the servants, and Eden could stay there. But his sister met this proposal with a cold stare.

So it fell out that between selfishness and greed, Eden got a summer all her own—which really did a great deal toward making her an artist and whatever else she was afterward to become. She had time to look about, to watch without being watched; to select diamonds in one window and furs in another, to select shoulders and mustaches in the big hotels where she went to lunch. She had the easy freedom of obscurity and the consciousness of power. She enjoyed both. She was in no hurry.

While Eden Bower watched the pigeons, Don Hedger sat on the

other side of the bolted doors, looking into a pool of dark turpentine at his idle brushes, wondering why a woman could do this to him. He, too, was sure of his future and knew that he was a chosen man. He could not know, of course, that he was merely the first to fall under a fascination which was to be disastrous to a few men and pleasantly stimulating to many thousands. Each of these two young people sensed the future, but not completely. Don Hedger knew that nothing much would ever happen to him. Eden Bower understood that to her a great deal would happen. But she did not guess that her neighbour would have more tempestuous adventurês sitting in his dark studio than she would find in all the capitals of Europe, or in all the latitude of conduct she was prepared to permit herself.

CHAPTER V

One Sunday morning Eden was crossing the Square with a spruce young man in a white flannel suit and a Panama hat. They had been breakfasting at the Brevoort and he was coaxing her to let him come up to her rooms and sing for an hour.

"No, I've got to write letters. You must run along now. I see a friend of mine over there, and I must ask him about something before I go up."

"That fellow with the dog? Where did you pick him up?" The young man glanced toward the seat under a sycamore where Hedger was reading the morning paper.

"Oh, he's an old friend from the West," said Eden easily. "I won't introduce you because he doesn't like people. He's a recluse. Good-by. I can't be sure about Tuesday. I'll go with you if I have time after my lesson."

She nodded, left him and went over to the seat littered with newspapers. The young man went up the Avenue without looking back.

"Well, what are you going to do today? Shampoo this animal all morning?" Eden inquired teasingly.

He made room for her on the seat. "No, at twelve o'clock I'm going out to Coney Island. One of my models, a fine girl, is going up in a balloon this afternoon. I've often promised to go and see her, and now I'm going."

Eden asked if models usually did such stunts. No, Hedger told her, but Molly Welch added to her earnings in that way.

"I believe," he added, "she likes the excitement of it. She's got a good deal of spirit. That's why I like to paint her. So many models have flaccid bodies."

"And she hasn't, eh? Is she the one who comes to see you? I can't help hearing her, she talks so loud."

"Yes, she has a rough voice, but she's a fine girl. I don't suppose you'd be interested in going?"

"I don't know," Eden sat tracing patterns on the asphalt with the end of her parasol. "Is it any fun? I got up feeling I'd like to do something different today. It's the first Sunday I've not had to sing in church. I had that engagement for breakfast at the Brevoort, but it wasn't very exciting. That chap can't talk about anything but himself."

Hedger warmed a little. "If you've never been to Coney Island, you ought to go. It's nice to see all the people; tailors and bartenders and prize-fighters with their best girls, and all sorts of folks taking a holiday."

Eden looked sidewise at him. So one ought to be interested in people of that kind, ought one? He was certainly a funny fellow. Yet he was never, somehow, tiresome. She had seen a good deal of him lately, but she kept wanting to know him better, to find out what made him different from men like the one she had just left—whether he really was as different as he seemed.

"I'll go with you," she said at last, "if you'll leave that at home."

She pointed to Cæsar's flickering ears with her sunshade.

"But he's half the fun. You'd like to hear him bark at the waves when they come in."

"No, I wouldn't. He's jealous and disagreeable if he sees you talking to anyone else. Look at him now."

"Of course, if you make a face at him. He knows what that means and he makes a worse face. He likes Molly Welch, and she'll be disappointed if I don't bring him."

Eden said decidedly that he couldn't take both of them. So at twelve o'clock when she and Hedger got on the boat at Desbrosses Street, Cæsar was lying on his pallet with a bone.

Eden enjoyed the boat ride. It was the first time she had been on the water and she felt as if she were embarking for France. The light, warm breeze and the plunge of the waves made her feel wide awake, and she liked crowds of any kind. They went to the balcony of a big, noisy restaurant and had a shore dinner with tall steins of beer. Hedger had got a big advance from his advertising firm since he first lunched with Miss Bower ten days ago, and he was ready for anything.

After dinner they went to the tent behind the bathing beach, where the tops of two balloons bulged out over the canvas. A red-faced man in a linen suit stood in front of the tent, shouting in a hoarse voice and telling the people that if the crowd was good for five dollars more a beautiful young woman would risk her life for their entertainment. Four little boys in dirty red uniforms ran about taking contributions in their pill-box hats. One of the balloons was bobbing up and down in its tether and people were shoving one another to get nearer the tent.

"Is it dangerous, as he says?" Eden asked.

"Molly says it's simple enough if nothing goes wrong with the balloon. Then it would be all up, I suppose."

"Wouldn't you like to go up with her?"

"I? Of course not. I'm not fond of taking foolish risks."

Eden sniffed. "I shouldn't think sensible risks would be very much fun."

Hedger did not answer, for just then everyone began to shove the other way and shout, "Look out. There she goes!" And a band of six pieces began playing furiously.

As the balloon rose from its tent enclosure, they saw a girl in green tights standing in the basket, holding carelessly to one of the ropes with one hand and with the other waving to the spectators. A long rope trailed behind to keep the balloon from blowing out to sea.

As it soared, the figure in green tights in the basket diminished to a mere spot, and the balloon itself, in the brilliant light, looked like a big silver-gray bat, with its wings folded. When it began to sink, the girl stepped through the hole in the basket to a trapeze that hung below, and gracefully descended through the air, holding to the rod with both hands, keeping her body taut and her feet close together. The crowd—it had grown very large by this time—cheered vociferously. The men took off their hats and waved, little boys shouted, and fat old women, shining with the heat and a beer lunch, murmured admiring comments upon the balloonist's figure.

"Beautiful legs, she has!"

"That's so," Hedger whispered. "Not many girls would look well in that position."

Then, for some reason, he blushed a slow, dark, painful crimson.

The balloon descended slowly, a little way from the tent, and the red-faced man in the linen suit caught Molly Welch before her feet touched the ground and pulled her to one side. The band struck up "Blue

Bell" by way of welcome, and one of the sweaty pages ran forward
and presented the balloonist with a large bouquet of artificial flowers.
She smiled and thanked him, and ran back across the sand to the
tent.

"Can't we go inside and see her?" Eden asked. "You can explain to
the door man. I want to meet her."

Edging forward, she herself addressed the man in the linen suit and
slipped something from her purse into his hand.

They found Molly seated before a trunk that had a mirror in the lid
and a "make-up" outfit spread upon the tray. She was wiping the cold
cream and powder from her neck with a discarded chemise.

"Hello, Don," she said cordially. "Brought a friend?"

Eden liked her. She had an easy, friendly manner, and there was
something boyish and devil-may-care about her.

"Yes, it's fun. I'm mad about it," she said in reply to Eden's ques-
tions. "I always want to let go, when I come down on the bar. You don't
feel your weight at all, as you would on a stationary trapeze."

The big drum boomed outside, and the publicity man began shouting
to newly arrived boat-loads. Miss Welch took a last pull at her cigarette.
"Now you'll have to get out, Don. I change for the next act. This time I
go up in a black evening dress, and lose the skirt in the basket before I start
down."

"Yes, go along," said Eden. "Wait for me outside the door. I'll stay
and help her dress."

Hedger waited and waited, while women of every build bumped
into him and begged his pardon, and the red pages ran about holding out
their caps for coins, and the people ate and perspired and shifted parasols
against the sun. When the band began to play a two-step all the bathers
ran up out of the surf to watch the ascent. The second balloon bumped
and rose, and the crowd began shouting to the girl in a black evening dress
who stood leaning against the ropes and smiling.

"It's a new girl," they called. "It ain't the Countess this time. You're
a peach, girlie!"

The balloonist acknowledged these compliments, bowing and looking down over the sea of upturned faces, but Hedger was determined she
should not see him, and he darted behind the tent-fly. He was suddenly
dripping with cold sweat, his mouth was full of the bitter taste of anger,
and his tongue felt stiff behind his set teeth. Molly Welch, in a shirt-waist
and a white tam-o'-shanter cap, slipped out from the tent under his arm

and laughed up in his face. "She's a crazy one, you brought along. She'll get what she wants!"

"Oh, I'll settle with you, all right!" Hedger brought out with difficulty.

"It's not my fault, Donnie. I couldn't do anything with her. She bought me off. What's the matter with you? Are you soft on her? She's safe enough. It's as easy as rolling off a log, if you keep cool." Molly Welch was rather excited herself, and she was chewing gum at a high speed as she stood beside him, looking up at the floating silver cone.

"Now watch," she exclaimed suddenly. "She's coming down on the bar. I advised her to cut that out, but you see she does it first rate. And she got rid of the skirt, too. I don't think those black tights show off her legs very well, she's got fine legs. But she keeps her feet together like I told her, and makes a good line along the back. See the light on those silver slippers—that was a good idea of mine. Come along to meet her. Don't be a grouch; she's done it fine!"

Molly tweaked his elbow, and then left him standing like a stump while she ran down the beach with the crowd, which was flowing over the sand like a thick liquid and gazing upward at the slowly falling silver star.

Though Hedger was sulking, his eye could not help seeing the low blue welter of the sea, the arrested bathers, standing in the surf, their arms and legs stained red by the dropping sun, shading their eyes and looking shoreward while the great bird settled down.

Molly Welch and the red-faced man caught Eden under the arms and lifted her aside, a red page dashed up with a bouquet, and the band struck up "Blue Bell." Eden laughed and bowed, took Molly's arm and ran up the sand in her black tights and silver slippers, dodging the friendly old women and the gallant sports who wanted to offer their homage on the spot.

When she emerged from the tent, dressed in her own clothes, that part of the beach was almost deserted. She stepped to her companion's side and said, carelessly, "Hadn't we better try to catch this boat? I hope you're not sore at me. Really, it was lots of fun."

Hedger looked at his watch.

"Yes, we have fifteen minutes to get to the boat," he said politely.

As they walked toward the pier, one of the red-imp pages ran up panting.

"Lady, you're carrying off the bouquet," he said aggrievedly.

Eden stopped and looked at the bunch of spotty cotton roses in her hand. "Of course. I want them for a souvenir. You gave them to me yourself."

"I give 'em to you for looks, but you can't take 'em away. They belong to the show."

"Oh, you always use the same bunch?"

"Sure we do. There ain't too much money in this business."

She laughed and tossed them back to him.

"Why are you angry?" she asked Hedger. "I wouldn't have done it if I'd been with some fellows, but I thought you were the sort who wouldn't mind. Molly didn't for a minute think you would."

"What possessed you to do such a fool thing?" he asked roughly.

"I don't know. When I saw Molly coming down, I wanted to try it. It looked exciting. Didn't I hold myself as well as she did?"

Hedger shrugged his shoulders, but in his heart he instantly forgave her.

The return boat was not crowded, though the boats that passed them, going out, were packed to the rails. The sun was setting. Boys and girls sat on the long benches with their arms about each other, singing.

Eden felt a strong wish to propitiate her companion, to be alone with him. She had been curiously wrought up by her balloon trip; it was a lark, but not very satisfying unless one came back to something after the flight. She wanted to be admired and adored.

Though Eden said nothing, and sat with her arms limp on the rail in front of her, looking languidly at the rising silhouette of the city and the bright path of the sun, Hedger felt a strange drawing near to her. If he but brushed her white skirt with his knee, there was an instant communication between them, such as there had never been before. They did not talk at all, but when they went over the gang-plank she took his arm and kept her shoulder close to him. He felt as if they were enveloped in a highly charged atmosphere, an invisible network of subtle, almost painful sensibility. They had somehow taken hold of each other.

An hour later, they were dining in the back garden of a little French hotel on Ninth street, long since passed away. It was cool and leafy there, and the mosquitoes were not very numerous. A party of South Americans at another table were drinking champagne, and Eden murmured that she thought she would like some, if it were not too expensive. "Perhaps it will make me think I am in the balloon again. That was a very nice feeling. You've forgiven me, haven't you?"

Hedger gave her a quick straight look from under his black eyebrows, and something went over her that was like a chill, except that it was warm and feathery. She drank most of the wine; her companion was indifferent to it. He was talking more to her tonight than he had ever done before. She asked him about a new picture she had seen in his room, a queer thing full of stiff, supplicating female figures. "It's Indian, isn't it?"

"Yes. I call it Rain Spirits, or maybe, Indian Rain. In the Southwest, where I've been a good deal, the Indian traditions make women have to do with the rainfall. They were supposed to control it, somehow, and to be able to find springs and make moisture come out of the earth. You see I'm trying to learn to paint what people think and feel; to get away from all that photographic stuff. When I look at you, I don't see what a camera would see, do I?"

"How can I tell?"

"Well, if I should paint you, I could make you understand what I see." For the second time that day Hedger crimsoned unexpectedly, and his eyes fell and steadily contemplated a dish of little radishes. "That particular picture I got from a story a Mexican priest told me; he said he found it in an old manuscript book in a monastery down there, written by some Spanish missionary. He got his stories from the Aztecs. This one he called 'The Forty Lovers of the Queen,' and it was more or less about rain-making."

"Aren't you going to tell it to me?" Eden asked.

Hedger fumbled among the radishes. "I don't know if it's the proper kind of story."

Eden smiled; "Oh, forget about that! I've been balloon riding today. I like to hear you talk."

Her low voice was flattering. She had seemed like clay in his hands ever since they got on the boat to come home. He leaned back in his chair, forgot his food and, looking at her intently, began to tell his story, the theme of which he somehow felt was dangerous tonight.

The tale began, he said, somewhere in Ancient Mexico, and concerned the daughter of a king. The birth of this Princess was preceded by unusual portents. Three times her mother dreamed that she was delivered of serpents, which betokened that the child she was to bear would have power with the rain gods. The serpent was the symbol of water. The Princess grew up dedicated to the gods, and wise men taught her the rain-making mysteries. She was guarded from men at all times, for it was the law of Thunder that she be so until her marriage. In the years of her adolescence, rain was abundant with her people. The oldest man could not remember such fertility.

When the Princess had counted eighteen years, her father went to drive out a war party that harried his borders on the north and troubled his prosperity. The King destroyed the invaders and brought home many prisoners. Among the prisoners was a young chief, taller than any of his captors, of such strength and ferocity that the King's people came a day's journey to look at him. When the Princess beheld his great stature, and saw that his arms and breast were covered with the figures of wild animals, bitten into the skin and coloured, she begged his life from her father. She desired that he should practise his art upon her, and prick upon her skin the signs of Rain and Lightning and Thunder, and stain the wounds with herb-juices, as they were upon his own body. For many days, upon the roof of the King's house, the Princess submitted herself to the bone needle, and the women with her marvelled at her fortitude.

But the Princess was without shame before the Captive, and it came about that he threw from him his needles and his stains, and embraced the Princess; and her women ran down from the roof screaming, to call the guard which stood at the gateway of the King's house, and none stayed to protect their mistress. When the guard came, the Captive was thrown into bonds, and he was maimed, and his tongue was torn out and he was given for a slave to the Rain Princess.

The country of the Aztecs to the east was tormented by thirst, and their king, hearing much of the rain-making arts of the Princess, sent an embassy to her father, with presents and an offer of marriage. So the Princess went from her father to be the Queen of the Aztecs, and she took with her the Captive, who served her in everything with entire fidelity and slept upon a mat before her door.

The King gave his bride a fortress on the outskirts of the city, whither she retired to entreat the rain gods. This fortress was called the Queen's House, and on the night of the new moon the Queen came to it from the palace. But when the moon waxed and grew toward the round, then the Queen returned to the King. The drought abated in the country and rain fell abundantly by reason of the Queen's power with the stars.

When the Queen went to her own house she took with her no servant but the Captive, and he slept outside her door and brought her food after she had fasted. The Queen had a jewel of great value, a turquoise that had fallen from the sun, and had the image of the sun upon it. And when she admired a young man whom she had seen in the army or among the slaves, she sent the Captive to him with the jewel, for a sign that he should come to her at the Queen's House upon business concerning the welfare of all. And some, after she had talked with them, she sent away with rewards; and some she took in and kept them by her for one day or two.

Afterward she called the Captive and bade him conduct the youth by the secret way he had come, underneath the chambers of the fortress. But for the going away of the Queen's visitors the Captive took out the bar that was beneath a stone in the floor of the passage and put in its stead a rush-reed, and the youth stepped upon it and fell through into a cavern that was the bed of an underground river, and whatever was thrown into it was not seen again. In this service and in all others the Captive did not fail the Queen.

But when the Queen sent for the Captain of the Archers, she detained him four days, and on the fourth day she went to the Captive outside her door and said: "Tomorrow take this man up by the sure way, by which the King comes, and let him live."

In the Queen's door were arrows, purple and white. When she desired the King to come to her publicly, with his guard, she sent him a white arrow, but when she sent the purple, he came secretly and covered himself with his mantle to be hidden from the stone gods at the gate. When the Queen thus detained the Captain of the Archers, and moreover purposed to let him live, the Captive took a purple arrow to the King, and the King came secretly and found them together. He killed the Captain with his own hand, but the Queen he brought to public trial. The Captive, when he was put to the question, told on his fingers forty men that he had let through the underground passage into the river. The Captive and the Queen were put to death by fire, both on the same day, and afterward there was scarcity of rain.

★   ★   ★   ★   ★

Eden Bower sat shivering a little while she listened. Hedger was not trying to please her, she thought, but to antagonize and frighten her by his fantastic story. She had often told herself that his lean, big-boned lower jaw was like his bulldog's, but tonight his face made Cæsar's most savage and determined expression seem an affectation. Now she was looking at the man he really was. Nobody's eyes had ever defied her like this. They were searching her and seeing everything: all she had concealed from Livingston, and from the millionaire and his friends, and from the newspaper men. He was testing her, trying her out, and she was more ill at ease than she wished to show.

"That's quite a thrilling story," she said at last, rising and winding her scarf about her throat. "It must be getting late. Almost everyone has gone."

They walked down the Avenue like people who have quarrelled, or who wish to get rid of each other. Hedger did not take her arm at the street crossings and they did not linger in the Square. At her door he tried none of the old devices of the Livingston boys. He stood like a post, having forgotten to take off his hat, gave her a harsh, threatening glance, muttered "good-night," and shut his own door noisily.

There was no question of sleep for Eden Bower. Her brain was working like a machine that would never stop. After she undressed she tried to calm her nerves by smoking a cigarette, lying on the divan by the open window. But she grew wider and wider awake, combating the challenge that had flamed all evening in the strange man's eyes. The balloon had been one kind of excitement, the wine another; but the thing that had roused her, as a blow rouses a proud man, was the doubt, the contempt, the sneering hostility with which this violent man had looked at her when he told his savage story. Crowds and balloons were all very well, she reflected, but woman's chief adventure is man. With a mind overactive and a sense of life over-strong, she wanted to walk across the roofs in the starlight; to sail over the sea and face at once a world of which she had never been afraid.

Hedger must be asleep; his dog had stopped sniffing under the double doors. Eden put on her wrapper and slippers and stole softly down the hall over the old carpet; one loose board creaked just as she reached the ladder. The trapdoor was open, as always on hot nights. When she stepped out on the roof she drew a long breath and walked across it, looking up at the stars. Her foot touched something soft; she heard a low growl, and on the instant Cæsar's sharp little teeth caught her ankle and waited. His breath was like steam on her leg. Nobody had ever intruded upon his roof before, and he panted for the movement or the word that would let him spring his jaw. Instead, the hand that held it closed on his throat, as Hedger reached out from his blankets.

"Wait a minute. I'll settle with him," he said grimly.

He dragged the dog toward the manhole and disappeared. When he came back he found Eden standing over by the dark chimney, looking away in an offended attitude.

"I caned him unmercifully," he panted. "Of course, you didn't hear anything; he never whines when I beat him. He didn't nip you, did he?"

"I don't know whether he broke the skin or not," she answered aggrievedly, still looking off into the west.

"If I were one of your friends in white trousers, I'd strike a match to find whether you were hurt, though I know you are not, and then I'd see your ankle, wouldn't I?"

"I suppose so."

He shook his head and stood with his hands in the pockets of his old painting jacket. "I'm not up to such boy-tricks. If you want the place to yourself, I'll clear out. But if you stay here and I stay here—" he shrugged his shoulders.

Eden did not stir, and she made no reply. Her head drooped slightly, as if she were considering. But the moment he put his arms about her they began to talk, both at once, as people do in an opera. The instant avowal of each brought out a flood of trivial admissions. Hedger confessed his crime, was reproached and forgiven, and now Eden knew what it was in his look that she had found so disturbing of late.

Standing against the black chimney, with the sky behind and blue shadows before, they looked like one of Hedger's own paintings of that period; two figures, one white and one dark, and nothing whatever distinguishable about them but that they were male and female. The faces were lost, the contours blurred in shadow, but the figures were a man and a woman, and that was their whole concern and their mysterious beauty— it was the rhythm in which they moved, at last, along the roof and down into the house. She came down very slowly. The excitement and bravado and uncertainty of that long day and night seemed all at once to tell upon her. When his feet were on the carpet and he reached up to lift her down, she twined her arms about his neck as after a long separation, and turned her face to him, and her lips, with their perfume of youth.

CHAPTER VI

In time they quarrelled, of course, and about an abstraction—as young people often do, as mature people almost never do. Eden came in late one afternoon. She had been with some of her musical friends to lunch at Burton Ives' studio, and she began telling Hedger about that beautiful place. He listened a moment and then threw down his brushes.

"I know exactly what it's like," he said impatiently. "A very good department store conception of a studio. It's one of the show places."

"Well, it's a gorgeous place, and he said I could bring you to see him. The boys tell me he's awfully kind about giving people a lift, and you might get something out of it."

Hedger started up and pushed his canvas out of the way. "What could I possibly get from Burton Ives? He's almost the worst painter in the world; the stupidest, I mean."

Eden was annoyed. Burton Ives had been very nice to her and had begged her to sit for him.

"You must admit that he's a very successful one," she said coldly.

"Of course he is. Anybody can be successful who will do that sort of thing. I wouldn't paint his pictures for all the money in New York."

"Well, I saw a lot of them, and I think they are beautiful."

Hedger bowed stiffly.

"What's the use of being a great painter if nobody knows about you?" Eden went on persuasively. "Why don't you paint the kind of pictures people can understand, and then, after you're successful, do whatever you like."

"As I look at it," said Hedger brusquely, "I am successful."

Eden looked about the dark hole. "Well, I don't see any evidences of it," she said, biting her lip. "He has a Japanese servant and a wine cellar and keeps a riding horse."

Hedger melted a little. "My dear, I have the most expensive luxury in the world, and I am much more extravagant than Burton Ives, for I work to please nobody but myself."

"You mean you could make money and don't? That you don't try to get a public?"

"Exactly. A public only wants what has been done over and over. I'm painting for painters—who haven't been born."

"What would you do if I brought Mr. Ives down here to see your things?"

"Well, for God's sake, don't! Before he left I'd probably tell him what I thought of him."

Eden rose. "I give you up. You know very well there's only one kind of success that's real."

"Yes, but it's not the kind you mean. So you've been thinking me a scrub painter, who needs a helping hand from some fashionable studio man? What the devil have you had anything to do with me for, then?"

"There's no use talking to you," said Eden, walking slowly toward the door. "I've been trying to pull wires for you all afternoon, and this is what it comes to."

She had expected that the tidings of a prospective call from the great man would be received very differently, and had been thinking as she came home in the stage how, as with a magic wand, she might gild Hedger's future, float him out of his dark hole on a tide of prosperity, see his name in the papers and his pictures in the windows on Fifth Avenue.

Hedger mechanically snapped the midsummer leash on Cæsar's collar and they ran downstairs and hurried through Sullivan street off toward the river. He wanted to be among rough, honest people, to get down where the big drays bumped over stone paving blocks, and the men wore corduroy trousers and kept their shirts open at the neck. He stopped for a drink in one of the sagging bar-rooms on the water front. He had never in his life been so deeply wounded; he did not know he could be so hurt. He had told this girl all his secrets. On the roof, in these warm, heavy summer nights, with her hands locked in his, he had been able to explain all his misty ideas about an unborn art the world was waiting for; had been able to explain them better than he had ever done to himself. And she had looked away to the chattels of this uptown studio and coveted them for him! To her he was only an unsuccessful Burton Ives.

Then why, as he had put it to her, did she take up with him? Young, beautiful, talented as she was, why had she wasted herself on a scrub? Pity? Hardly; she wasn't sentimental. There was no explaining her. But in this passion that had seemed so fearless and so fated-to-be, his own position now looked to him ridiculous. Hedger ground his teeth so loud that his dog, trotting beside him, heard him and looked up.

While they were having supper at the oysterman's, Hedger planned his escape. Whenever he saw her again, everything he had told her, that he should never have told anyone, would come back to him; ideas that he had never whispered even to the painter whom he worshipped and had gone all the way to France to see. To her they must seem his apology for not having horses and a valet, or merely the puerile boastfulness of a weak man. He would catch the train out to Long Beach tonight, and tomorrow he would go on to the north end of Long Island, where an old friend of his had a summer studio among the sand dunes, and he would stay until things came right in his mind. And she could find a smart painter, or take her punishment.

When he went home, Eden's room was dark; she was dining out

somewhere. He threw his things into a hold-all he had carried all about the world with him, strapped up some colours and canvases, and ran downstairs.

CHAPTER VII

Five days later Hedger was a restless passenger on a dirty, crowded Sunday train, coming back to town. Of course he saw now how unreasonable he had been in expecting a Huntington girl to know anything about pictures; here was a whole continent full of people who knew nothing about pictures and he didn't hold it against them. What had such things to do with him and Eden Bower? When he lay out on the dunes, watching the moon come up out of the sea, it had seemed to him that there was no wonder in the world like the wonder of Eden Bower. He was going back to her because she was older than art, because she was the most overwhelming thing that had ever come into his life.

He had written her yesterday, begging her to be at home this evening, telling her that he was contrite, and wretched enough.

Now that he was on his way to her, his stronger feeling unaccountably changed to a mood that was playful and tender. He wanted to share everything with her, even the most trivial things. He wanted to tell her about the people on the train, coming back tired from their holiday with bunches of wilted flowers and dirty daisies; to tell her that the fish-man, to whom she had often sent him for lobsters, was among the passengers, disguised in a silk shirt and a spotted tie, and how his wife looked exactly like a fish, even to her eyes.

He could tell her, too, that he hadn't even unstrapped his canvases—that ought to convince her.

In those days passengers from Long Island came into New York by ferry. Hedger had to be quick about getting his dog out of the express car in order to catch the first boat. The East River, and the bridges, and the city to the west, were burning in the conflagration of the sunset; there was that great home-coming reach of evening in the air.

The car changes from Thirty-fourth Street were too many and too perplexing; for the first time in his life Hedger took a hansom cab for Washington Square. Cæsar sat bolt-upright on the worn leather cushion beside him, and they jogged off, looking down on the rest of the world.

It was twilight when they drove down lower Fifth Avenue into the Square, and through the Arch behind them were the two long rows of pale violet lights that used to bloom so beautifully against the gray stone and asphalt. Here and yonder about the Square hung globes that shed a radiance not unlike the blue mists of evening, emerging softly when daylight died, as the stars emerged in the thin blue sky. Under them the sharp shadows of the trees fell on the cracked asphalt and the sleeping grass. The first stars and the first lights were growing silver against the gradual darkening, when Hedger paid his driver and went into the house—which, thank God, was still there! On the hall table lay his letter of yesterday, unopened.

He went upstairs with every sort of fear and every sort of hope clutching at his heart; it was as if tigers were tearing him. Why was there no gas burning in the top hall? He found matches and the gas bracket. He knocked, but got no answer; nobody was there. Before his own door were exactly five bottles of milk, standing in a row. The milk-boy had taken spiteful pleasure in thus reminding him that he forgot to stop his order.

Hedger went down to the basement; it, too, was dark. The janitress was taking her evening airing on the basement steps. She sat waving a palm-leaf fan majestically, her dirty calico dress open at the neck. She told him at once that there had been "changes." Miss Bower's room was to let again, and the piano would go tomorrow. Yes, she left on Saturday, she sailed for Europe with friends from Chicago. They arrived on Friday, heralded by many telegrams. Very rich people they were said to be, though the man had refused to pay the nurse a month's rent in lieu of notice—which would have been only right, as the young lady had agreed to take the rooms until October.

Mrs. Foley had observed, too, that he didn't overpay her or Willy for their trouble, and a great deal of trouble they had been put to, certainly. Yes, the young lady was very pleasant, but the nurse said there were rings on the mahogany table where she had put tumblers and wine glasses. It was just as well she was gone. The Chicago man was uppish in his ways, but not much to look at. She supposed he had poor health, for there was nothing to him inside his clothes.

Hedger went slowly up the stairs—never had they seemed so long, or his legs so heavy. The upper floor was emptiness and silence. He unlocked his room, lit the gas and opened the windows. When he went to put his coat in the closet, he found, hanging among his clothes, a pale, flesh-tinted dressing gown he had liked to see her wear, with a perfume— oh, a perfume that was still Eden Bower! He shut the door behind him and there, in the dark, for a moment he lost his manliness. It was when he held this garment to him that he found a letter in the pocket.

The note was written with a lead pencil, in haste: She was sorry that he was angry, but she still didn't know just what she had done. She had thought Mr. Ives would be useful to him; she guessed he was too proud. She wanted awfully to see him again, but Fate came knocking at her door after he had left her. She believed in Fate. She would never forget him and she knew he would become the greatest painter in the world. Now she must pack. She hoped he wouldn't mind her leaving the dressing gown; somehow, she could never wear it again.

After Hedger read this, standing under the gas, he went back into the closet and knelt down before the wall; the knot hole had been plugged up with a ball of wet paper—the same blue notepaper on which her letter was written.

He was hard hit. Tonight he had to bear the loneliness of a whole lifetime. Knowing himself so well, he could hardly believe that such a thing had ever happened to him; that such a woman had lain happy and contented in his arms. And now it was over. He turned out the light and sat down on his painter's stool before the big window. Cæsar, on the floor beside him, rested his head on his master's knee. We must leave Hedger thus, sitting in solitude with his dog, looking up at the stars.

CHAPTER VIII

Coming, Eden Bower!

This legend, in electric lights over the Manhattan Opera House, for weeks announced her return to New York, after years of spectacular success in Paris. She came at last, under the management of an American Opera Company, but bringing her own *chef d'orchestre*.

One bright December afternoon Eden Bower was going down Fifth Avenue in her car, on the way to her broker in William Street. Her thoughts were entirely upon stocks—Cerro de Pasco, and how much she should buy of it—when she suddenly looked up and realized that she was skirting Washington Square. She had not seen the place since she rolled out of it in an old-fashioned four-wheeler to seek her fortune, eighteen years ago.

"*Arrêtez, Alphonse. Attendez-moi,*" she called, and opened the door before he could reach it. The children who were streaking over the asphalt on roller skates saw a lady in a long fur coat and short, high-heeled shoes alight from a French car and pace slowly about the Square, holding her muff to her chin. This spot, at least, had changed very little, she reflected; the same trees, the same fountain, the white arch, and over yonder Garibaldi, drawing the sword for freedom. There, just opposite her, was the old red brick house.

"Yes, that is the place," she was thinking. "I can smell the carpets now, and that dog—what was his name? That grubby bathroom at the end of the hall, and that dreadful Hedger—Still, there was something about him, you know—"

She glanced up and blinked against the sun. From somewhere in the crowded quarter south of the Square a flock of pigeons rose, wheeling quickly upward into the brilliant blue sky. She threw back her head, pressed her muff closer to her chin, and watched them with a smile of amazement and delight. So they still rose, out of all that dirt and noise and squalor, fleet and silvery, just as they used to rise that summer when she was twenty and went up in a balloon on Coney Island!

Alphonse opened the door and tucked her robes about her. All the way down town her mind wandered from Cerro de Pasco, and she kept smiling and looking up at the sky.

When she had finished her business with the broker, she asked him to look in the telephone book for the address of M. Gaston Jules, the picture dealer, and slipped the paper on which he wrote it into her glove. It was five o'clock when she reached the French Galleries, as they were called. On entering, she gave the attendant her card, asking him to take it to M. Jules. The dealer appeared very promptly and begged her to come into his private office, where he pushed a great chair toward his desk for her and signalled his secretary to leave the room.

"How good your lighting is in here," she observed, glancing about. "I met you at Simon's studio, didn't I? Oh, no! I never forget anybody who interests me." She threw her muff on his writing table and sank into the deep chair. "I have come to you for some information that's not in my line. Do you know anything about an American painter named Hedger?"

He took the seat opposite her. "Don Hedger? But, certainly! There are some very interesting things of his in an exhibition at V—'s. If you would care to—"

She held up her hand. "No, no. I've no time to go to exhibitions. Is he a man of any importance?"

"Certainly. He is one of the first men among the moderns. That is to say, among the very moderns. He is always coming up with something different. He often exhibits in Paris, you must have seen—"

"No, I tell you I don't go to exhibitions. Has he had great success? That is what I want to know."

M. Jules pulled at his short gray mustache. "But, Madame, there are many kinds of success," he began cautiously.

Madame gave a dry laugh. "Yes, so he used to say. We once quarrelled on that issue. And how would you define his particular kind?"

M. Jules grew thoughtful. "He is a great name with all the young men, and he is decidedly an influence in art. But one can't definitely place a man who is original, erratic, and who is changing all the time."

She cut him short. "Is he much talked about at home? In Paris, I mean? Thanks. That's all I want to know." She rose and began buttoning her coat. "One doesn't like to have been an utter fool, even at twenty."

"*Mais, non!*" M. Jules handed her her muff with a quick, sympathetic glance. He followed her out through the carpeted showroom, now closed to the public and draped in cheesecloth, and put her into her car with words appreciative of the honour she had done him in calling.

Leaning back in the cushions, Eden Bower closed her eyes, and her face, as the street lamps flashed their ugly orange light upon it, became hard and settled, like a plaster cast; so a sail, that has been filled by a strong breeze, behaves when the wind suddenly dies. Tomorrow night the wind would blow again, and this mask would be the golden face of Clytemnestra. But a "big" career takes its toll, even with the best of luck.

Smart Set 92 (August 1920): 3–25

Appendix

VARIANTS IN "COMING, EDEN BOWER!" AND "COMING, APHRODITE!"

✳ ✳ ✳

Although differences between the texts of "Coming, Eden Bower!," as it appeared in the *Smart Set* (August 1920), and "Coming, Aphrodite!," in *Youth and the Bright Medusa* (New York: Alfred A. Knopf, 1920), do exist in punctuation, spelling, paragraphing, and minor details of styling, these are mechanical matters that will be omitted in this summary of the variants in the two versions of the story. Only substantive changes—substitutions, additions, and deletions—are noted, in order to suggest to the general reader something of the nature of the differences between the stories and to assist the scholar by indicating page and line references for further checking. Pagination given for "Coming, Eden Bower!" refers to the present volume; for convenience, pagination given for "Coming, Aphrodite!" refers to the current rather than the first printing of *Youth and the Bright Medusa* (New York: Alfred A. Knopf, 1951).

The substantive variants in the two texts may be divided into three types: those relating to sexuality and, presumably, efforts to keep "Coming, Eden Bower!" free from censorship (see the discussion in the Introduction); those relating to style, including some amplifications; and those relating to other changes in the facts or details of the narrative. Following are examples of each kind and a record of the principal substantive variants in the order in which they appear.

Examples

"Coming, Eden Bower!"		"Coming, Aphrodite!" (*Youth and the Bright Medusa*)	
Sexuality			
151:1–2	his new neighbour, clad in a pink chiffon cloud of some sort,	17:12–13	his new neighbour, wholly unclad,
151:4	a woman in negligée was not an improper object	17:15–16	Nudity was not improper
151:6	a human body	17:18	a woman's body
151:12	now an arm, now a shoulder,	17:25	now an arm, now a shoulder, now a thigh,

[177]

APPENDIX

151:17	light.	18:3–5	light, from a foot or shoulder, from the up-thrust chin or the lifted breasts.
165:38–39	She was guarded from men at all times,	43:3–5	She was with difficulty restrained from men and was guarded at all times,
166:17–18	embraced the Princess;	43:27–28	fell upon the Princess to violate her honour;
166:21	he was maimed	44:4	he was gelded
167:8	the Queen's visitors	45:9	the Queen's lovers
169:30	their perfume of youth.	49:20–21	their perfume of youth and passion.

Style

144:30	aroma	6:12	smell
145:8–9	babies who were being held up	7:7	babies that were being supported
145:12–13	fresh, bright, unsmoked leaves	7:12	bright, sticky leaves
152:3	perspiration	19:11	sweat
155:32–33	this was the man with whom he wanted to study,	26:3	this was the man for him,
167:32	fantastic story	46:10	brutal story
170:21	Eden looked about the dark hole.	52:17	Eden glanced about.

One stylistic variant between the American and English editions of *Smart Set* in which "Coming, Eden Bower!" appeared should be noted: 163:34 "I hope you're not sore at me" was changed to "I hope you're not angry with me" in the English version.

Other Changes

147:13–14	woman he knew.	10:28–11:1	woman who always cheated him.
156:10	goat-butter, which was very strong.	26:22–23	goat-butter, which was strong and full of hair, as it was churned in a goat skin.
174:21	sitting in solitude	59:22–23	sitting in his tank
174:22	*Coming, Eden Bower!*	59:24	COMING, APHRODITE!
174:23	Manhattan Opera House	59:25	Lexington Opera House
176:23–24	the golden face of Clytemnestra.	63:9	the golden face of Aphrodite.

Record of Substantive Variants

Longer passages with substitutions or additions are not given here in full. See the text in *Youth and the Bright Medusa* for complete collations.

144:11	around the hall	5:17	about the hall
144:30	aroma	6:12	smell
145:8–9	babies who were being held up	7:7	babies that were being supported

145:12–13	fresh, bright, unsmoked leaves	7:12	bright, sticky leaves
146:3	that of lilacs	8:20–21	that of the lilacs
146:17	night job as a packer	9:9	night job as packer
146:28–29	Remington, then a great man in American art,	9:24–25	Remington, then at the height of his popularity,
146:32	something	10:1	experiments
146:32–33	and they put him out of the shop.	10:2–3	that made them put him out of the shop.
146:34	commercial work because he	10:4	commercial work; he
147:13–14	woman he knew.	10:28–11:1	woman who always cheated him.
147:38	soft trail of light	12:4	soft little trail of light
151:1–6	his new neighbour . . . body	17:12–18	his new neighbour . . . body
151:10–12	the gold . . . shoulder,	17:22–25	the gold . . . thigh,
151:17	disc of light.	18:3–5	disc of light . . . breasts.
151:20	come down;	18:8–10	come down . . . arm-pit.
151:23	Hedger was staring	18:13–14	Hedger was crouching on his knees, staring
151:24	gold on the faded	18:15–16	gold sleeping on the faded
151:25	spot seemed enchanted	18:16	spot was enchanted
151:29	stuffed with laundry.	18:20–21	stuffed with laundry, not knowing what had happened to him.
151:33	three frying pans	18:26–27	three greasy frying pans
152:3	perspiration	19:11	sweat
152:9	third box of cigarettes	19:17	fifth box of cigarettes
152:28–29	this girl . . . for the stage.	20:12–14	this unclad girl . . . for a purpose.
152:37	made him start.	20:24–25	made him start and brought out the sweat on his forehead.
153:1	came out of his closet	21:1	came slinking out of his closet
153:6–8	the beauty of women . . . burned with it.	21:8–16	a woman's body . . . without tenderness.
153:13	shirtwaist factory girls	21:22	silk-skirt factory girls
153:15	into the country	21:24	in the country
153:33–35	he had seen a woman emerge and give herself up to the primitive poetry of motion.	22:21–24	he had seen a woman who emerged naked . . . but his own.
154:21	looked	23:27	peered
155:32–33	this was the man with whom he wanted to study,	26:3	this was the man for him,
156:10	goat-butter, which was very strong.	26:22–23	goat-butter, which was strong and full of hair, as it was churned in a goat skin.
157:27	grown up in that prairie town	29:11	grown up
157:28	outside of it.	29:11–12	outside of that prairie town.
159:31	He	32:24	Hedger
159:32	One of my models, a fine girl,	32:25	One of my models

160:35	feel wide awake	34:18	very wide awake
161:8	shoving one another	35:5	shoving forward
161:9	as he says	35:6	as he pretends
161:11	it would be all up	35:8	it would be all over
161:18	began playing	35:16	commenced playing
161:28	The crowd—it had	36:2	The crowd, which had
162:38	his set teeth	38:3	his teeth
163:12–13	I don't think those black tights show off her legs very well, she's got fine legs.	38:19	Those black tights show off her legs very well.
163:15	a good idea of mine.	38:22	a good idea I had.
163:18–20	the crowd, which was flowing over the sand like a thick liquid and gazing upward at the slowly falling silver star.	38:25–26	the crowd.
163:23–24	dropping sun, shading their eyes and looking shoreward while the great bird settled down.	39:2–3	dropping sun, all shading their eyes and gazing upward at the slowly falling silver star.
163:25	red-faced man	39:4	manager
163:37	red-imp pages	39:18	pages
164:13	Molly	40:8	her
164:15–16	he instantly forgave her.	40:11–12	he forgave her.
164:30	her shoulder close to him.	41:1	her shoulder close to his.
165:20	missionary. He got	42:10–11	Missionary, who got
165:24–25	the proper kind of story."	42:16	the proper kind of story to tell a girl."
165:35	the child she was to bear	42:28	the child she carried
165:38	She was guarded from men at all times,	43:3–5	She was with difficulty restrained from men and was guarded at all times,
165:39	law of Thunder that she be so	43:5–6	law of the Thunder that she be maiden
166:3	eighteen years	43:9	eighteen summers
166:17–18	embraced the Princess;	43:27–28	fell upon the Princess to violate her honour;
166:21	maimed	44:4	gelded
166:32	grew toward the round, then	44:17–19	grew toward the round, because the god of Thunder had had his will of her, then
166:39	admired	44:27	desired
167:2	come to her	45:2	come to her secretly
167:4	she took in	45:5	she took into her chamber
167:4–5	for one day or two	45:5–6	for one night or two
167:8	the Queen's visitors	45:9	the Queen's lovers
167:12–13	In this service and in all others the Captive did not fail the Queen.	45:14–15	In this service nor in any other did the Captive fail the Queen.
167:15	four days, and on	45:17–19	four days . . . with him. On
167:22–23	When the Queen . . . live,	45:27–28	On the fifth night . . . lover,

167:30	while she listened	46:8	as she listened
167:32	fantastic story	46:10	brutal story
168:16	the strange man's eyes	47:10	Hedger's eyes
168:19	this violent man	47:14	the painter
168:30	looking up at the stars.	47:27	looking up at the sky.
168:34–35	Instead . . . blankets.	48:5	Instead . . . throat.
169:5	trousers	48:15	pants
169:11	I'll clear out.	48:21–23	I'll clear out. . . . it.
169:16	of each brought	49:1	brought
169:26	into the house.	49:14	into the dark hole; he first, drawing her gently after him.
169:30	perfume of youth.	49:20– 51:8	perfume of youth and passion. / One Saturday afternoon . . . permitted it.
169:34–35	that beautiful place.	51:13	its splendours.
170:3	a gorgeous place	51:18	gorgeous
170:21	Eden looked about the dark hole.	52:17	Eden glanced about.
171:26	ridiculous.	54:15–17	ridiculous; a poor . . . favours.
171:28	Hedger planned	54:20–21	he planned
171:30	ideas that he	54:23	ideas he
171:34	man. He	54:27– 55:2	man. Yet if . . . danger. He
171:36	sand dunes, and he	55:5	sand dunes. He
172:1	carried all about	55:10	carried about
172:23	even to her eyes.	56:12–13	even to her eyes, on which cataracts were forming.
172:24	hadn't even unstrapped	56:13–14	hadn't as much as unstrapped
173:21	left on Saturday	58:1	left yesterday
174:21	sitting in solitude	59:22–23	sitting in his tank
174:22	*Coming, Eden Bower!*	59:24	COMING, APHRODITE!
174:23	Manhattan Opera House	59:25	Lexington Opera House
174:23–24	for weeks announced her return	59:25–26	had long announced the return of Eden Bower
175:7	that dog	60:23	the dog
176:23–24	the golden face of Clytemnestra.	63:9	the golden face of Aphrodite.

A Note on the Editing

✣ ✣ ✣

The stories in this volume have been lightly edited to correct obvious misspellings and typographical errors; to normalize the capitalization of compound place names (streets, buildings, and rivers); to avoid obtrusively old-fashioned word-forms (such as, in "Ardessa," 113:34 *sky-scraper*] *skyscraper*) or spaced contractions (*I 've, he 'll*), which appeared throughout the *Century* texts of "The Bookkeeper's Wife" and "Ardessa"; and to follow present publishing practice in the placing of quotation marks and in other points of styling.

With only a few exceptions, there has been no attempt to make all forms consistent throughout the book. Each story has been treated as a unit. Generally, when inconsistencies in spelling (*theatre, theater*) or hyphenation in compound words appear within the text of a single story, the rule was to take the form most often used, or, if the usage was evenly divided, to choose the form most consistent with Willa Cather's usage elsewhere. For the following frequently used words, the closed rather than the hyphenated forms were used consistently throughout the book: *today, tonight, tomorrow; downtown, uptown; downstairs, upstairs.*

The stories have had no substantive editing. In only two instances words have been changed to fit meaning: in "Ardessa," 102:38 *mental message*] *mental massage;* in "Her Boss," 135:29 *Manning*] *Wanning.* In "Coming, Eden Bower!" Willa Cather for the first time used the English spelling in words like *neighbour* (rather than *neighbor*). A few inconsistencies in this usage in the *Smart Set* text have been regularized. Since "Coming, Eden Bower!" is the only story with two somewhat parallel texts, that of "Coming, Aphrodite!" in *Youth and the Bright Medusa* has been used to determine some usages. Two typographical errors were recognized by comparing texts: 144:13 *woman*] *women*; 149:30 *shaft*] *soft.* In all texts of the Eden Bower story, including later printings of "Coming, Aphrodite!," *Livingston* has twice been used for *Huntington.* These two appearances, at 167:37 and 168:9, have been allowed to stand. Other notes on the variants in "Coming, Eden Bower!" are in the Appendix.